CW00376276

2000

architects

K-Z

First published in Australia in 2006 by
The Images Publishing Group Pty Ltd
ABN 89 059 734 431
6 Bastow Place, Mulgrave, Victoria 3170, Australia
Telephone: +61 3 9561 5544 Facsimile: +61 3 9561 4860
Email: books@images.com.au
Website: www.imagespublishinggroup.com

Copyright © The Images Publishing Group Pty Ltd 2006
The Images Publishing Group Reference Number: 645

All rights reserved. Apart from any fair dealing for the purposes
of private study, research, criticism or review as permitted
under the Copyright Act, no part of this publication may be
reproduced, stored in a retrieval system or transmitted in any
form by any means, electronic, mechanical, photocopying,
recording or otherwise, without the written permission of the
publisher.

National Library of Australia Cataloguing-in-Publication data

2000 architects

2nd ed.
Includes index.
ISBN 1 920744 93 2

1. Architects – Directories.
2. Architectural firms – Directories.

720.92

Editor: Aisha Hasanovic

Designed by The Graphic Image Studio Pty Ltd, Mulgrave, Australia
www.tgis.com.au

Printing & binding by Pimlico Book International, Hong Kong

IMAGES has included on its website a page for special notices
in relation to this and our other publications.
Please visit www.imagespublishinggroup.com

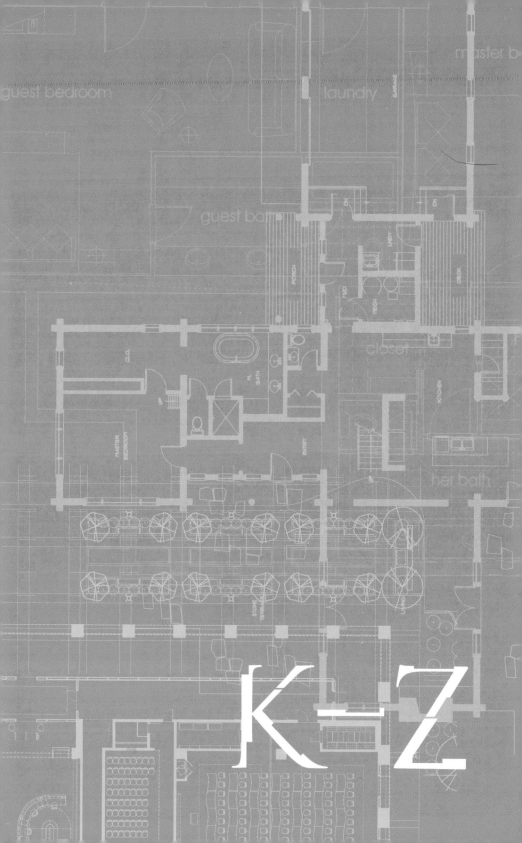

K–Z

KAA DESIGN GROUP, INC.

brandieh@kaadesigngroup.com www.kaadesigngroup.com

1 Weldon Brewster 2 Weldon Brewster 3 Weldon Brewster

Partners Grant Kirkpatrick and Steven Straughan united in their passion for integrating aesthetics and function with the inception of Kirkpatrick Associates Architects in 1988. In the years since, KAA has grown from a two-man team into a thriving office of 60.

KAA has committed itself to landscape, architectural, graphic, and interior design that accommodates client needs while bearing in mind the well-being of the environment and community. With a portfolio comprised of high-profile projects such as Banana Republic, Nicole Miller, Inc., Hugo Boss Fashions, Geary's of Beverly Hills, Christie's of London, and the Los Angeles County Museum of Art, it's no wonder that KAA commands such respect in the architecture community.

KAA affiliates believe this success owes to the intimate involvement of the clientele with all facets of a project. Clients range from private owners pursuing their dream home to CEOs looking to breathe new life into their businesses. KAA has helped realize the dreams of more than 250 such clients by remaining faithful to their vision: "Elevating the Human Spirit Through Design."

4 Weldon Brewster

5 Weldon Brewster

1 18th Walkstreet Residence, Manhattan Beach, California; custom, single family beachside residence
2 Los Angeles County Museum of Art, Los Angeles, California; renovation of multi-phased museum campus
3 Christie's of London, Beverly Hills, California; west-coast headquarters for international auction house
4 Beverly Park Residence, Beverly Hills, California; renovation of a custom single family estate
5 Via Arriba Residence, Palos Verdes, California; custom, single family hillside residence

● 4201 Redwood Avenue, Los Angeles, California 90066 USA Tel: +1 310 821 1400 Fax: +1 310 821 1440

KALLMANN MCKINNELL & WOOD ARCHITECTS, INC.

info@kmwarch.com   www.kmwarch.com

1   Robert Benson

Kallmann McKinnell & Wood Architects, Inc. offers comprehensive design services including feasibility studies, programming, master planning, architectural design, interior design and landscape architecture. In 1984, KMW received the AIA Firm of the Year Award, in recognition of KMW's stature among a select group of firms whose work exemplifies the highest standards of the profession. The citation notes the firm's "capacity to produce work of human value and lasting significance. Its continuing exploration of the potential of architecture to serve public needs will ensure the place of this small firm as a true giant of American design."

As the firm has matured over the last 20 years, it has invited into the practice a group of architects and directors who share its outlook on architecture as well as its commitment to a demanding set of design and construction standards. Together, they have created a notable diversity of award-winning projects for government, business, education, and the arts.

2   Steve Rosenthal

3   Steve Rosenthal

5   Richard Bryant/Arcaid

4   P&G Morison

1   Carl B. Stokes United States Courthouse & Federal Office Building, 2002, Cleveland, Ohio; view from southwest
2   Boston City Hall, 1969, Boston, Massachusetts; view from New Congress Street
3   American Academy of Arts & Sciences, 1981, Cambridge, Massachusetts; formal arcade and rustic structure above
4   Organisation for the Prohibition of Chemical Weapons, 1998, The Hague, The Netherlands; view from garden side
5   National Institute of Education at the Nanyang Technological University, 2001, Republic of Singapore; Library and School of the Arts

● 939 Boylston Street, Boston, Massachusetts 02115 USA Tel: +1 617 267 0808 Fax: +1 617 267 6999

KAMAL AMIN ASSOCIATES

kaminarch@aol.com   www.architect-kamin.com

1   Kamal Amin

2   Kamal Amin

3   Kamal Amin

5   Kamal Amin

Kamal Amin, Architect, Structural Engineer, was born in Egypt. He obtained a bachelor degree in architecture from the University of Cairo.

He came across the work of Frank Lloyd Wright at the cultural center in the United States Embassy in Cairo in 1948. Fascinated by Wright's work, he flew from Cairo to Phoenix immediately after his graduation in 1951, where he joined Wright at Taliesin near Scottsdale, Arizona. He worked with Wright during his crowning decade until Wright's death in 1959, and continued with the firm for the next 18 years.

During his years at Taliesin, he became convinced that working knowledge of structural engineering would enhance his abilities as an architect. He acquired certification as a structural engineer, studying under Mendel Glickman, chairman of the Engineering Department at the University of Oklahoma.

In 1977, Amin founded his own architectural engineering office in Scottsdale where he continues to practice.

Amin paints with watercolors, produces limited-edition silk screen serigraphs, and writes. His buildings stand in Arizona, California, Texas, Wisconsin, Virginia, Michigan, and Louisiana. His work has been published in Italy, Japan, Egypt, Sweden, and the United States.

4   Kamal Amin

1   Scottsdale Cardiovascular Center, Scottsdale, Arizona
2&3 Residence, Marion, Virginia; 6,000-square-foot residence with local granite laid in horizontal courses, all furniture, rugs and glass screens designed by Kamal Amin
4   Residence, Lake Geneva, Wisconsin; 5,500-square-foot residence has local limestone laid in horizontal courses
5   Residence, Fountain Hills, Arizona; 5,400-square-foot residence on steep hill has stump block and copper roof

● PO Box 4087, Scottsdale, Arizona 85261-4087 USA Tel: +1 480 837 9556 Fax: +1 480 816 8779

KANNER ARCHITECTS

kanner@kannerarch.com   www.kannerarch.com

1   Kanner Architects

2   Kanner Architects

Kanner Architects believes that every project is a special endeavor and that superior architecture can be achieved through creative planning and problem solving—thinking 'outside of the box.' The firm's design philosophy embraces the notion that buildings are meant to be places of joy, open and accessible, cutting-edge and inspirational. Every project must enhance the built environment.

Kanner Architects is an internationally recognized design firm located in Los Angeles, California. Its buildings have garnered over two dozen design awards in recent years, 20 of these being from the American Institute of Architects.

The firm's work has been widely published and has been featured in articles in the magazines *Abitare*, *Architecture*, *Architectural Record*, *Architectural Digest*, *Interior Design*, *L.A. Architect*, *Metropolis*, *Blueprint*, the *Los Angeles Times* and *The New York Times*. A monograph on Kanner Architects' work was published by The Images Publishing Group in 1998.

3   Kanner Architects

4   Kanner Architects

5   John Linden

1   Seacliff Homes, Malibu, California
2   Sagaponac Lot 30 Residence, Long Island, New York
3   High-rise Condominiums, Los Angeles, California
4   East Los Angeles Court House, Los Angeles, California
5   511 House, Pacific Palisades, California

● 10924 Le Conte Avenue, Los Angeles, California 90024 USA Tel: +1 310 208 0028 Fax: +1 310 208 5756

KAYA ARIKOGLU

arikoglu_arkitekt@yahoo.com   www.arikoglu.com

1   K. Arikoglu

Kaya Arikoglu received his architectural degree from the University of Maryland and his urban design degree from Cornell University. After teaching and practicing in the USA, Arikoglu Arkitekt Ltd. relocated to Turkey in 1992.

Mr Arikoglu practices architecture and urban design in a unique environment where east and west meet to join into one cultural mosaic. His design concepts filter through the social and natural context of Anatolia. His firm maintains highly tectonic universal aspirations, while preserving the respect and affection for hand-crafted traditional building systems. This allows his architecture to be site-specific to its context and its time period.

The process of his architecture is an accumulation of forms that are first tested for relevance and commodity, before being evolved and unified for implementation.

His work is underlined with the spirit that architecture as an art form can be attained under all circumstances in all environments.

2   K. Arikoglu

3   K. Arikoglu

4   K. Arikoglu

1 Tarsus American College Sports Hall, Tarsus, Turkey
2 Chamber of Maritime Trade, Mersin, Turkey; detail
3 SASA Technology and Research Center, Adana, Turkey
4 Tarsus American College Faculty Residence, Tarsus, Turkey
5 Temsa Cafeteria Building, Adana, Turkey

5   K. Arikoglu

● 11 Toros Caddesi, Cemalpasa 01120 Adana, Turkey Tel: +90 322 454 4082 Fax: +90 322 459 2019

KEBBELL DAISH

hello@kebbelldaish.co.nz   www.kebbelldaish.co.nz

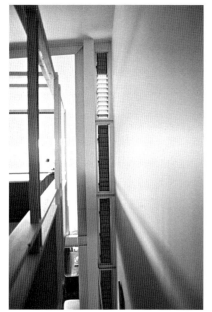

1   Daniel Watt

2   Sam Kebbell

John Daish and Sam Kebbell have been working together since 1996 and formed Kebbell Daish at the beginning of 2002. Daish and Kebbell both hold Masters degrees from the University of California at Berkeley and the Harvard School of Design respectively, and both partners teach and research at the Victoria University School of Design. The office produces a range of work including houses, offices, and public buildings and has been recognized at regional and national levels. The firm's work has been exhibited and published on many occasions in New Zealand and internationally.

3   Sarah Connor

1   Kebbell House, Te Horo, New Zealand; interior detail
2   Kebbell House, Te Horo, New Zealand; part elevation
3   Great Egyptian Museum Competition Entry, Giza, Egypt; exhibition model
4   Saatchi & Saatchi, Wellington, New Zealand

4   Jono Rotman

● PO Box 6356, Marion Square, Wellington, New Zealand Tel: +64 4 384 5866

KEITH WILLIAMS ARCHITECTS

studio@keithwilliamsarchitects.com   www.keithwilliamsarchitects.com

Keith R Williams BA(Hons) DipArch(Hons) RIBA was born in London in 1958. Educated at Kingston and Greenwich Schools of Architecture, and diplomating with first class honors for design portfolio, Williams worked first for Sheppard Robson and then Terry Farrell before founding Pawson Williams Architects when aged 29, subsequently becoming the firm's intellectual and creative driving force.

In 2001, he formed Keith Williams Architects to concentrate more effectively on a singular creative approach to architecture against a background of a dynamic and expanding portfolio of high-profile commissions.

Williams' architecture, with its concerns for space, light, form and material, exhibits a close consideration for scale, history and context, thereby achieving an aesthetic balance between his own contemporary, visionary architecture, and that which exists.

Designs for theaters, concert halls, museums, galleries, libraries, and civic buildings have been proposed in many countries throughout Europe.

He has judged national design awards and won a significant number of architectural competitions, both national and international. He has acted as architectural assessor to competition juries for major public projects and his work has been published worldwide.

1   Keith Willliams Architects

2   Eamonn O'Mahony   3   Eamonn O'Mahony

4   David Gandorg

5   Keith Willliams Architects

1   Private House, Abercorn Close, London, UK
2   Town Hall & Library, Athlone, Ireland
3   Town Hall & Library, Athlone, Ireland
4   Centro Culturale Di Torino, Turin, Italy
5   Irish World Music Center, University of Limerick, Ireland

● 17 – 21 Emerald Street, Holborn, London WC1N 3QN UK Tel: +44 020 7841 5810 Fax: +44 020 7841 5811

KEN TATE ARCHITECT

tate@kentatearchitect.com   www.kentatearchitect.com

1   Gordon Beall

2   Gordon Beall and Peter Howson

In 1984, Ken Tate Architect was established in Mississippi as a practice focused on the demand for traditional houses. The firm grew to become an important regional practice, winning numerous awards and being published over 50 times. The projects included hundreds of designs and well over 50 built residences ranging from a large Tennessee farmhouse on 1,000 acres to a Normandy-style estate on 2,000 acres.

In 1999, the firm relocated near New Orleans, Louisiana, and has since taken commissions in a wider variety of styles, including an Adirondack clubhouse, a modern beach house, a Georgian mansion, an Italian townhouse, and a French Colonial compound. These recent projects have also taken the firm to more distant locales, including Boston, Denver, the mountains of North Carolina, and Nashville.

Publications include: *The Classicist* (published by the Institute of Classical Architecture), *Southern Accents*, *Period Homes*, *Veranda*, and *Traditional Home*.

3   Carlos Studio

4   Gordon Beall and Peter Howson

5   Dan Bibb

1   Norton Residence, Madison, Mississippi; a French-style lake house with a 30-foot drop to the water
2   Young Residence, Baton Rouge, Louisiana; a Palladian-style villa enveloped by live oaks in Bayou country
3   Private Residence, Northern Mississippi; a stone and slate roof Normandy-style farmhouse on 2,000 acres
4   Private Residence, Central Mississippi; a Spanish Colonial-style estancia on a family compound in an established neighborhood
5   Private Residence, Southern Capital City; a French-style semi-urban walled enclave on a small lake

● 206 Covington Street, PO Box 550, Madisonville, Louisiana 70447 USA
Tel: +1 985 845 8181 Fax: +1 985 845 8182

KENGO KUMA & ASSOCIATES

kuma@ba2.so-net.ne.jp www02.so-net.ne.jp/~kuma/

Kengo Kuma was born in Kanagawa, Japan in 1954 and completed his masters degree at Tokyo University in 1979. He was a visiting scholar at Columbia University from 1985 to 1986.

In 1990, he established Kengo Kuma & Associates. Since 2001, he has been a professor at the Faculty of Science and Technology, Keio University.

Among his major works are the Kirosan Observatory (1995), Water/Glass (1995, for which he received the AIA Benedictus Award), Venice Biennale/Space Design of Japanese Pavilion (1995), Stage in Forest, and Toyoma Center for Performance Arts (1997, for which he received the 1997 Architectural Institute of Japan Annual Award), Stone Museum (2000, for which he received the International Stone Architecture Award 2001), and the Museum of Hiroshige Ando (2000, for which he received The Murano Prize). He was awarded the International Spirit of Nature Wood Architecture Award in 2002 for his major wooden architectures.

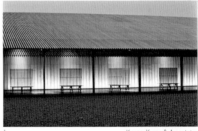

1   Kengo Kuma & Associates

2   Kengo Kuma & Associates

3   Kengo Kuma & Associates

4   Kengo Kuma & Associates

5   Kengo Kuma & Associates

1 Museum of Hiroshige Ando, Batou, Nasu-gun, Tochigi Prefecture, Japan
2 Plastic House, Meguro-ku, Tokyo, Japan
3 Stone Museum, Nasu, Tochigi Prefecture, Japan
4 Water / Glass, Atami, Shizuoka Prefecture, Japan
5 Great (Bamboo) Wall, Beijing, PRC

● 2-12-12-9F Minami Aoyama, Minato-ku, Tokyo 107-0062 Japan Tel: +81 3 3401 7721 Fax: +81 3 3401 7778

KIM YOUNG-SUB + KUNCHOOK-MOONHWA ARCHITECT ASSOCIATES

kunchook@hanmail.net   www.kimarch.com

1   Kim Jae Kyeong

2   Mun Jeong Sik

3   Kim Jae Kyeong

Kim Young-Sub was born in Korea in 1950 and graduated from Sungkyunkwan University, Department of Architectural Engineering in 1974. In 1982, Mr Kim established Kim Young-Sub + Kunchook-Moonhwa Architect Associates.

Kim Young-Sub's works have been shown at many exhibitions, including SIAC in Rome, Italy (1986); IAA (Innovative Architecture in Asia) in Bangalore, India (1998), and Beijing, China (2002); East Wind 2000; and Pacific Rim Architects in Tokyo, Japan (2000).

In addition to its well-known church projects, the firm has also undertaken a wide variety of projects including office buildings, university facilities, recreational centers, and residential buildings, many of which have been honored with design awards, including Grand Prize in the Annual Korean Institute of Registered Architects Award (1988), First Prize in the Annual Korean Architectural Culture Award (1992/93/96/97), Architectural Award of Seoul City (1992/96/2002), 7th Kim Swoo-Geun Architectural Award (1996), Korean Institute of Architects Award (1997), Grand Prize in the Annual Korean Environmental Design & Architectural Award (1995/99), and 5th Catholic Church Arts Award (2000).

Kim Young-Sub has recently lectured at the International Symposium of AIJ in Tokyo (2002); the International Symposium 'Cultural Diversity in Historic Cities' in Kazan, Russia (2002); the Fukushima International Colloquium 'New Capital City of Japan' (2001); and Tokyo University (2000).

4   Kim Jae Kyeong

1   Cheongyang Catholic Church, Cheongyang, Chungcheongnam-do, Korea
2   Chodang Catholic Church, Gangneung, Gangwon-do, Korea
3   Joong Ang Catholic Church, Anyang, Gyeonggi-do, Korea
4   Korea Life Insurance, Gangnam Building, Seocho-dong, Seoul, Korea
5   Sim Gok Resurrection Catholic Church, Buchon, Korea

5   Kim Jae Kyeong

● 287–3 Yangjae-dong Seocho-gu, Seoul 137-130 Republic of Korea Tel: +82 2 574 3842 Fax: +82 2 579 4172

KIMMERLE ARCHITECTS

kimmerle@kimmerle.com www.kimmerle.com

The Kimmerle Group is a multifaceted organization located in Morristown, New Jersey, USA. There are several operating divisions growing out of the business requirements of the Kimmerle organization:

Kimmerle Architects, PA is a design, planning and urban design firm established in 1990. Kimmerle Architects enjoys the benefits of ongoing relationships with many *Fortune 500* corporations, providing design and planning services to these organizations on a local and a national basis. Project areas include corporate office and education, downtown redevelopment, historic preservation, public and private educational, and justice. The firm maintains professional relationships with local and regional institutions, as well as a long list of major development companies in the northern New Jersey area.

The firm is the winner of three national design awards in the past four years and has been published in the *New York Times* and in numerous national design and industry publications.

Workspace, Inc. is a division of the company devoted to providing procurement services to corporate and institutional users in the areas of office equipment, furnishings, furniture, move management, and related services.

South Street Associates, LLC is the development company which owns and operates the company-owned headquarters site in Morristown. South Street Associates has recently completed the development and construction of an additional 5,500-square-foot office structure on site, which is fully leased. The firm continues to seek other opportunities both independently and in joint-venture partnerships.

1   Kimmerle Architects

2   Grace Marotti

4   Paul S Newman

1 The Great Swamp Environmental Science Center, Harding, New Jersey; a unique environmental center devoted to public education
2 Trilegiant, Norwalk, Connecticut; an old warehouse and addition were fully renovated to create new corporate office
3 Suburban Propane Corporation, Whippany, New Jersey; building houses corporate facility, warehouse and record storage archives
4 10 Park Place, Morristown, New Jersey; full restoration of historic structure in Morristown CBD
5 The Deidre O'Brien Child Advocacy Center, Morristown, New Jersey; center provides assistance and support for child victims of violence and abuse

3   Otto Baetz

5   Kimmerle Architects

●   264 South Street, Morristown, New Jersey 07960 USA Tel: +1 973 538 8885 Fax: +1 973 829 6270

KINGSLAND + ARCHITECTS INC.

C.Kingsland@kingslandplus.com   www.kingslandplus.com

Kingsland + Architects Inc. is the present version of a practice that originated in 1910. Since that time, the name of the firm has changed as partners departed or retired.

Kingsland + Architects Inc. is the culmination of knowledge and experience gathered over the past 75 years. It offers a complete and comprehensive package of services to suit all architectural and interior design needs. The firm has had the pleasure of working with a variety of different clients with varying and sometimes unusual needs.

The firm is a multidisciplined, progressive organization with knowledgeable and enthusiastic professionals who have an insuperable desire to take on challenge and succeed. It has had extensive experience in the design and construction of elementary, secondary, and post-secondary schools, private learning academies, ecclesiastic buildings, libraries, restaurants, retail and community centers. Its experience also includes renovations and additions as well as completely new multi-million dollar facilities.

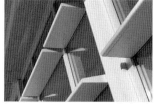

1   Insightmedia

2   Insightmedia

3   Insightmedia

4   Insightmedia

5   Insightmedia

Malvern District Library, Scarborough, Ontario
1   Sun shading devices
2   Tree structure detail
3   Front façade
4   Central axis, adult reading lounge
5   Central axis at circulation desk

● 2 Toronto Street, 4th Floor, Toronto, Ontario M5C 2B6 Canada Tel: +1 416 203 7799 Fax: +1 416 203 7763

KIRKSEY

info@kirksey.com   www.kirksey.com

Kirksey has maintained consistent growth since its founding in 1971 by providing its clients with superior architecture through innovative thinking, exceptional design, and unmatched client service in an environment that fosters professional growth, personal fulfillment, stability, and a commitment to the community.

What began as a small commercial architecture firm has evolved into a diverse organization of more than 100 design professionals belonging to ten architectural teams—Commercial, Education, Government, Healthcare, Hospitality, Interior Architecture, Renovation, Residential, Retail, and Special Use. It is this diversity of project types that allows Kirksey to provide its clients with a full complement of services, carried out by experts whose knowledge and talents best match their clients' business strategies and objectives. With this team-based approach, every project benefits from individual expertise while leveraging the collective knowledge of the entire firm.

1   Hickey-Robertson Photography

2   Aker/Zvonkovic Photography

3   Kirksey

4   Aker/Zvonkovic Photography

5   Aker/Zvonkovic Photography

1   Idea Integration, Houston, Texas; 25,000-square-foot build-out for a national e-business solutions provider; 2002 Houston AIA Award of Honor
2   One BriarLake Plaza, Houston, Texas; 20-story office building with 7-level parking garage
3   HEALTHSOUTH Medical Center, Birmingham, Alabama; a 219-bed 'Digital Hospital of the Future'
4   Ripley House Neighborhood Complex, Houston, Texas; non-profit community center, 2002 Houston AIA Award of Honor
5   Park Towers, Houston, Texas; two 18-story office towers with 6-level parking garage

●   6909 Portwest Drive, Houston, Texas 77024 USA   Tel: +1 713 850 9600   Fax: +1 713 850 7308

KISHO KUROKAWA ARCHITECT & ASSOCIATES

kurokawa@kisho.co.jp

2   Koji Kobayashi

2   KKAA

Kisho Kurokawa architect & associates (KKAA) has provided technical expertise in the fields of architecture, urban design, regional and new town planning, landscape design, socio-economic planning, long-range development planning, and futures forecasting for government and private agencies both in Japan and abroad.

When approaching a particular project, the group of architects, planners and engineers focus on the concepts of the 'symbiotic theory', postulating that architecture as well as urban and social structures should enhance the ambivalent, heterogeneous nature of man.

In applying these concepts, the practicing consultant includes in each project plan an understanding of how the structural and causal variables are integrated within a constantly changing environment. The group thus strives to discover the best possible solutions for concrete social needs.

Based on the above-described organization and design approach, Kisho Kurokawa architect & associates has executed more than 100 projects over the past 40 years.

2   Koji Kobayashi

4   KKAA

1   National Art Center, Roppongi, Tokyo, Japan
2   Zhengzhou CBD Landscape, Zhengzhou, PRC
3   Japan Nursing Association Building, Omotesando, Tokyo, Japan
4   Astana International Airport, Astana, Kazakhstan

● 11F, Aoyama Building, 1-2-3 Kita Aoyama, Minato-ku, Tokyo 107-0061 Japan
Tel: +81 3 3404 3481 Fax: +81 3 3404 6222

KKS INTERNATIONAL
KKS GROUP

info@kkstokyo.co.jp www.kkstokyo.co.jp/kks/english.html

For 40 years Kanko Kikaku Sekkeisha, with KKS International, has been a leader in professional architectural and interior design services for the hospitality industry. The firm's credentials have been well established by creating distinctive environments that enrich the lives of everyone, while providing superior, far-reaching design strategies for the client.

KKS International commits the same attention to large and small projects, while mastering the most demanding situations with equal ease. From lush resorts in the tropics and opulent city hotels, to the scenic ski resorts in the northern alps of Japan, it is KKS's ingenuity and high standards that describe the essence of its work. The firm carefully tends to the total environmental design of all its projects, enhancing not only the guest's experience, but also the convenience and comfort for the client, management and staff, enhancing their efficiency and work quality.

1   KKS International

2   Kenchiku Gaho

3   Shenzhen Our Space Digital Video Co., ltd

4   Studio Murai   5   Kenchiku Gaho

1 Hilton Otaru Hotel, Otaru, Hokkaido Prefecture, Japan; 5-star hotel
2 Pan Pacific Hotel KLIA, Kuala Lumpur, Malaysia; 5-star hotel at Kuala Lumpur International Airport
3 Fuzhou Shangri-La Hotel, Fuzhou, PRC; 5-star hotel
4 Cerulean Tower, Tokyu Hotel, Sakuragaoka-cho, Shibuya District, Tokyo, Japan; worm's-eye view
5 Hilton Dalian Hotel; Dalian, PRC; 5-star hotel

● 17 Mori Building, 1-26-5 Toranomon, Minato-ku, Tokyo 105-0001 Japan
Tel: +81 3 3507 0374 Fax: +81 3 3507 0386

KLEIHUES + KLEIHUES

berlin@kleihues.com www.kleihues.com

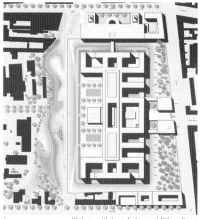

1   Kleihues + Kleihues Archive and Dülmen-Rorup

Initially established by architect and urban planner Professor Josef P Kleihues in 1962, the architectural office Kleihues + Kleihues was founded as a limited company by the partners Prof. Josef P. Kleihues and Jan Kleihues with Norbert Hensel in 1996. The award-winning practice has operated successfully on a national and international level, providing the whole range of architectural services.

A responsible approach to designing high quality inhabitable space is the underlying philosophy of this office. As a result, the buildings by Kleihues + Kleihues distinguish themselves through a timeless though modern design that respects the context of the location; the buildings are functional and enduring.

2   Stefan Lotz

3   Stefan Lotz

4   Christian Richters

5   Hélène Binet

1&2 Federal Intelligence Service Headquarters, Berlin, Germany
3   Concorde Hotel, Augsburger Strasse, Berlin, Germany
4   Fiege Engineering Headquarters, Greven, Germany
5   Museum of Contemporary Art, Chicago

● Helmholtzstrasse 42, Berlin D-10587 Germany Tel: +49 30 399 7790 Fax: +49 30 399 779 77

KLING

info@kling.us www.kling.us

1   Kling

2   Jeff Goldberg/Esto

Kling is an integrated, full-service, architecture, engineering, interiors and planning firm based in Philadelphia, Pennsylvania. Since its founding as a sole architectural proprietorship in 1946, the firm has grown to more than 400 employees with branch offices in Washington, DC; Iselin, New Jersey; and Raleigh, North Carolina.

Its clients are located across the United States and around the world, and include financial services companies, pharmaceutical corporations, information technology providers, US federal government agencies, and institutions of higher learning.

Its work has garnered more than 300 design and industry awards, as well as the accolades of its clients and the public. The focus of the practice, from inception to the present, remains completely committed to the issues of social responsibility and the advocacy of artistry upon which it was founded.

3   Dennis Gilbert

4   Kling

5   David Sundberg/Esto

1 University of Colorado, Health Sciences Center, Aurora, Colorado
2 SAP America, Inc., Corporate Headquarters, Newtown Square, Pennsylvania
3 GlaxoSmithKline Medicines Research Centre, Stevenage, UK
4 Center-City High Rise Study, Philadelphia, Pennsylvania
5 Merck & Co., Inc., Building 800, Rahway, New Jersey

● 2301 Chestnut Street, Philadelphia, Pennsylvania 19103 USA Tel: +1 215 569 2900 Fax: +1 215 569 5963

KMD ARCHITECTURE

super@kmd.ie www.kmd.ie

KMD Architecture is an Irish architectural practice dedicated to quality of design, service and efficiency. It takes as its objective in every project the challenge to achieve not only functional and budgetary objectives of the client but also to fulfill its responsibility as an architectural practice towards the final occupants of the building and society by respecting the building context and creating sustainable environments.

It approaches each project through research and analysis of both the program (the brief) and the context (the site). The organization promotes 'total' involvement of the abilities of the 45-plus staff within the practice through design reviews, in-house discussion and the transfer of successful experiences from other projects through to current work.

KMD Architecture has considerable experience in masterplanning and takes the same innovative design approach to masterplanning as it does to individual building projects.

1   Barry Mason Photography

3   Eamonn O'Mahony, Studioworks

2   Eamonn O'Mahony, Studioworks

1 City Quay Office Development,
   Dublin
2 Xerox Technology Park, Dundalk
3 George's Quay Office
   Development, Dublin
4 James Ussher Library, Trinity
   College Dublin
5 IBM SSD Facility, Dublin

4   Eamonn O'Mahony, Studioworks   5   Eamonn O'Mahony, Studioworks

● 4 Prince's Street South, City Quay, Dublin 2, Ireland Tel: +353 1 677 0077 Fax: +353 1 677 1186

KOHN PEDERSEN FOX ASSOCIATES

info@kpf.com   www.kpf.com

1   Timothy Hursley

2   H.G. Esch

Through 26 years of practice, the philosophy of KPF has always been the insistence on design excellence, principal commitment, superior management, and outstanding service to its clients. KPF recognizes the civic responsibility of buildings, as well as the importance of engineering technology and sustainability, in shaping our built environment.

The firm provides full architecture, masterplanning, space planning, programming, building analysis, and interior design services for clients in both the public and private sectors. It operates globally, bringing an informed perspective to local issues and fulfilling the unique functional, aesthetic, and social goals of each project. The firm believes that design emerges from an intensive dialogue with the client, the site, and the program. For KPF, the architectural response to its clients' aspirations is the true measure of the success of its work.

KPF's strong body of work has earned the firm recognition as one of the most respected architectural design firms in the world. The firm has been the recipient of numerous awards, recognizing its wide range of design and technical accomplishments.

5   Peter Cook

3   H.G. Esch

4   Michael Moran

1 Gannett/USA Today Headquarters, McLean, Virginia; overall view from the south
2 Thames Court, London, UK; trading floor at base of high atrium with long span trusses and motorized shading device
3 745 Seventh Avenue, New York, New York; night shot looking east
4 New Academic Complex, City University of New York, Baruch College, New York, New York; aerial view from the west
5 Rothermere Institute for American Studies, Oxford, UK; south elevation seen from new garden quadrangle

● 111 West 57th Street, New York, New York 10019 USA Tel: +1 212 977 6500 Fax: +1 212 956 9526

KONING EIZENBERG ARCHITECTURE

info@kearch.com www.kearch.com

Since its establishment in 1981, the Koning Eizenberg practice has become well-known for its buildings of everyday living, including affordable housing, community centers, recreation centers, schools, custom homes, hotels, stores, and work places.

Many of its buildings have won multiple awards and have been published in architectural and other publications in the USA and abroad. The influence of Koning Eizenberg's approach to design can also be measured by the numerous invited speaking engagements and teaching appointments at universities around the world.

Hank Koning and Julie Eizenberg have refocused architects' attention on the value and design potential of socially responsible projects by demonstrating architectural excellence in the design of many tight-budget affordable housing projects and community buildings. Their buildings might best be described as 'brilliantly sensible'.

In Koning Eizenberg's buildings, one is encouraged to discover space and architecture for oneself, guided by compositional cues, landscape strategies, spatial sequence and scale change. The result is innovative architecture with a rare kind of humanism.

1   Benny Chan, Fotoworks

2   Benny Chan, Fotoworks

3   Grant Mudford   4   Tim Griffith

1 PS#1 Elementary School, Santa Monica, California; a progressive elementary school expansion; AIA California Council Honor Award, AIA Los Angeles Merit Award
2 25th Street Studio, Santa Monica, California; mixed-use commercial/studio; Savings by Design Energy Efficiency Award
3 5th Street Family Housing, Santa Monica, California; 32 units of affordable family housing; AIA California Merit Award, AIA Los Angeles Merit Award
4 31st Street House, Santa Monica, California; single family residence; National AIA Award

● 1454 25th Street, 2nd Floor, Santa Monica, California 90404 USA
Tel: +1 310 828 6131 Fax: +1 310 828 0719

KONIOR & PARTNERS

mail@konior.com www.konior.com

1   Konior & Partners Architects

2   Konior & Partners Architects

3   Konior & Partners Architects

4   Konior & Partners Architects

1 Wlodarzewska, Warsaw, Poland
2 Trinity Business Park, Warsaw, Poland
3 Orbis, Gand, Belgium
4&5 Crown Tower, Warsaw, Poland

A Belgian architect born in Krakow (Poland) in 1944, Ludwik Konior received his Civil Engineer-Architect diploma in 1968 from the Polytechnical School of Krakow where he was assistant teacher at the faculty of architecture until 1973. That year, he started collaborating with famous Belgian architect Henri Montois and became a partner in 1983 when the firm was transformed into Bureau d'Architecture Henri Montois s.p.r.l.

Konior is now active in his own studio, Konior & Partners. He has worked on large-scale projects such as major international competitions (Parc de la Villette in Paris; special mention); headquarters projects such as Kompass and Space Research Corporation and embassy projects such as the Polish Missions to the European Union and to NATO.

Ludwik Konior has designed and co-designed projects in Belgium, Cameroon, Congo, France, Italy and Poland, including the 140,000-square-meter Council of Europe in Brussels and the Embassies of Italy, Luxembourg and Poland, also in Brussels. He was responsible for the design of headquarters for Citibank, Pfizer and Worldcom, and for recent projects in Warsaw for Carlsberg, Heineken, Securitas and Shell.

5   W. Krynski

● Avenue Maurice 1, B-1050 Brussels, Belgium Tel: +32 2 647 9947 Fax: +32 2 647 9888

364

KUBOTA ARCHITECT ATELIER

info@katsufumikubota.jp www.katsufumikubota.jp

Born in 1957 in Yamaguchi Prefecture, Kubota formed Kubota Architect Atelier in 1988. Kubota's architectural concept is concerned with creating abstract spaces. His original, strong and elegant designs of structure are based on simple, honest materials, and thoughtfully resolved details. He strives to devise minimal yet complex details by studying the relationship between construction materials and possible displacements of the structure. Environmental factors such as light and the flow of air play a major role in his designs.

Main works include, M-Clinic, 2005; M-House and I-House, 2004; Yamaguchi Prefecture Pavilion, 2001; Y-House, 1998; and Crystal Unit series between 1993–1998. His works have been widely featured in international publications such as *Case in Giappone*, *Houses on the Edge*, *Minimalism*, *PreFab*, *Architectural Digest*, *Casabella*, *GA Houses*, and *Minimalist Houses*.

1 H. Ueda

2 H. Ueda   3 H. Ueda

4 H. Ueda   5 H. Ueda

M-CLINIC, Hiroshima, Japan
1 Exterior of eye clinic building
2 Sharp edge of white structure
3 Main lobby facing water
4 Water garden
5 Clinic interior

● 1-8-24 Imazu-cho, Iwakuni, Yamaguchi 740-0017 Japan Tel: +81 827 22 0092 Fax: +81 827 22 0079

KUTH/RANIERI ARCHITECTS

contact@kuthranieri.com www.kuthranieri.com

Kuth/Ranieri Architects is a full-service architectural firm based in San Francisco, California. Established in 1990 by Byron Kuth AIA, and Elizabeth Ranieri AIA, Kuth/Ranieri has earned a national and international reputation for its innovative architectural projects that integrate client needs with contemporary issues of design and technology.

Kuth/Ranieri has received numerous regional, state and national awards from the American Institute of Architects; I.D. Magazine's Awards for Environments; and the Architectural League of New York's Young Architects and Emerging Voices awards. Its work has been featured in publications in the United States, Japan, and Europe and has been displayed in commercial, university and museum galleries in New York, Boston, Houston, and San Francisco. Byron Kuth and Elizabeth Ranieri graduated from the Rhode Island School of Design with degrees in Fine Arts and Architecture. They are on the Faculty at the California College of Arts and Crafts, and have also taught at the Harvard Graduate School of Design.

The design produced by Kuth/Ranieri is distinguished by innovation within industry standards of construction and fabrication and an efficient and proactive project delivery. Kuth/Ranieri is dedicated to sustaining collaborative relationships with its clients, technical associates, builders and manufacturers, providing a full range of service at every phase of the project.

1   David Wakely Photography

2   Kuth/Ranieri

4   Kuth/Ranieri

5   Cesar Rubio Photography

1 Iann Stoltz Residence; front façade
2 Lodi Bunkhouse; exterior
3 Park Presidio Residence; back façade
4 Park Presidio Residence; stairway
5 Iann Stlotz Residence; dining room

Portrait credit: Kuth/Ranieri

3   Kuth/Ranieri

● 340 Bryant Street, Suite #300, San Francisco, California 94107 USA
Tel: +1 415 543 9235 Fax: +1 415 543 9237

KUWABARA PAYNE MCKENNA BLUMBERG ARCHITECTS

kpmb@kpmbarchitects.com www.kpmbarchitects.com

Kuwabara Payne McKenna Blumberg Architects (KPMB) was founded in 1987 by Bruce Kuwabara, Thomas Payne, Marianne McKenna and Shirley Blumberg. The portfolio encompasses cultural, civic, education, hospitality, and performing arts projects located across Canada and, increasingly, in the USA and Europe. Completed projects include the Goodman Theatre in Chicago, the Star Alliance Lounge at the Zurich International Airport, and the Canadian Embassy in Berlin, Germany.

The studio is recognized for its commitment to the design of the public realm, cultural institutions, and the tectonics of interior architecture. Future projects include the corporate headquarters for Manitoba Hydro in Winnipeg, the Celia Franca Training Centre for the National Ballet School of Canada, and the Festival Centre and Tower for the Toronto International Film Festival Group.

The work has received more than 70 awards, including nine Governor General's awards—Canada's most prestigious architecture award, and is published in the *Contemporary World Architect series* (Rockport Publishers, 1997) and *The Architecture of Kuwabara Payne McKenna Blumberg Architects* (Birkhauser, 2004).

1   Tom Arban

2   Tom Arban

3   Tom Arban

4   Tom Arban

1 James Stewart Centre for Mathematics, McMaster University, Hamilton, Ontario; view through architectural void into classroom
2 Le Quartier Concordia, Concordia University, Montreal, Quebec; west elevation showing stacked atria (with Fichten Soiferman et Associes)
3 University of Toronto at Scarborough Campus, Management Building, Toronto, Ontario; interior view of central atrium
4 Centennial HP Science and Technology Centre, Scarborough, Ontario; south elevation (with Stone McQuire Vogt Architects)
5 Festival Centre and Tower, Toronto International Film Festival Group, Toronto, Ontario; model of mixed-use cultural facility and residential development

5   Ben Rahn/A Frame

● 322 King Street West, 3rd Floor, Toronto, Ontario M5V 1J2 Canada Tel: +1 416 977 5104 Fax: +1 416 598 9840

LAB ARCHITECTURE STUDIO

info@labarchitecture.com   www.labarchitecture.com

Lab architecture studio operates a critical design approach which recognizes the inherent complexity in building and construction and which harnesses this complexity to produce projects that are robust and adaptable. It is a practice where design and tactical decisions operate alongside the numerous constraints and unforeseen developments of any project, whether large or small. The ability to not only accept change and alteration, but to use these critical events in a productive and reinvigorating manner is central to any progressive architectural practice.

Lab architecture studio was founded in 1994 in London, UK, by architects Peter Davidson and Donald L. Bates. The Melbourne office was opened in 1997 as a consequence of winning the Federation Square architectural design competition. In 2004, the studio opened a third office in Beijing and since that time the two directors have been dividing their time between the UK, PRC and Australia. The Federation Square project is critically considered to be amongst the most innovative architectural projects to be constructed in the history of Australia.

1

Lab architecture

3   Matt Johnson

2

Lab architecture

4   Peter Clarke

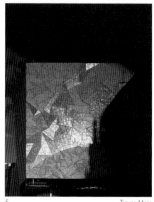

5   Trevor Mein

1&2   Sotto shang du, Beijing, PRC
   3   Federation Square, Melbourne, Victoria
   4   Federation Square, Melbourne, Victoria; south atrium at night
   5   Federation Square, Melbourne, Victoria; National Gallery of Victoria façade

Portrait credit: Trevor Mein

● Level 4, 325 Flinders Lane, Melbourne, Victoria 3000 Australia Tel: +61 3 9612 1026 Fax: +61 3 9620 3088
Unit 300 Curtain House, 134–146 Curtain Road, London EC2A 3AR UK
Tel: +44 20 7033 9193 Fax: +44 20 7729 3071

LAWRENCE W. SPECK
OF PAGE SOUTHERLAND PAGE

aus@pspaec.com   www.pspaec.com

Lawrence W. Speck received both undergraduate and graduate degrees from MIT where he also served on the faculty for three years after graduation. In 1975, he began teaching at the University of Texas, Austin, where he served as dean from 1992–2001. His practice grew from residential projects in the 1970s to large urban plans by the mid-1980s when he began his association with PageSoutherlandPage.

The oldest architectural firm in Texas, PageSoutherlandPage has a staff of over 250 design professionals, with offices in Austin, Houston, Dallas and Washington, DC. The firm's widely diversified practice has included almost every building type in locations around the world.

Lawrence W. Speck and PageSoutherlandPage allied initally as two separate firms combining a strong design talent and capability with a long-standing track record of solid professional performance for several high-profile public projects. In 1999, Speck joined the firm as a design principal.

The practice is committed to exploring four areas of particular interest: dealing with the paradoxes of contemporary urbanism; reinforcing the locality and diversity inherent in the different communities, cities and regions it deals with; applying a broad view of sustainability; and concentrating on a high quality of construction through careful use of materials and detailing.

1   Tim Griffith

2   Tim Griffith

3   Tim Griffith

1 Austin Convention Center Expansion, Austin, Texas;
   400,000-square-foot addition completes renewal plan
   of derelict downtown district
2 Austin City Lofts, Austin, Texas; 82-unit mixed-use
   residential complex
3 Seton Medical Center Expansion and Renovation Austin,
   Texas; large surgery expansion and renovation to
   1970's hospital

● 400 West Cesar Chavez Street, Suite 500, Austin, Texas 78701 USA
Tel: +1 512 472 6721 Fax: +1 512 477 3211

LEERS WEINZAPFEL ASSOCIATES ARCHITECTS

marketing@lwa-architects.com www.lwa-architects.com

Leers Weinzapfel is a firm distinguished by an exceptional quality of design, founded on a commitment to the public realm and to the craft of building. The firm's work has been widely recognized in more than 40 national and regional awards by the profession, by exhibitions and lectures at numerous local and international schools of architecture, and by the architectural press in the USA, Europe, and Japan.

A commitment to an enriched modernism, closely fitted to the particular nature of the program and site context distinguishes the firm's design work. The design team approaches each problem with a clear set of core principles, a passion for material and detail exploration, and a desire to create meaningful places for social interaction. The result is a tailor-made response to each set of conditions, which conveys both conceptual consistency and specific character.

1   Anton Grassl

2   Chuck Choi

3   Chuck Choi

4   Chuck Choi

5   Alan Karchmer/Esto

1 Smith College Fitness Center, Northampton, Massachusetts; fitness center unites two existing gymnasiums
2 University of Cincinnati University Pavilion, Cincinnati, Ohio; new student services center
3 Blue Hill Avenue Youth Development Center, Boston, Massachusetts; new youth and community center
4 Mugar Center for the Performing Arts, Cambridge School of Weston, Weston, Massachusetts; center includes theater, performance, and classroom space
5 Harvard University Science Center Expansion, Cambridge, Massachusetts; additions to Josep Lluis Sert's 1970 original Science Center

● 280 Summer Street, Boston, Massachusetts 02210 USA Tel: +1 617 423 5711 Fax: +1 617 482 7257

LEIGH & ORANGE LTD.

info@leighorange.com.hk www.leighorange.com

Founded in Hong Kong in 1874, Leigh & Orange is a large, well-established, international architectural design practice offering high quality design and project management services, to major local and overseas clients on a wide range of building types, in both public and private sectors.

Services include architecture, interior design, urban planning and project management. The practice, which operates throughout China, East Asia and the Middle East, is certified under ISO 9001 and ISO 14001. Leigh & Orange operates an integrated quality management system covering quality, environment and safety.

The practice adopts an innovative design approach for all projects, incorporating the latest intelligent building ideas in addition to the green concepts of sustainability, energy conservation and minimal environmental footprint.

1   Lin Yan

2   Lin Yan

3   Jolans Fung

4   Eric Chan   5   Eric Chan

1 C.E.O. Building, Beijing, PRC
2 Beijing Lan Hua International Building, Beijing, PRC
3 Isola Bar & Grill, Hong Kong, SAR, PRC
4 Jeddah Riviera Mall, Jeddah, Kingdom of Saudi Arabia
5 Hong Kong Science Park Phase 2, Hong Kong, SAR, PRC

● 19/F East, Warwick House, TaiKoo Place, 979 King's Road, Hong Kong, PRC
Tel: +852 2899 9000 Fax: +852 2806 0343

LENHARDT LOLLI & RODGERS ARCHITECTS

www.LLRA.net

2   Gregory Benson Photography

3   Gregory Benson Photograph

1   Ruhi Vargha Photography

Lenhardt Lolli & Rodgers Architects (LLRA) is a full-service design firm providing comprehensive planning, architectural, and engineering services from programming through construction phase administration. The firm is committed to understanding the goals and aspirations of its clients and providing them with architecture that integrates their needs with the latest technology and design theory. These collaborations result in buildings that are as functional as they are aesthetically pleasing—on time and on budget.

4   Sabatino Photograph

The firm's partnership of Joyce Lenhardt, AIA, James C. Lolli, AIA, and Philip J. Rodgers, AIA, ensures that with every project one principal is the primary contact person and maintains crucial involvement among the core group supported by project architects, intern architects, design, and technical staff. The firm organizes a design team of appropriate consultants for each project. Along with consultants, LLRA represents an architectural/engineering design team of up to 40 people.

5   Gregory Benson Photography

1   Saint Luke Evangelical Lutheran Church, Devon, Pennsylvania
2   Cokesbury Village, Hockessin, Delaware
3   Meadowood Community, Worcester, Pennsylvania
4   Saint Joseph's University, Philadelphia, Pennsylvania; collaboration with Sabatino Architects
5   Simpson Gardens, Lansdowne, Pennsylvania

● 550 Pinetown Road, Suite 490, Fort Washington, Pennsylvania 19034 USA
Tel: +1 215 653 0935 Fax: +1 215 653 0938

LEO A DALY

info@leoadaly.com www.leoadaly.com

LEO A DALY is an internationally renowned architecture, planning, engineering, and interior design firm with corporate headquarters located in Omaha, Nebraska. The company's portfolio includes award-winning projects in 50 countries, all 50 states, and the District of Columbia in the USA. The firm currently employs more than 1200 architects, planners, engineers, and interior designers in 20 offices worldwide. It is consistently ranked in the top five largest architecture/engineering firms and top 10 interior design firms in the USA, and is listed among the top 20 global architecture firms.

LEO A DALY projects reflect imagination and intelligence, creating exceptional solutions that enhance the quality of the human experience and the environment. Current market sectors include health care, aviation, hospitality, and federal USA government.

LEO A DALY was founded in Omaha, Nebraska, in 1915 by Leo A. Daly, Sr. The firm is currently led by president and chairman Leo A. Daly III, FAIA, RIBA, RAIA.

1   Fu Xing

2   Maxwell MacKenzie

3   Robert Royal

4   Prakesh Patel

5   Stuart Woods

1 Haitong Securities Building, Shanghai, PRC; intelligent building mixing technology with fluid design
2 Pope John Paul II Cultural Center, Washington, DC; building paying homage to the late pope
3 Repsol YPF Research and Development Complex, Mostoles, Spain; laboratory and educational campus for petrochemical company
4 National World War II Memorial, Washington, DC
5 White Pond Resort and Training Center, Baiyangdian, Hebei, PRC; educational, recreational, and leisure facilities

● 8600 Indian Hills Drive, Omaha, Nebraska 68114 USA Tel: +1 402 391 8111 Fax: +1 402 391 8564

LEVIN & ASSOCIATES ARCHITECTS

blevin@levinarch.com www.levinarch.com

1   Alex Vertikoff

2   Alex Vertikoff

Levin & Associates Architects, the Los Angeles architecture firm founded in 1980 by Harvard-educated architect Brenda A. Levin, FAIA, has preserved and renovated Los Angeles' most beloved landmarks, including City Hall, Oviatt and Bradbury Buildings, Grand Central Market, and Wiltern Theater.

The firm's work also includes urban design and master planning (Barnsdall Park, Autry Museum, Oakwood School) and the design of new institutional, commercial and multi-family housing facilities (buildings at Occidental and Scripps Colleges; galleries at the University of California, Santa Barbara and The Huntington; housing at the Downtown Women's Center and Adams Congress Apartments).

The firm is currently working on the Griffith Observatory, Frank Lloyd Wright buildings at Barnsdall Park, National Center for the Preservation of Democracy, and Library Court. Levin & Associates has been honored and recognized by, among others, the American Institute of Architects, Urban Land Institute, City of Los Angeles, State of California, and Los Angeles Conservancy.

3   Lisa Romerein

4   Grant Mudford

5   Gary Krueger

1 The MaryLou and George Boone Gallery, The Huntington, San Marino, California; night view of restored carriage house
2 Johnson Student Center, Occidental College, Los Angeles, California; quadrangle plaza elevation of new addition
3 Los Angeles City Hall, Los Angeles, California; City Hall rotunda with restored chandelier
4 Bradbury Building, Los Angeles, California
5 Music, Dance and Athletic Center, Oakwood School, North Hollywood, California

● 811 West Seventh Street, Suite 900, Los Angeles, California 90017 USA
Tel: +1 213 623 8141 Fax: +1 213 623 9207

LEWIS / SCHOEPLEIN ARCHITECTS

mail@lewisschoeplein.com   www.lewisschoeplein.com

1   Lewis / Schoeplein

2   Art Gray

The partnership of Lewis / Schoeplein Architects was founded in 1998 by Toni Lewis and Marc Schoeplein, to produce environments that seamlessly combine beauty and functionality as an end product, using effective team relationships as a means to that end. Each project is seen as an opportunity to architecturally engage a unique social and physical context, accomplished though an interactive design process that encourages client participation.

In keeping with the partners' interest in architecture as it relates to the larger community, the firm's work includes a variety of project types, including fire stations, churches, community centers, offices, restaurants, apartments, and single-family homes. The partners each have backgrounds in some of Los Angeles' best known design firms, and are now being recognized on their own in national and international publications for work which is expressive and pragmatic, inspirational and humanistic.

3   Art Gray

4   Art Gray

5   Art Gray

1   Venice Japanese Community Center, Los Angeles,
California; new classroom and gymnasium building
2   Feminist Majority Foundation / Ms. Magazine,
Beverly Hills, California; main lobby
3   Feminist Majority Foundation / Ms. Magazine,
Beverly Hills, California; view from street
4   Kaplan Residence, Silverlake, California;
view from street below
5   Kaplan Residence, Silverlake, California; entry

●   10590 1/2 W. Pico Boulevard, Los Angeles, California 90064 USA
Tel: +1 310 842 8620   Fax: +1 310 842 8190

LEWIS.TSURUMAKI.LEWIS (LTL)

office@LTLwork.net   www.LTLwork.net

1   Michael Moran

3   Michael Moran

Lewis.Tsurumaki.Lewis (LTL) is an architecture and research partnership founded in 1993 by Paul Lewis, Marc Tsurumaki, and David J. Lewis. The firm has received numerous awards, including the Emerging Voice award from the Architectural League of New York, and was selected to exhibit work in the USA Pavilion at the 2004 Venice Architecture Biennale. LTL's work is contained in the permanent collections of the San Francisco Museum of Modern Art and The Heinz Architectural Center.

Paul Lewis is a fellow of the American Academy in Rome, winner of the 1999 Mercedes T. Bass Rome Prize in Architecture. He is the Director of Graduate Studies at Princeton University School of Architecture. Marc Tsurumaki teaches at the Columbia University Graduate School of Architecture and David J. Lewis is the Director of the M.Arch Program at Parsons School of Design.

2   Rudolph Janu

1 Fluff Bakery, New York, New York; stacked felt dining
   area with custom chandelier
2 Bornhuetter Residence Hall, The College of Wooster,
   Wooster, Ohio; entry courtyard with cantilevered
   study areas
3 Xing Restaurant, New York, New York; front bar and
   dining area with acrylic canopy
4 Ini Ani Coffee Shop, New York, New York; cardboard
   and steel volume with custom furniture

4   Michael Moran

● 147 Essex Street, New York, New York 10002 USA Tel: +1 212 505 5955 Fax: +1 212 505 1648

LHOAS & LHOAS

pablo@lhoas-lhoas.com   www.lhoas-lhoas.com

1   Lhoas & Lhoas Architects

Lhoas & Lhoas was established 1994 and specializes in the transformation of existing buildings in Belgium and France.

The firm defends the necessity to create contemporary architecture in an uninhibited and pleasant manner. Each project is considered differently, affirming a free attitude toward heritage, as well as generally trying to transcend the functional, technical, and economic data of the projects to give them extra dimensions.

2   Lhoas & Lhoas Architects

3   Lhoas & Lhoas Architects

4   Lhoas & Lhoas Architects

1 Les Grignoux, Movie Theater, Liége, Belgium; competition entry
2 Socialist Party Headquarters; Brussels, Belgium
3 Leo Burnett Advertising Agency, Brussels, Belgium; offices
4 Atomium Basement, Brussels, Belgium; competition entry

● 40 Avenue Montana, Brussels 1180 Belgium Tel: +32 023 720 875 Fax: +32 023 720 876

LINE AND SPACE

studio627@lineandspace.com www.lineandspace.com

1   Henry Tom, AIA

2   Henry Tom, AIA

4   Henry Tom, AIA

For 27 years, Line and Space has studied and perfected its understanding of the climate and the land. Extensive programming assists in defining the true needs of both the client and the site.

The firm's architecture shows reverence to the textures and forms of the fragile environment, recognizing the cooling effects of shade, shadow, and the efficient use of water and wind in harsh surroundings. Buildings take advantage of affordable native materials while stone, masonry, and stucco, are sensitively juxtaposed with wood, metal, and color. Such indigenous materials play an important role in the organic relationship that welds structure to the earth and how buildings that touch the sky contribute to their visual success.

Line and Space's projects demonstrate that architecture is like art—it should please the senses while uplifting the spirit.

3   Les Wallach, FAIA

1 Boyce Thompson Arboretum Visitor Center Superior, Arizona; stone veneer helps center grow from site
2 Arizona Sonora Desert Museum, Restaurant and Gallery Complex, Tucson, Arizona; natural materials strengthen the connection to the earth
3 Campbell Cliffs, Tucson, Arizona; residence is an extension of the land
4 Hansen Residence, Tucson, Arizona; entry approach with existing undisturbed natural vegetation

● 627 East Speedway Tucson, Arizona 85701 USA Tel: +1 520 623 1313 Fax: +1 520 623 1303

LINESYNC ARCHITECTURE

Julie@LineSync.com   www.LineSync.com

LineSync Architecture creatively expresses the desires and needs of its clients in spatial dimensions that invigorate and inspire. Each unique project manifests an aesthetic of self-definition derived from personal investigation, collaboration, and invention.

Whether grand or intimately personal, creating unique and rewarding spaces is the hallmark of the distinctive aesthetic that is LineSync Architecture.

1   Gary Hall

3   Joseph Cincotta

2   Luis Ruiz Matus

5   Julie Lineberger

4   Kersey

1 RG Niederhoffer, Capital Management, Inc., New York, New York; client entrance to trading floor, custom glass wall
2 Geodesic D'Home, Halifax, Vermont; personalized retirement Geodesic D'Home, inspired by R. Buckminster Fuller
3 Gate House Pool Grotto, Wilmington, Vermont; children's wading pool fountain alongside spa
4 Al Turki Enterprises Headquarters, Muscat, Oman; night lighting of national landmark
5 Strawbale Home, Wilmington, Vermont; entry into chiropractic office

● 14 Castle Hill, Wilmington, Vermont 05363 USA Tel: +1 802 464 2526 Fax: +1 802 464 8788

LIPPMANN ASSOCIATES

laa@lippmannassociates.com.au www.lippmannassociates.com.au

Ed Lippmann's work is intrinsically linked to the place and time in which he operates. His architecture is a response to its physical context—Sydney, Australia—the spectacular Asian/Pacific city where he grew up and is now established. His work is at the forefront of the search for appropriate technologies and in that respect, contributes to the global zeitgeist at the commencement of the 21st century.

Ed Lippmann acknowledges the influence of his modern heroes. Nevertheless, for him, modernism is not a fixed style or static dogma but rather a continuously evolving historical phenomenon affected by developing social, economic and technical conditions.

An appreciation and interpretation of site, whether it be that of a suburban dwelling or a public building in an urban 'conservation area', has led to the realization of projects considered by others to be merely a dream.

Lippmann Associates has been involved in a range of residential, commercial, retail, industrial and institutional projects in Australia, the USA, and Southeast Asia. The consistent ability to satisfy, and in many cases exceed, the client brief through an understanding of constructability, structure and aesthetics has led to Lippmann Associates' emergence as an innovative force in contemporary architecture.

A commitment to innovation, and the search for and implementation of fresh, viable and environmentally sympathetic solutions are the hallmarks of this organization.

1   Ross Honeysett

2   Ross Honeysett

3   Ross Honeysett

4   Ross Honeysett

5   Farshid Assassi

1 RTA Pedestrian Footbridge, Fairfield
2 Andrew 'Boy' Charlton Pool, Sydney
3 Tree House, Sydney
4 King George V Recreation Centre, Sydney
5 Cashman/Pickes House, Wombarra

● 570 Crown Street, Surry Hills, New South Wales 2010 Australia
Tel: +61 2 9318 0844 Fax: +61 2 9319 2230

LIPSKY + ROLLET

archi@lipsky-rollet.com   www.lipsky-rollet.com

Lipsky + Rollet specializes in educational and cultural projects. The firm is committed to the creation of spaces, specifically adapted to the transmission of knowledge and the discovery of new paths for intuition and invention.

Lipsky + Rollet defines architecture as the complex art of organizing matter and space in order to enhance life. The firm believes humanity has reached a crucial development phase where education and scientific research has become the key to the future of the world and its people.

The firm is currently working on a new campus in the center of the old town of Troyes and renovating a graphic arts college in Paris. The firm has been involved in cultural projects such as the construction of the new choreographic center in Montpellier and an industrial museum for Cristal St Louis.

1   Guy Depollier

2   Paul Raftery

4   Paul Raftery

3   Paul Raftery

1   ESISAR, Valence, France
2&3   The Grand Ateliers, Isle d'Abeau, France
4&5   University Library of Sciences, France

5   Paul Raftery

● 18, rue de la Perle, Paris 75003 France Tel: +33 1 48 87 16 33 Fax: +33 1 48 87 42 77

LONG & ASSOCIATES
ENGINEERS/ARCHITECTS, INC.

Lex@longandassociates.com   www.longandassociates.com

Long & Associates is the essence of a full-service firm. Established in 1974, the firm has matured with architecture leading the way to include planning, programming, project design, cost estimating, interior design, educational specifications, electrical engineering, mechanical engineering, plumbing design, structural engineering, speciality engineering, contract administration, construction management, and environmental engineering. The firm's greatest strength is its team diversity.

Service is the core of the firm's existence. It seeks a long-standing relationship with each of its clients and to provide service unmatched in the industry. One way this is accomplished is through team diversity. Long & Associates offers its clients one-stop shopping and responsibility, which cannot be matched through standard consulting practices. The firm works closely with its clients and has tailored its project management process to building consensus at every stage.

1   Red Kite Studios

2   Long & Associates

3   Red Kite Studios

4   George Cott

1 Liberty Middle School, New Tampa, Florida
2 Lake Buena Vista Palace Hotel, Lake Buena Vista, Florida
3 Bayshore High School, Bradenton, Florida
4 Recreation Sports Facility @ University of Florida, Gainesville, Florida
5 Hendry County Public Health Unit, Clewiston, Florida

5   Red Kite Studios

● 4525 S. Manhattan Avenue, Tampa, Florida 33611-2305 USA Tel: +1 813 839 0506 Fax: +1 813 839 4616

LORCAN O'HERLIHY ARCHITECTS

loh@loharchitects.com www.loharchitects.com

Lorcan O'Herlihy Architects (LOh/a) is an award-winning firm based in Culver City, California. LOh/a is creating a body of work that operates in high contrast to the formal spectacle and populist artifice prevalent today, experimenting with an architecture of removal. The work strips away the visual and spatial excesses of the 1980s and 90s to expose a purity and authenticity of construction and craft.

O'Herlihy's achievements—his devotion to his craft, and his dedication to building—have garnered him praise within the critical press and from his architectural colleagues. In over 22 residential and commercial projects, he has also brought simple yet challenging ideas to form. O'Herlihy has set out to bring relief to a culture saturated with images, advertising and artificiality. The result is a stripped-down approach to design that can be applied to almost anything: the city, a building, a park.

Previously, Lorcan worked at I.M.Pei and Partners on the celebrated Louvre Museum in Paris, and as an associate at Steven Holl Architects, where he was responsible for several projects including the award-winning Hybrid building in Seaside, Florida, which received a National Honor Award from the American Institute of Architects.

1   Marvin Rand

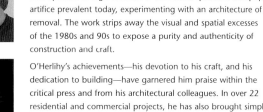

2   LOh/a

3   Conrad Johnson

4   LOh/a

1 Youbet.com, Woodland Hills, California; collaboration
   with Pugh+Scarpa Architects
2 Queens Museum, Queens, New York
3 R & B Delicatessen, Santa Monica, California
4 Shijiazhuang Planning Building, Shijiazhuang, PRC
5 Lexton MacCarthy House, Silver Lake, California

5   Douglas Hill

● 5709 Mesmer Avenue, Culver City, California 90230 USA Tel: +1 310 398 0394 Fax: +1 310 398 2675

LOUISE BRAVERMAN, ARCHITECT

louise.braverman@att.net

Louise Braverman, Architect is committed to creating projects that interweave light, texture, and the movement of the body through space into a poetic whole that speaks to those who inhabit it. Each project registers the impact of extensive individual research, a thorough investigation of site, program, and cultural milieu. That process is combined with a parallel exploration of innovative structural systems, technology and materials to create a design that strives to be elemental in both form and construction. Complementing the design capabilities of the firm, Louise Braverman, Architect provides a high degree of service and professionalism on all projects that range in scale, type, and complexity.

1   Scott Frances/Esto

2   Michael Moran

3   Louise Braverman

1 House at Ninevah Beach, Sag Harbor, New York; new waterfront house construction facing Long Island Sound
2 *Maps + Movies* at Grand Central Terminal, New York City; 42nd Streetfront light installation of NYC cinematic images
3 Chelsea Court, New York City; 18 units of SRO low-income housing
4 Renovated Apartment, New York City; stainless steel-fiberglass light/display operable room divider
5 *Poetic Light* at Grand Central Terminal, New York City; light/video installation of lines of poetry

4   Scott Frances

5   Scott Frances

● 16 East 79th Street, Suite 43, New York, New York 10021 USA Tel: +1 212 879 6155 Fax: +1 212 879 3492

LP ARCHITECTS

lp.architekten@aon.at   www.lparchitekten.at

LP architects defines quality with economy and ecology. Since its foundation in 2000, this young architecture office aims to offer an alternative to everyday alpine design, by providing innovative and modern architecture. Recent awards and prizes have encouraged the team to maintain its current direction.

1   Susanne Reisenberger

2   Susanne Reisenberger

3   Karl Schurl

4   Karl Schurl

5   Karl Schurl

1 Residential House Reisenberger, Bischofshofen, Austria; southwest elevation
2 Residential House Reisenberger, Bischofshofen, Austria; living room
3 Furniture Studio Reiter, Altenmarkt, Austria; entrance
4 Furniture Studio Reiter, Altenmarkt, Austria; information desk
5 Energy systems Kramer, Wagrain, Austria; office box

● Matthäus-Lang-Gasse 7, A-5550 Radstadt Austria
Tel: +43 6 4522 0429 Fax: +43 6 4522 0429 50

LS3P ASSOCIATES LTD.

johnmack@ls3p.com   www.ls3p.com

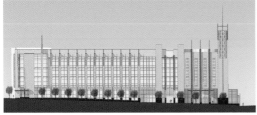

1   LS3P ASSOCIATES LTD.

3   LS3P ASSOCIATES LTD.

2   Risden McElroy

4   LS3P ASSOCIATES LTD.

At LS3P ASSOCIATES, LTD. the client is integral to the process. The practice is built around three tenets:

- SOLUTIONS THROUGH LISTENING is the LS3P way of attentively synthesizing the client's vision, goals and program into a project concept.
- SERVICE BY DESIGN is the consistent methodology of practice, project and quality control that ensures every LS3P service is delivered effectively, expeditiously and in accordance with the client's expectations for the successful delivery of the building experience.
- SUCCESS FROM EXPERIENCE defines the concentration of leadership, talent, expertise and enthusiasm that constitutes an LS3P studio. Unleashing the power of experts who practice with excellence, integrity, caring, respect and balance is what LS3P Associates is committed to providing for its clients.

The practice is based on an interwoven methodology that creates a great source of pride in its principals and associates. This total integration of talent and resources includes the clients who play a significant role in the LS3P process of total project delivery.

5   LS3P ASSOCIATES LTD.

Johnson & Wales University Academic Building
Charlotte Campus, Charlotte, North Carolina, USA
1   North elevation
2   View from Trade Street (rendering)
3   View from adjacent building
4   View from interior courtyard
5   Aerial view of interior courtyard

● 205 1/2 King Street, Charleston, South Carolina 29401 USA
Tel: +1 843 577 4444 Fax: +1 843 722 4789
112 South Tryon Street, Suite 200, Charlotte, North Carolina 28284 USA
Tel: +1 704 333 6686 Fax: +1 704 333 2926

LUBOWICKI • LANIER ARCHITECTURE

info@lubowickilanier.com   www.lubowickilanier.com

Lubowicki • Lanier was established by Paul Lubowicki and Susan Lanier in 1988. Together they have designed several award-winning residential and commercial projects. They have also lectured at Harvard University Graduate School of Design, The Architectural League of New York, The International Design Center of British Columbia, UCLA School of Architecture, the Los Angeles Forum, California College of Architecture at CALPOLY Pomona, Southern California Institute of Architecture, USC School of Architecture, Tulane University School of Architecture, and the University of Texas School of Architecture in Arlington.

Lubowicki • Lanier approaches the design of each project as an opportunity to bring together the program, site, context, and client, into a dynamic set of relationships. The creation of a common language integrates these relationships, so that each project's unique character reveals itself. Attention to these principles makes its practice of architecture an art.

1   Tom Bonner

2   Erich Koyama

3   Tim Street-Porter   4   Tom Bonner

1 Stringfellow Residence, West Los Angeles, California; contemporary addition to a 1920's Spanish-revival house
2 O'Neill Guesthouse, West Los Angeles, California
3 Hardy Residence, West Hollywood, California; contemporary addition to a 1930's Spanish-revival house
4 Chiat/Day Advertising Agency, Venice, California; interior
5 Angels and Franciscans: Innovative Architecture from Los Angeles and San Francisco, Gagosian/Castelli Gallery, New York City; exhibition design

5   Michael Moran

● 141 Sierra Street El Segundo, California 90245 USA Tel: +1 310 322 0211 Fax: +1 310 322 3620

LUNDBERG DESIGN STUDIO

info@lundbergdesign.com www.lundbergdesign.com

Lundberg Design specializes in high-end modern design, with no particular emphasis on any specific building type. While the core of the practice remains architectural, it remains committed to providing design at many levels and is often involved in product, landscape, graphic, and sculpture design. The firm's signature style is characterized by sculptural form, simply and elegantly executed, highlighting the importance of details.

In 1996, the firm designed Oracle CEO Larry Ellison's San Francisco residence and has continued to work for individuals and corporations seeking a reflection of their own individuality. Lundberg Design also has its own dedicated 4000-square-foot metal fabrication facility for custom design work and experimentation.

1   Cesar Rubio

2   Cesar Rubio   3   Cesar Rubio

1 Jackson Street Suite, San Francisco, California; floating translucent glass subtly defines areas for bathing, dressing, and sleeping
2 The Slanted Door Restaurant, San Francisco; natural materials expressed in an elegant, simple statement
3 Barnes Pool House and Pool, Calistoga, California; house and pool extend into forest beyond
4 Ninth Street Stair, San Francisco, California; materials and details form stair into sculpture
5 Lundberg Cabin and Pool, Sonoma, California

4   Cesar Rubio   5   JD Peterson

● 2620 Third Street, San Francisco, California 94107-3115 USA
Tel: +1 415 6951 1018 Fax: +1 415 695 0379

LUNZ PREBOR FOWLER ARCHITECTS

www.lunz.com

1   George Cott, Chroma, Inc.

Lunz Prebor Fowler Architects is an award-winning architectural firm headquartered in Lakeland, Florida. Its professional services consist of master planning, site analysis, programming, graphics, building design, interior design, space planning, facilities management and construction phase administration.

Edward G. Lunz, AIA established the firm in 1987, after concluding a successful 12-year partnership with the Smith-Lunz Group. The staff now includes principals Mr Lunz, Mr Daniel Fowler, AIA, and Mr Victor Prebor, AIA, and additional staff architects, a CADD manager, CADD operator/draftsmen, administrative staff, a construction coordinator and an interior designer.

Lunz Prebor Fowler Architects has successfully designed and managed over $200 million of work over the past five years. Its customer-oriented philosophy, attention to detail and quality of designs, have resulted in 90 percent of its clients becoming repeat or referred customers.

The office has a diverse portfolio of design experience that includes: corporate offices, government projects, higher education, master planning, design and renovations, recreation facilities, museums, fine arts centers, historic restorations and renovations, transportation/distribution facilities, and multiple-unit and single family residences.

2   George Cott, Chroma, Inc.

3   George Cott, Chroma, Inc.

4   George Cott, Chroma, Inc.

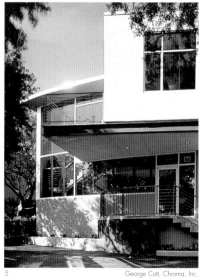

5   George Cott, Chroma, Inc.

1&2 Aviation Museum Pavilion, Lakeland, Florida; design of a sport aviation museum for experimental aircraft and memorabilia
3   Publix Charities Commons Residence Halls, Florida Southern College, Lakeland, Florida; design of three new campus residence halls
4   Polk County Science Building, Florida Southern College, Lakeland, Florida; refurbishment of a Frank Lloyd Wright-designed science building
5   Design Studio, Lakeland, Florida; renovation of multiple offices into a single design studio

● 58 Lake Morton Drive, Lakeland, Florida 33801 USA Tel: +1 863 682 1882 Fax: +1 863 687 6346

MACK SCOGIN MERRILL ELAM ARCHITECTS
FORMERLY SCOGIN ELAM AND BRAY ARCHITECTS

office@msmearch.com www.msmearch.com

Mack Scogin Merrill Elam Architects was formed in order to take full advantage of the complimentary skills and talents of the two principals. Projects by Mack Scogin and Merrill Elam have received more than 50 design awards, including six national AIA Awards of Excellence. Together they received the 1995 Academy Award in Architecture from the American Academy of Arts and Letters, and the 1996 Chrysler Award for Innovation in Design.

Mack Scogin and Merrill Elam have worked with some of the most prestigious and respected clients in the world. Project types include: office buildings, factories, warehouses, stadia, airports, health facilities, laboratories, houses, dormitories, classroom and studio facilities, campus centers, libraries, museums, galleries, exhibitions, and schools.

Current projects include: the Wang Campus Center and Davis Garage for Wellesley College in Massachusetts; the United States Federal Courthouse in Austin, Texas; a School of Architecture for The Ohio State University in Columbus, Ohio; a Music Library for The University of California at Berkeley in California; the Herman Miller Cherokee Operations facility in Canton, Georgia; the Gates Center for Computer Science for Carnegie Mellon University in Pittsburgh, Pennsylvania; and the Graduate Engineering Center for Clemson University, Greenville, South Carolina.

1   Timothy Hursley

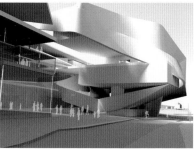

2   Mack Scogin Merrill Elam Architects

3   Timothy Hursley

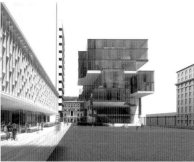

4   Mack Scogin Merrill Elam Architects

5   Timothy Hursley

1 Jean Gray Hargrove Music Library, University of
   California, Berkeley, USA
2 Fine Arts Center Invited Competition, University of
   Connecticut, Storrs, USA
3 Mountain Tree House, Dillard, Georgia, USA
4 Nexus Invited Competition, Barnard College, New York,
   New York, USA
5 Knowlton School of Architecture, The Ohio State
   University, Columbus, Ohio, USA

● 111 John Wesley Dobbs Avenue, Atlanta, Georgia 30303 USA Tel: +1 404 525 6869 Fax: +1 404 525 7061

MACKEY MITCHELL ASSOCIATES

kathy_u@mackeymitchell.com www.mackeymitchell.com

1   Barclay Goeppner

2   Alise O'Brien

Mackey Mitchell Associates is an award-winning professional design services firm, which provides services in planning, architecture and interior design. Founded in 1968, MMA is known for its client and user-oriented approach to the collaborative design process. The firm has a portfolio of wide-ranging projects from work in Saudi Arabia to major universities and *Fortune 500* companies.

For two consecutive years, the *St. Louis Business Journal* has chosen Mackey Mitchell as one of the area's Best Places to Work; in 2001, First Place Laclede Award for People Development, and in 2000, for Corporate Culture. In 1999, the firm was recognized by *Architectural Record* as one of 'America's Best Managed Firms.'

Mackey Mitchell Associates maintains a high-level of professionalism, approaching each commission with respect, integrity, and sincerity. The firm embraces design as an extension of the community, while expressing the client's spirit and intent. The firm recognizes that what is done today lays the groundwork for tomorrow.

3   Alise O'Brien

4   Sam Fentress

5   Sam Fentress

1 The Highlands @ Forest Park, St. Louis, Missouri
2 St. Mary's Emergency Room Addition, St. Louis, Missouri
3 McDonnell Pediatric Research Building, St. Louis, Missouri
4 Small Group Housing, Washington University, St. Louis, Missouri
5 Herman Stemme Office Building, St. Louis, Missouri

● 800 St. Louis Union Station, St. Louis, Missouri 63103-2257 USA
Tel: +1 314 421 1815 Fax: +1 314 421 5206

MADDOX NBD ARCHITECTURE

maddoxnbd@maddoxnbd.com   www.maddoxnbd.com

1   Jason Meyer (Brad Feinknopf studio)

2   Brad Feinknopf

3   Brad Feinknopf

4   Brad Feinknopf

5   Ed Knuff

1 Delaware County Administrative Services Building,
   Delaware, Ohio; Rutherford B. Hayes County Services
   Building
2 Ohio Department of Transportation Headquarters,
   Columbus, Ohio; new office headquarters for the
   Ohio Department of Transportation
3 Memorial Hall, Columbus, Ohio; former science
   exhibition hall renovated for government offices
4 Center for Technology and Learning, Columbus State
   Community College; new 3-story laboratory/classroom
   facility
5 Assumption Village, Assisted Living Residence, North Lima
   (Youngstown), Ohio; sitting area adjacent to dining room

'Specialized clients need specialized services.' This simple axiom
compels Maddox NBD Architecture to provide a higher level of
service to its clients.

Maddox NBD provides architectural services for a wide range
of building types. It creates responsive, award-winning designs,
ranging from corporate and public facilities, to educational
environments, to senior living communities, to interior spaces.

The firm delivers its services through a focused approach to its
target markets. Its goal is to provide its clients the specialized
services and attention their projects require.

Maddox NBD challenges its project teams to find innovative
solutions that meet and exceed clients' goals and expectations.
The staff of architects, planners, interior designers and landscape
architects form the firm's creative core.

Maddox NBD is positioned to successfully guide its clients
as markets continue to evolve into more specialized niches.

● 4945 Bradenton Avenue, Dublin (Columbus), Ohio 43017 USA Tel: +1 614 764 3800 Fax: +1 614 764 4522

MAK ARCHITECTS

design@makarchitects.co.uk www.makarchitects.co.uk

1   Niall Clutton

MAK Architects has been at the forefront of contemporary design, working predominantly in the world of interiors and architecture for 15 years.

As the practice has matured, it has undertaken an increasing number of interior design, new build and refurbishment projects to which it applies a keen commercial awareness and quality design.

MAK Architects continues to produce award-winning interiors for clients such as Valtech Ltd, which won the FX Award for Best Medium Office in 2001.

The firm has in place an innovative education and research program which involves a close working relationship with establishments including the D&AD, RCA Helen Hamlyn Centre for Inclusive Design, and Central St Martin's College.

As MAK Architects looks to the future and its range and experience of projects evolves, the firm will constantly challenge people's perceptions of what it does and will continue to apply commercial awareness with its innovative design quality to the benefit of its clients.

2   Chris Gascoigne

3   MAK Architects   4   Michael Frantzis   5   Todd Eberle

1   Deloitte Consulting, London; corporate interiors employing creative and innovative elements
2   M & C Saatchi, London; award-winning dramatic interiors optimizing calm and stillness
3   Lumina Building, London; elegant yet flexible mixed-use office development
4   Goswell Road, London; award-winning residential development created on a derelict site
5   St. Martin's Lane Hotel, London; modern hotel refurbishment in collaboration with Philippe Starck

●   33-37 Charterhouse Square, London EC1M 6EA UK   Tel: +44 20 7600 5151   Fax: +44 20 7600 1092

MANCINI•DUFFY

info@manciniduffy.com   www.manciniduffy.com

Mancini•Duffy has been in business over 80 years, established in 1920 as the corporation of Halsey, McCormack & Helmer, architects of such landmark buildings as the Williamsburgh Savings Bank. The company operates under the name Mancini•Duffy, which was formed when Ralph Mancini Associates (established in 1981) and Duffy Inc. (established in 1955) combined forces to concentrate on the unique aspects of interior architecture. The firm is led by an executive committee composed of Chief Executive Officer Anthony P. Schirripa, AIA; President Dina Frank, AIA, IIDA, and David C. Hannaford, CPA.

Headquartered in New York City, the firm maintains additional offices in Washington, DC; Mountain Lakes, New Jersey and Stamford, Connecticut, while the firm's alliance with San Francisco-based Richard Pollack & Associates allows it to provide service capabilities on the west coast. In 2001 it entered into an alliance with the major London-based architecture firm TP Bennett to form Architects and Designers International Alliance (ADIA), allowing it to provide design service to clients throughout Europe.

1   Cesar Rubio Photography

2   Peter Paige

3   Durston Saylor

4   Michael Moran

5   Peter Paige

1   Exigen, San Francisco, California; reception
2   Condé Nast Publications, New York City; executive reception area
3   Lincoln Financial Group, Philadelphia, Pennsylvania; conference room
4   Airbus North America, Herndon, Virginia; main reception area
5   Condé Nast Publications, New York City; reception for Allure magazine

●   39 West 13th Street, New York, New York 10011 USA   Tel: +1 212 938 1260   Fax: +1 212 938 1267

MANUELLE GAUTRAND ARCHITECTS

contact@manuelle-gautrand.com www.manuelle-gautrand.com

1 Gizmo

Manuelle Gautrand was born in 1961 in France and in 1985 was awarded a Diploma of Architecture. In 1991, the office of Manuelle Gautrand Architects was established.

Since that time, approximately 15 buildings have been completed by the firm. The practice has also received several prizes and awards, including the 'Albums de la Jeune Architecture' in 1992; nomination at the French awards 'First Work of the Moniteur' for a movie complex in Villefontaine in 1994; nomination at the international Dupont Benedictus Awards for 5 toll stations on the A16 highway in 1999; prize winner of the French awards 'A.M.O. 2000' for a catering project at Nantes airport in 2000; and French awards 'Delarue' of the Académie of Architecture in 2002.

Teaching appointments include: architecture consulting at MICQP (Mission for the Quality of Public Constructions) since 1999; teacher at the School of Architecture of Paris-Val de Seine since 1999; and visiting teacher at the 'Ecole Spéciale d'Architecture' in Paris, 2000–2001. Mr Gautrand has also been a member of the Renne architecture school's Administration Council since 2002.

2 Philippe Ruault

3 Philippe Ruault

4 Gizmo

5 Philippe Ruault

1 Citroën Showroom on Champs-Elysées, Paris, France
2 5 toll stations on A16 motorway, France
3 Theater and movie complex, Saint-Louis, France
4 F. Pinault Contemporary Art Foundation , Ile Seguin, Paris, France
   (competition)
5 National Drama Center, Béthune, France

● 36 Boulevard de la Bastille, F-75012 Paris, France Tel: +33 156 950 646 Fax: +33 156 950 647

MARBLE FAIRBANKS ARCHITECTS

info@marblefairbanks.com www.marblefairbanks.com

1   Arch Photo/Eduard Hueber

2   Marble Fairbanks Architects

MFA Marble Fairbanks Architects is an award-winning practice in New York City. Scott Marble and Karen Fairbanks began collaborating in 1990 and have worked on a wide range of residential, commercial, and institutional projects since that time. They have been teaching at Columbia University and Barnard College since 1989, investigating themes and issues present in their built work. Honors and awards received by MFA include a PA Award by *Architecture Magazine* for the Chicago Public Schools Design Competition, an *ar+d* Award for MoMA ticket booths, three projects selected as American Architecture Awards by the Chicago Athenaeum, numerous design awards from the New York Chapter of the AIA, and finalists in the Nara Convention Hall Design Competition. They were selected for Forty under Forty, both Emerging Architects and Young Architects by the Architectural League of New York, and Fellows of the New York State Foundation for the Arts. Their work has been exhibited worldwide and is included in the museum collections of the Museum of Modern Art and the Nara Prefectural Museum of Art.

3   Gregory Goode

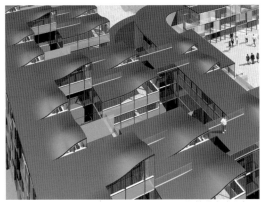

4   Marble Fairbanks Architects

5   Arch Photo/Eduard Hueber

1 Museum of Modern Art, New York; moveable ticket booths and entry lobby
2 Housing Ecologies, Arverne, New York; expanded roofscape
3 Tenri Cultural Institute, New York; visual continuities at classrooms
4 Chicago Public School, Chicago; building and landscape continuities, model
5 Open Loft, New York; sliding glass wall under skylight

● 66 West Broadway, #600, New York, New York 10007 USA Tel: +1 212 233 0653 Fax: +1 212 233 0654

MARIO BELLINI ASSOCIATI

mba@bellini.it www.bellini.it

Mario Bellini was born in 1935 and graduated from the Politecnico di Milano. His activities range from architecture and urban design to furniture and industrial design.

His fame dates from 1963 when he became design consultant and department head at Olivetti. He has since worked with a variety of firms in and outside Italy. Many of his designs are now in the permanent collection of the MoMA in New York, which honored him with a one-man show in 1987.

He has won eight Compasso d'Oro and many other international architectural awards. Since the 1980s he has worked chiefly as an architect in Europe, United Arab Emirates, Japan, USA and Australia. His competition-winning extension to the National Gallery of Victoria in Melbourne was recently completed.

An avid art lover and collector, he is also well known as an art exhibition designer. From 1986 to 1991 he was editor of *Domus*.

1
Antonio Tartaglione

2
Zabban

3
Mario Bellini Associati

4
Fregoso/Basalto

5
Yoshio Shiratori

1 Natuzzi Americas Headquarters, 1998, High Point, North Carolina, USA; new headquarters for a leading international furniture company
2 Milan Trade Fair, new fair district, 1997, Milan, Italy
3 Cultural Centre with public library and theater, 2001/in progress, Turin, Italy; international competition-winning project
4 International Exhibition and Congress Centre in the historical Park of Villa Erba, 1990, Cernobbio (Como), Italy
5 Tokyo Design Center, 1992, Tokyo, Japan; multistory building for furniture showrooms

● 4, Piazza Arcole, Milano 20143 Italy Tel: +39 02 5810 3877 Fax: +39 02 5811 3466

MARIO BOTTA ARCHITETTO

info@botta.ch www.botta.ch

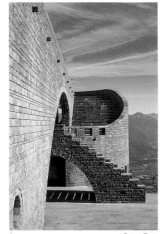

1   Enrico Cano

After an apprenticeship with the architects Carloni and Camenisch in Lugano, Mario Botta attended the Art College in Milan, then studied at the University Institute of Architecture in Venice. Directed by Carlo Scarpa and Giuseppe Mazzariol, he graduated in 1969. In Venice, he was given the opportunity to meet and work for Le Corbusier and Louis I. Kahn. Since 1970, he has designed buildings all over the world, including family houses, museums and churches. He teaches extensively, giving lectures and seminars in different architectural schools in Europe, Asia, and in North and South America. He was visiting professor at the Federal Polytechnic School in Lausanne in 1976, and at the Yale School of Architecture, New Haven in 1987. In 1983, he was appointed Professor of the Swiss Polytechnic Schools, and since 1996 has been Professor and mentor of the new Architecture Academy Ticino in Mendrisio, Switzerland.

His work has achieved international renown and numerous awards, including 'Merit Award for Excellence in Design' by the AIA for the Museum of Modern Art in San Francisco.

2   Ralph Richter

3   Pino Musi

4   Pino Musi

1 Chapel of Saint Mary of the Angels, Monte Tamaro, Ticino, Switzerland
2 Municipal Library, Am Königswall, Dortmund Germany
3 San Francisco Museum of Modern Art, Third Street, San Francisco, California USA; collaboration with HOK Inc.
4 The Cymbalista Synagogue and Jewish Heritage Center, University Campus, Tel Aviv, Israel
5 Watari-um Museum of Contemporary Art, Shibuya-ku, Tokyo, Japan; collaboration with Takenaka Co.

Portrait credit: Marco D'Anna

5   Pino Musi

● Via Ciani 16, 6904 Lugano, Switzerland Tel: +41 91 972 86 25 Fax: +41 91 970 14 54

MARK ENGLISH ARCHITECTS

inglese@aol.com

Mark English established Mark English Architects in 1992.

He received a Bachelor of Architecture degree from California Polytechnic University in San Luis Obispo and was awarded a Masters in Architecture from Syracuse University after studying in Florence, Italy. He became registered in California in 1987 and later practiced architecture at the renowned San Francisco firm House + House.

Since its founding, Mark English Architects has strived to produce spaces that enhance the lives of those who inhabit them and, as completed products, are exceptional examples of well-crafted residential and commercial architecture.

The process of design is one in which the owner's concerns and desires are of primary importance. As chief design lead on all projects, Mark English develops his clients' ideas about space and transforms them into reality. His responsibilities are comprehensive and do not conclude until the project becomes inhabited and every detail is accounted for.

Built projects include countless residences in San Francisco and throughout the Bay Area, as well as commercial projects such as restaurants, offices, product demonstration rooms, and entertainment spaces.

2   Alan Geller

3   Alan Geller

1   Claudio Santini

4   Claudio Santini

1   Buena Vista Residence, San Francisco, California; interior
2   Buena Vista Residence, San Francisco, California; façade,
3   Dirickson Residence Novato, California; interior
4   Robertson Residence, San Francisco, California; interior

● 250 Columbus Avenue, Suite 200, San Francisco, California 94133 USA
Tel: +1 415 391 0186 Fax: +1 415 362 9104

MARMOL RADZINER AND ASSOCIATES

info@marmol-radziner.com www.marmol-radziner.com

Leo Marmol and Ron Radziner formed their partnership in 1989 in Santa Monica, launching a unique design-build practice led by architects. Marmol Radziner and Associates currently employs over 40 architects, landscape architects, planners and interior designers, and a construction crew of over 40. Since its inception, the firm has developed a growing reputation for its innovative design approach, research, and precision in applying construction standards.

A breadth of projects distinguishes the firm, from small, intimately scaled residences to large public and urban projects for community based and non-profit organizations and schools. Design projects include new office spaces for ad agency TBWA\Chiat\Day in San Francisco, a preK-12 campus for The Accelerated School of Los Angeles, boutiques for Costume National and Chan Luu in Los Angeles, Tree People's Center for Community Forestry including an environmental learning center and conference center, Santos Plaza for special needs housing, and several residences for Tom Ford, former Creative Director of Gucci and Yves Saint Laurent.

1   Benny Chan

2   Benny Chan

3   Marmol Radziner and Associates

1 TBWA\Chiat\Day, San Francisco, California;
   renovation of a warehouse into an advertising office
2 Ward Luu Residence, Los Angeles, California;
   4,000 square-foot new residence with landscape
3 The Accelerated School, Los Angeles, California;
   urban K-12 school in South Central Los Angeles
4 Glencoe Residence, Venice, California; 2800 square-
   foot new residence with landscape

4   Benny Chan

● 12210 Nebraska Avenue, Los Angeles, California 90025 USA Tel: +1 310 826 6222 Fax: +1 310 826 6226

MARMON MOK

dror@marmonmok.com   www.marmonmok.com

Marmon Mok was established in 1953 in San Antonio, Texas and has grown into one of the most respected architecture/engineering firms in the southwest region of the USA with a staff that exceeds 60.

With more than 75 awards from the AIA and the construction industry, the firm has a strong reputation for award-winning designs and effective project delivery. The firm is organized into four studios to serve the specialized needs of both the public and private-sector clients

Marmon Mok regards the creation of architecture as a highly participatory process—one that is an intensive and ongoing collaboration of clients, architects, engineers, and contractors.

The firm's most significant projects include: San Antonio International Airport, Terminal 1, the 65,000-seat AlamoDome, Cancer Therapy and Research Center, and Security Service Federal Credit Union corporate headquarters.

1   Dror Baldinger

2   Dror Baldinger

3   Craig Blackmon

4   Craig Blackmon

1 Veterinary Hospital, San Antonio, Texas
2 Veterinary Hospital, San Antonio, Texas
3 Temple Beth El, San Antonio, Texas
4 San Antonio International Airport, San Antonio, Texas
5 Colonial Bank, Austin, Texas

5   Craig Blackmon

● 700 N. St. Mary's, Suite 1600, San Antonio, Texas 78205 USA
Tel: +1 210 223 9492 Fax: +1 210 223 2582

MARTE.MARTE ARCHITEKTEN ZT GMBH

architekten@marte-marte.com   www.marte-marte.com

1   Albrecht Immanuel Schnabel   2

Bruno Klomfar

3   Bruno Klomfar

Formed in 1993, Marte.Marte Architekten takes its inspiration from Heinrich von Tessenow's quote 'das Einfache ist nicht immer das Beste, aber das Beste ist immer einfach' (the simple thing is not always the best, but the best is always simple).

Marte.Marte specializes in residential and public architecture, and is currently completing an industrial building for the System Industrie Electronic AG in Lustenau. Its projects have been widely published in the magazines *architektur.aktuell*, Vienna; *a+u*, Japan; and *Wallpaper**, London.

4   Ignacio Martinez   5

Ignacio Martinez

1 Boathouse, Fussach, Austria
2 System Industrie Electronic AG, Lustenau, Austria
3 Extension and Chapel for Cemetery, Batschuns, Austria
4 Seewald, Furx, Austria
5 Residence, Dafins, Austria

● Totengasse 18, Weiler 6833 Austria Tel: +43 5523 52587 Fax: +43 5523 52587-9

MARTINEZ + CUTRI CORPORATION

www.mc-architects.com

Martinez + Cutri Corporation is a multidisciplinary firm whose practice is based on the concept that the design of forms in space should be generated by the context of their surroundings, while the principles of design should enhance our culture.

Since its inception in 1980, its portfolio of work has included educational facilities; mixed-use urban centers; convention and public assembly facilities; high density, mixed-use housing; luxury hotels and waterfront resorts; as well as industrial and R&D developments. These buildings and spaces are innovative while being cost-effective and within prescribed construction schedules.

The intent of Martinez + Cutri is to create good design, that is, to create spaces and structures which exhibit a timeless quality. Martinez + Cutri designs environments that are inviting regardless of typology and locale. It is the firms' contention that the vitality and beauty of the built environment plays a crucial role in creating a productive and healthy community and, as design professionals, they must assume responsibility for that role.

1
Jim Brady

2
Larry Bates

3
Jim Brady

4
Joe Cordelle, La Jolla Group

5
Jimmy Flucker

1 National City Adult Education Center, National City, California; 27,000-square-foot transit-oriented school
2 Southwestern College Masterplan, Otay Mesa, California; 40-acre, 10,000 student campus
3 Rancho Del Rey Middle School, Chula Vista, California; 132,600-square-foot facility for 1,400 students
4 Manchester Grand Hyatt, San Diego, California; 800-guestroom luxury hotel
5 VillageWalk, San Diego, California; 72-unit, mixed-use housing project

● 750 B Street, 1700 Symphony Towers, San Diego, California 92101 USA
Tel: +1 619 233 4857 Fax: +1 619 233 7417

MASAYOSHI SETOGAWA + ART–SESSION

post@rsession.com   www.rsession.com

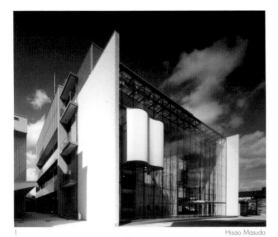

1

Hisao Masuda

After graduating from Kyoto University, Masayoshi Setogawa worked at the Architecture Bureau of Nippon Telegraph & Telephone Corporation (now NTT Facilities) for eight years before establishing ART–SESSION in 1988. Based in Kyoto, the firm's work includes private residences, multifamily housing, offices, and aged-care facilities throughout Japan.

Masayoshi Setogawa is currently an associate lecturer at Tokyo Denki University.

2

Hisao Masuda

3

Kei Sugino

4

Hisao Masuda

5

Hisao Masuda

1 Takii Seed Quality Control Center, Kyoto, exterior
2 Takii Seed Fukuoka Branch, Fukuoka, Japan; night view of slope with potted plants along glass façade
3 North-Cottage, Kyoto, Japan; housing for four
4 Kourien Residence, Osaka, Japan; living room facing the courtyard
5 Higashioji Residence, Kyoto, Japan; exterior

● AOI Building, 5F Takoyakushi-dori Karasuma-nishi-iru, Nakagyo-ku, Kyoto 604-8151 Japan
Tel: +81 75 251 1490 Fax: +81 75 251 1620

MASSIMILIANO FUKSAS ARCHITECT

office@fuksas.it m.fuksas@fuksas.fr www.fuksas.it

Massimiliano Fuksas was born in Rome in 1944, where he graduated in architecture from La Sapienza University in 1969.

In 1967, 1989 and 1993 he established practices in Rome, Paris and Vienna, respectively. In 1998 he received an award in recognition of his professional career at Vitruvio International a la Trayectoria in Buenos Aires.

From 1998 to 2000 he was director of the VII Biennale Internazionale di Architettura di Venezia, 'Less Aesthetics, More Ethics'. In 1999 he was awarded the Grand Prix d'Architecture Française, and the following year was appointed 'National Academic of San Luca and Commandeur de l'Ordre des Arts et des Lettres de la République Française'.

He has been a visiting professor at a number of universities, in Stuttgart, Paris, Vienna and New York and has a special interest in the study of urban problems in large metropolitan areas.

Among his latest projects are: Trade Fair Center, Milan; MAB mall, Frankfurt; Aquadeus water park, Salzburg; Erlangen Arcaden mall; Nardini headquarters, Bassano del Grappa; Twin Towers, Vienna; Ferrari SpA head office, Maranello; Italian Space Agency (ASI), Rome; Italia Congress Centre, Rome-Eur; and head office of Piemonte's Region, Turin.

1   A. Furudate

2   A. Furudate 3   A. Furudate

1–3 Twin Towers, Vienna, Austria;
      two towers for office use with
      entertainment center, cinema,
      restaurants and car parking
4&5 Peace Centre, Jaffa, Israel;
      commissioned by Shimon
      Peres, a home port for all
      sailors and a haven for
      the shipwrecked

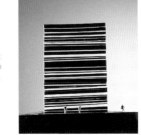

4   M. Mesa 5   M. Mesa

● Piazza del Monte di Pietà 30, 00186 Rome, Italy Tel: +39 06 6880 7871 Fax: +39 06 6880 7872
   85, rue du Temple, 75003 Paris, France Tel: +33 1 4461 8383 Fax: +33 1 4461 8389

MCA INTEGRATED DESIGN

mca@mcarchitects.it   www.mcarchitects.it

1   MCA

MCA Mario Cucinella Architects, founded in 1992, is a company with solid experience at the forefront of contemporary design and research. MCA has an integrated approach to design work, based on close collaboration with multidisciplinary consultants to create innovative and appropriate design responses for every project.

Sustainable building design and the rational use of energy are central concerns of MCA's work and research. The environmental quality of its designs is analyzed and developed using specialized software and testing models in order to produce buildings of architectural quality with state-of-the-art energy performance.

Mario Cucinella, founder of MCA, has 15 years experience as an architect and product designer. His work is internationally recognized and he has won many competitions and awards, including the prestigious Outstanding Architect Award 2004 by the World Renewable Energy Council. He graduated from the University of Genoa and worked with the Renzo Piano Building Workshop for five years. He teaches technology studio at Ferrara University and lectures regularly on his work in schools of architecture around Europe.

He opened a second office, MCA Integrated Design, with associate Elizabeth Francis in Bologna, Italy in 1999.

2   MCA

3   MCA   4   Jean de Calan   5   Jean de Calan

1 Bergognone 53, Milan, Italy; study model of new façade for a Milan office building renovation
2 Bergognone 53, Milan, Italy; computer rendering of internal court, Milan office renovation project
3 Ex casa di Bianco, Cremona, Italy; study model of façade for a palazzo renovation
4 Ferry Terminal Building, Otranto, Italy; main entrance and steps to roof terrace
5 Ferry Terminal Building, Otranto, Italy; view from northeast

● Via Matteotti 21, 40129 Bologna, Italy Tel: +39 51 6313 381 Fax: +39 51 6313 316

MCCULLOUGH MULVIN ARCHITECTS

macmul@eircom.net www.mcculloughmulvin.com

Christian Richters   2   Christian Richters

3   Christian Richters

Based in Dublin, McCullough Mulvin Architects is one of Ireland's most prestigious and award winning young architectural practices. Established in the late 1980s by Valerie Mulvin and Niall McCullough, it now includes a number of the country's best young architects.

The office has worked on major cultural projects like the Abbey Theatre, in the Temple Bar regeneration area (where the practice designed Temple Bar Galleries, Black Church Print Studios and the Music Centre) and in the recently completed Model Arts and Niland Gallery in Sligo. Other projects include new civic office buildings, including Dun Laoghaire-Rathdown County Hall and civic offices in Donegal and Sligo; a continuous thread of residential design in houses and apartments; and new libraries such as the Waterford City Library and the joint design for the Ussher Library in Trinity College (with KMD Architecture).

The practice tries to keep an open mind on how architecture might reflect thought about living and working in Ireland. Many of the projects are either in sensitive contexts and reflect a specific response to site and place or are modern interventions into existing buildings, an open-ended exploration of scale, materials and form.

4   Christian Richters

Christian Richters

1   Model Arts and Niland Gallery, Sligo, County Sligo
2   Sligo Courthouse, Sligo, County Sligo
3   Ussher Library, Trinity College, Dublin
4   Tubbercurry Civic Offices and Library, County Sligo
5   Dungloe District Offices, Dungloe, County Donegal

● 2 Leeson Park, Dublin 6, Ireland Tel: +353 1 497 2266 Fax: +353 1 497 9592

MCINTOSH PORIS ASSOCIATES

mporis@mcintoshporis.com www.mcintoshporis.com

1   Balthazar Korab

McIntosh Poris Associates provides architectural, interior, and urban design to institutional, commercial, and residential clients. Douglas McIntosh and Michael Poris, AIA, approach every project through close collaboration with clients, consultants, contractors, and associates.

The firm's goal is to transform cities and create interactive buildings, communities, and urban centers with architecture arrived at through vision and dialogue. They aim to affect how we perceive and interact at multiple scales through the transformation of buildings, sites, neighborhoods, and districts.

These talented architects have built more than 100 diversified residential, mixed-use commercial, institutional, and arts projects in Michigan, California, Connecticut, New York, Ontario, and Illinois. The firm designs what its founders call 'architecture that strives to create new relationships and meanings.'

Both principals received Bachelor of Science degrees in Architecture from University of Michigan. Poris earned a Masters of Architecture from Southern California Institute of Architecture (SCI-Arc); McIntosh received a Masters of Architecture from Yale University.

2   McIntosh Poris Associates

3   Balthazar Korab   4   Balthazar Korab   5   Laszlo Regos

1 Steinhardt residence, Birmingham, Michigan; modern home in a neighborhood of mostly traditional elements
2 Lafayette Park, Detroit, Michigan; new town homes complete urban mixed-use plan originated by Mies van der Rohe
3 Private residence, Bloomfield Hills, Michigan; the 9,000-square-foot, two-story house is designed in relationship to its landscape
4 Private residence, Bloomfield Hills, Michigan; interior elements are delineated in mahogany wood
5 Panacea nightclub, Detroit, Michigan; curved niches echo the building's historic exterior arches

● 36801 Woodward Avenue, Suite 200, Birmingham, Michigan 48009 USA
Tel: +1 248 258 9346 Fax: +1 248 258 0967

MCMANUS ARCHITECTS & CONSULTANTS

kevin@mcmanusarchitects.com.au   www.mcmanusarchitects.com.au

McManus Architects is a boutique firm, founded by Kevin McManus in 1987. Prior to establishing his practice, Kevin worked in London and Limerick (Ireland), as a government and airline architect. He is a graduate of Melbourne University with postgraduate study at RMIT University, Melbourne.

The firm provides a personal service, fast response and has on call various skilled personnel.

The office is centrally located in Melbourne and the firm carries out both metropolitan work and state-wide projects. Kevin has featured in several press articles and has also written articles on architectural matters.

Projects vary from low-rise commercial (three-story offices) to community (Doxa Youth Complex, police stations) and residential (single- and multi-unit housing).

The aims of the practice are the provision of detailed briefing, the exploration of all possibilities, and the last project leading into the next.

1   KMM

2   KMM

3   KMM

4   KMM

5   Max Loudon

1 Architect's Home, Maribyrnong River,
   Melbourne, Victoria
2 Birregurra Police Station, Victoria
3 Doxa Youth Complex, Malmsbury, Victoria
4 River House, Melbourne, Victoria
5 Office Building, North Melbourne, Victoria

● 331 Queensberry Street, North Melbourne, Victoria 3051 Australia
Tel: +61 3 9326 7997 Fax: +61 3 9326 7996

MDA JOHNSON FAVARO

jfavaro@johnsonfavaro.com   www.johnsonfavaro.com

MDA Johnson Favaro is dedicated to high quality, well-crafted buildings and plans that contribute positively to the larger social and physical environment through the integration of architecture, landscape, and urban design. In a time of excessive emphasis on specialization and isolation, it believes in the value of comprehensively interrelating these disciplines. The firm's work consists of a balance of architecture and urban design, but no matter what the starting point, the intent is to explore and enhance the uniqueness of place. Thus, although the principles remain constant, the particulars of any project may vary as they are always conditioned by local circumstance.

Established in 1989, MDA Johnson Favaro has since successfully executed over $400 million worth of construction projects. The firm utilizes research, innovative design and project management to meet project requirements and economics, as well as to achieve state-of-the-art technical excellence. Its Boston office is actively involved in all projects nationwide, with the Culver City office focusing on projects in the West and Pacific Coast. With the Southern California office, MDA Johnson Favaro is better able to maintain the close contact required with clients on the west coast from beginning to completion of the project.

1   Steve Johnson

2   Carlos Madrid

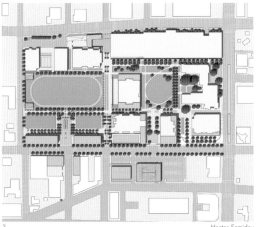

3   Hector Semidey

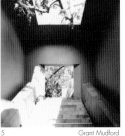

4   Steve Johnson   5   Grant Mudford

1   The Shops on South Lake Avenue, Pasadena, California; Building A @ Del Mar and Lake Avenue
2   LATTC/ Los Angeles Trade Technical College, South Campus Project, Los Angeles, California; grand entry at south campus
3   LATTC/ Los Angeles Trade Technical College, Campus Masterplan, Los Angeles, California
4   PMCA/ Pasadena Museum of California Art, Pasadena, California
5   Price Gallery, Los Angeles, California; entry court stair as seen from ground floor entrance

● 5898 Blackwelder Street, Culver City, California 90232 USA Tel: +1 310 559 5720 Fax: +1 310 559 8220

MECANOO ARCHITECTEN

info@mecanoo.nl www.mecanoo.nl

1   Christian Richters

2   Christian Richters

Mecanoo has produced several outstanding projects during its 20 years of existence. Director Francine Houben (1955) is opposed to too stringent interpretations of her professional area. For her, architecture is not only designing a building. The area of her attention is much wider: "Architecture is a combination of various elements, like town and landscape planning and interior design. Mecanoo's work is characterized by the integration of these disciplines".

In Mecanoo's designs technical, human and playful aspects are interwoven into one solution. Houben: "Architecture should touch the senses. Architecture can never be a purely intellectual, conceptual and visual game. What counts in the end is the interweaving of form and emotion."

With around 300 projects, over 100 realized, and various projects under construction or in preparation, the practice is very successful in the Netherlands and Europe. The concern for the expressive potential of space, form and material is combined with a reflective practice on the dialogue with clients and future users.

3   Christian Richters

4   DPI Animation House

5   Christian Richters

1 Maliebaan 16, Utrecht, The Netherlands; renovation and underground extension of an office villa
2 Chapel Saint Mary of the Angels, Rotterdam, The Netherlands; chapel with continuous wall and floating roof
3 Library, Technical University, Delft, The Netherlands; library of glass and grass with 1,000 workspaces
4 Montevideo, Rotterdam, The Netherlands; 152-meter tower for living and working
5 National Heritage Museum, Arnhem, The Netherlands; entrance building with interior museum and panoramic theater

● Oude Delft 203–2611 HD Delft, PO Box 3277–2601 DG Delft, The Netherlands
Tel: +31 15 279 8100 Fax: +31 15 279 8111

MEHMET KONURALP

konuralpm@superonline.com www.mehmetkonuralp.com

1   Mehmet Konuralp

Mehmet Konuralp was born in Istanbul in 1939. He studied architecture at the Architectural Association School of Architecture in London between 1960–65 and finished his studies in Urbanism at the Leverhulme Department of Planning and Urban Design of the same school in 1966. He returned to Istanbul in 1968 and worked in all fields of the profession, including architectural design, interior design, and contracting, as well teaching in various schools of architecture, in Istanbul and Bursa.

Among his major realized works are Istanbul Highways Zincirlikuyu Facilities, Ordu Sagra Facilities, A. Bristol Hospital, Sabah Media Plaza, ATV Television and Newspaper Center, and ATK Textile Factory. He has also realized many residential buildings and interior designs.

Mehmet Konuralp was one of the master jury members of the Aga Khan Architecture Awards during the 1993–95 cycle. His projects, as well as his professional contributions and lectures, are widely covered in national and international publications.

2   Mehmet Konuralp

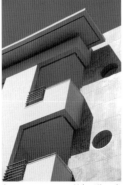

3   Mehmet Konuralp   4   Mehmet Konuralp

5   Mehmet Konuralp

1   ATK Textile Factory, Cerkezkoy, Turkey; production hall
2   Sabah Media Plaza, Istanbul, Turkey; entrance court
3   ATV Television and Newspaper Center, Istanbul, Turkey; façade detail
4   Residential Block, Istanbul, Turkey; façade detail
5   Sabah Media Plaza, Istanbul, Turkey; central court

● 9/4 Bostan Sokak, Tesvikiye 34367 Istanbul, Turkey Tel: +90 212 236 1681 Fax: +90 212 236 1680

MERKX + GIROD

arch@merkx-girod.nl   www.merkx-girod.nl

From its establishment in 1985, the Merkx + Girod portfolio has comprised many projects, including refurbishment, renovation, new development, expansion, exhibitions, styling and product development. Its work ranges from small residential assignments to strategies for large and complex interiors of public buildings in which the logistic and functional requirements are integrated in a spatial vision.

The firm's work involves groups of architects, interior architects, designers and graphic designers and is characterized by an analytical approach in which detail, quality and refinement are core values. This team approach, and the experience gained through many realized projects, ensures that the wishes and expectations of clients are met.

1   Roos Aldershoff

2   Roos Aldershoff

3   Roos Aldershoff

4   Roos Aldershoff

5   Roos Aldershoff

1   Young & Rubicam Advertising Agency, Amsterdam, Netherlands; refurbishment of head office and restaurant
2   Rijksmuseum, Amsterdam, Netherlands; "Masterpieces"
3   Lijnbaansgracht, Amsterdam, Netherlands; private house renovation
4   Interieur Biennale, Kortrijk, Belgium; imaginary materials library, trade-fair stand, 2004
5   City Hall, Alphen aan den Rijn, Netherlands; refurbishment of office and public areas

● Gietersstraat 23, 1015 HB Amsterdam The Netherlands Tel: +31 20 523 0052 Fax: +31 20 620 1329

MEUSER ARCHITEKTEN BDA

meuser@inter.net www.meuser-architekten.de

1   Atelier Kraut

Meuser Architekten BDA was founded in 1996 in Berlin, Germany. Since then, Natascha and Philipp Meuser have been working with a team of architects and editors at the interface between practice and theory. The firm carries out planning tasks in the areas of architecture, interior design, and furniture design. Natascha and Philipp also curate exhibitions and produce publications on architecture and urban planning in an international context. Meuser Architekten BDA has created projects for private clients and public contractors, both within Germany and abroad.

2   Hans-Peter Schmidt

3   Meuser Architekten BDA

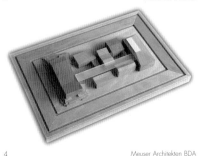

4   Meuser Architekten BDA

5   Matthias Broneske

1   Private Apartment, Berlin, Germany, 1996
2   Orientation System, Rhineland-Palatine, Germany, 2003–2006 (in cooperation with Adler & Schmidt Kommunikations-Design)
3&4 Sea Villa, near St. Petersburg, Russia, 2004–2007 (in cooperation with NPS Tchoban Voss Architekten)
5   ZDF Merchandising Shop, Berlin, Germany, 2000

● Meuser Architekten BDA, Schlueterstrasse 17, Berlin 10625, Germany
Tel: +49 30 3150 6315 Fax: +49 30 3150 6317

MHKW
MICHAEL H.K. WONG ARCHITECTS INC.

mhkw@mhkw.com   www.mhkw.com

1   MHKW

2   MHKW

Formed in 1976, MHKW is a coterie of ardent professionals committed to the ideals of architectural excellence. Since its inception, the firm's ongoing philosophy has been a practical yet sensitive approach to design, maintaining an innovative edge. The size of the firm remains such that personal participation, informed direction and professional dedication are maintained in all projects. The client is given personal attention to cover a wide range of services, by a core staff of highly skilled professionals. All design schemes promise to strike a balance between the client's demands and the complex restrictions of today's economic and political pressures.

Located in Toronto, the firm has been consistently expanding its clientele from North America and the Caribbean to Europe, Southeast Asia and China. Specializing in large-scale developments, MHKW has vast experience in commercial, residential, educational, institutional and recreational projects. Renowned for innovative design, MHKW is the winner of many international competitions.

3   MHKW

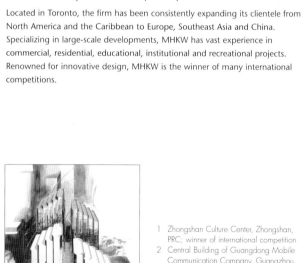

1 Zhongshan Culture Center, Zhongshan, PRC; winner of international competition
2 Central Building of Guangdong Mobile Communication Company, Guangzhou, PRC; winner of international competition
3 Mother Teresa Secondary School, Scarborough, Ontario, Canada
4 The Chongqing World Trade Center, Chongqing, PRC
5 Leadership Square, Oklahoma City, Oklahoma, USA; winner of international competition

4   MHKW   5   MHKW

● 878 Yonge Street, 4th Floor, Toronto, Ontario M4W 2J1 Canada Tel: +1 416 921 2331 Fax: +1 416 921 2336

MICHAEL DAVIES ASSOCIATES

design@mdassociates.com.au www.mdassociates.com.au

Established in 1975, Michael Davies Associates Pty Ltd provides the complete range of professional architectural services for small and large-scale projects: from initial feasibility study and site selection, through planning, design and documentation to construction and fitout. Over time the company's clients have varied significantly, from major builders and developers to local and state government agencies. In recent years, the practice has built upon Michael Davies' personal interest in aquatic centers and has developed a strong reputation for being at the forefront of design of this exciting and complex building type.

Michael Davies Associates endeavors to continually improve the service it provides to its clients in an ever-changing and increasingly competitive environment. MDA not only seeks to fulfil the design brief but also to make proactive contributions to the total success of each project. MDA has the people, the management skills and the technology to produce exceptional results on time and on budget.

In early 2003, MDA acquired the practice of Tompkins Shaw Evans Architects. Since its inception in 1890, this award-winning company has been responsible for many significant projects, both within Australia and internationally. The experience of the two companies is complementary and their combined resources are substantial, forming an organization capable of providing services to clients worldwide in any field of architectural practice.

1   Brett Boardman, Photographer

2   Brett Boardman, Photographer

3   Brett Boardman, Photographer   4   Brett Boardman, Photographer

1 Lane Cove Aquatic Leisure Centre, Lane Cove, New South Wales; indoor aquatic and leisure centre
2 Cabarita Ferry Wharf, Cabarita, New South Wales; transportation infrastructure: ferry wharf
3 Michael Davies Associates Offices, 49 York Street, Sydney, New South Wales; commercial interior fitout
4 Blacktown Olympic Centre, Aquilina Reserve, Rooty Hill, New South Wales; NSW state softball centre, baseball centre, athletics facilities
5 Auburn Civic Precinct, Queen and Susan Streets, Auburn, New South Wales; police command, council offices, central library, community facilities

5   Brett Boardman, Photographer

● Level 12, 49 York Street, Sydney, New South Wales 2000 Australia
Tel: +61 2 9262 6277 Fax: +61 2 9262 6369

MICHAEL ELLIS ARCHITECTS

michael@mearchitects.com.au www.mearchitects.com.au

Michael Ellis Architects provides dynamic architectural design and planning solutions for its clients. Its main activities are multi-unit developments, new residential buildings, and alterations to existing residences. The firm is committed to personal responsibility and innovative, technically inspired creativity that fashions architecture out of considered space.

1 YQ Photography 2 Michael Ellis Architects

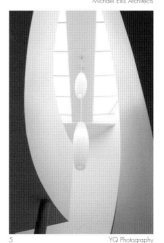

3 YQ Photography 4 YQ Photography 5 YQ Photography

Thornbury Residence, Melbourne, Victoria
1 Rear elevation highlighting spotted gum timber cladding
2 Angled bay window from first-floor master bedroom
3 Staircase and skylight detail
4 Staircase adjoining meals area
5 View from underneath staircase

● 1/171 Moray Street, South Melbourne, Victoria 3205 Australia
Tel: + 61 3 9696 9592 Fax: + 61 3 9696 9593

MICHAEL GRAVES & ASSOCIATES

info@michaelgraves.com www.michaelgraves.com

1   Tim Hursley

2   Daria Scagliola & Stijn Brakkee

Michael Graves & Associates' unique international practice encompasses planning, architecture, and interior design, and with its sister company Michael Graves Design Group, integrates those disciplines with product design and graphic design. Noted for design originality as well as functional innovation, the firms' influential designs infuse modern aesthetics with humanism.

Since its founding in 1964 by the renowned American architect, Michael Graves, FAIA, the firm has designed more than 300 buildings worldwide, including large-scale masterplans, mixed-use projects, corporate headquarters, offices, hotels, resorts, restaurants, retail stores, civic, and recreational projects.

More than 175 awards for design excellence have been won by the firm. Michael Graves was the recipient of the 1999 National Medal of Arts, and the 2001 Gold Medal of the American Institute of Architects.

3   Toyota Photo Studio

4   Andrew Lautman

5   John Donat

1 The Denver Central Library; Western History Reading Room
2 'Castalia', Headquarters for the Ministry of Health and Sport, The Hague, The Netherlands; recladding and renovation of an existing 1960s tower
3 Fukuoka Hyatt Regency Hotel and Office Building, Fukuoka, Japan; view from park
4 International Finance Corporation of the World Bank, Washington, DC; view from Washington Circle
5 Hyatt Regency Taba Heights Hotel, Taba Heights, Egypt; view from lagoon toward guestrooms

Portrait credit: Bill Phelps

● 341 Nassau Street, Princeton, New Jersey 08540 USA Tel: +1 609 924 6409 Fax: +1 609 924 1795

MIROGLIO ARCHITECTURE + DESIGN

Info@madarchitects.com www.madarchitects.com

1   Joel Gardner Photography

Miroglio Architecture + Design (M.a.+d), founded in 1993, challenges conventional thought about the genesis of built form. Its work has been recognized for innovative solutions to a variety of design challenges, including residential, commercial, and institutional buildings, interiors, furniture, and lighting.

Joel Miroglio, principal and founder of M.a.+d, graduated *summa cum laude* from Cal Poly University in San Luis Obispo, California, and obtained a Master of Architecture degree at Yale University, where he was awarded a graduate fellowship for a year of study in Rome, Italy.

Recently named one of the top 50 design firms in the world by *VM+SD* magazine, and one of the world's 12 most exciting design firms by *DDI* magazine, M.a.+d.'s projects and drawings have been featured in numerous other national and international publications. In total, M.a.+d. has received more than 22 international design awards, including an AIA award.

2   Joel Gardner Photography

3   Joel Gardner Photography

4   Joel Gardner Photography

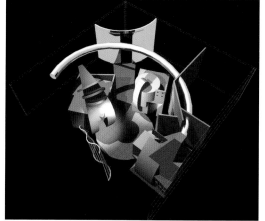

5   Miroglio Architecture + Design

1   Futuretronics, Orlando, Florida
2   Piazza Quercia, Yountville, California
3   Napa Community Bank Building, Napa, California
4   Patronik Designs Jewelry Gallery, Burlingame, California
5   Freemerchant.com Corporate Headquarters, Emeryville, California

●   381 Orange Street, Suite C, Oakland, California 94610 USA   Tel: +1 510 891 9145   Fax: +1 510 891 9107

MITCHELL/GIURGOLA ARCHITECTS, LLP

www.mitchellgiurgola.com

1   Jeff Goldberg/Esto

2   Jock Pottle/Esto

3   Jeff Goldberg/Esto

4   Jeff Goldberg/Esto

5   Mitchell/Giurgola Architects, LLP

Mitchell/Giurgola is committed to the belief that architecture is capable of enriching the daily experience. The firm's practice is a humanist one dedicated to the creation of comfortable, accommodating, enlightened, and efficient spaces appropriate to their function.

Good design is not a mysterious enterprise, but rather, a product of good listening, responsive planning, and close working relationships between designers and their clients. Mitchell/Giurgola's design approach is founded on the premise that building organization is derived from a precise interpretation of program and the careful calibration and integration of form to its surroundings. Professional services include masterplanning and urban design; research and programming; new buildings, additions, and renovations; interiors and graphic design.

1 Virginia Air and Space Center/Hampton Roads History Center, Hampton, Virginia; east façade
2 Joan and Joel Smilow Research Center, New York University, New York, New York; model view from FDR Drive
3 Applied Technology Center, Onondaga Community College, Syracuse, New York; view from west
4 Chancellors Hall, Southampton College, Long Island University, Southampton, New York; academic wing (left) and radio station (behind trees)
5 Patuxent River Naval Air Museum and Visitors' Center, Lexington Park, Maryland; entry view

● 170 West 97th Street, New York, New York 10025-6492 USA Tel: +1 212 663 4000 Fax: +1 212 866 5006

MITSURU SENDA + ENVIRONMENT DESIGN INSTITUTE

www.ms-edi.co.jp

Mitsuru Senda is a professor of the Tokyo Institute of Technology, and the honorary president of the Environment Design Institute (EDI) in Tokyo, Japan.

For the past 35 years he has specialized in designing play structures and play environments for children. He has won several design awards was awarded a doctorate in 1982 with his thesis entitled "The Research of the Structure of Children's Play Environment".

He states, "specialized design categories such as cities, buildings, landscape, play equipment, and interiors should not be designed separately; they must be designed totally. It is the environmental design". Based on this policy, when he designs a space or area, he values the story—such as history, life, animals, and people—being there, and he introduces himself as "the environment architect". His design policy has been explored in several publications, including *Design of Children's Play Environments*, *Play Space for Children*, and *Play Structure*.

1   Mitsuru Senda + Environment Design Institute

2   Mitsuru Senda + Environment Design Institute

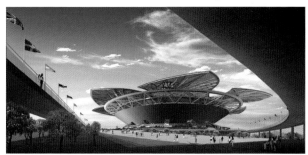

3   Mitsuru Senda + Environment Design Institute

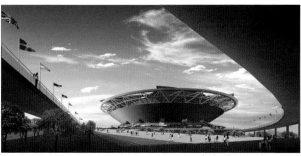

4   Mitsuru Senda + Environment Design Institute

Shanghai Qi Zhong Forest Sports City Tennis Center, Shanghai, PRC
1&4   Bird's-eye view of closed roof
2&3   Bird's-eye view of open roof

●   5-12-22, Roppongi, Minato-ku, Tokyo 106-0032 Japan   Tel: +81 3 5575 7171   Fax: +81 3 5562 9928

MONTALBA ARCHITECTS, INC.

david@montalbaarchitects.com   www.montalbaarchitects.com

1   Dominique Vorillon

2   Dominique Vorillon

Montalba Architects, Inc. is an award-winning practice, producing select architecture and urban design related projects in the USA and Europe. Projects emphasize conceptual experience, by creating environments that are both socially responsive and aesthetically progressive. The forces of volumetric landscapes, material integrity, the sculpting of natural light, and the purity of spatial volumes create solutions to pragmatic requirements of client, constructability, and context.

The depth of its work, innovative perspective, and collaboration with the client, highlight Montalba Architects' emphasis as a design-oriented architectural practice. Montalba Architects has compiled a prestigious and diverse collection of projects ranging in scale from residential homes, retail and commercial office interiors, to mixed-use building and master planning projects.

3   MA Inc. & Sharc

4   John Linden

1&2   Hazen Pool Pavilion, Beverly Hills, California
   3   North Beach House, Hobe Sound, Florida
   4   Monique L'Huillier, Beverly Hills, California
   5   OFW Duplex, Marina Del Rey, California

5   MA Inc.

● 451 San Vicente Boulevard, Suite 16, Santa Monica, California 90402 USA
Tel: +1 310 450 4054 Fax: +1 310 395 8623

MOORE RUBLE YUDELL
ARCHITECTS & PLANNERS

info@mryarchitects.com www.moorerubleyudell.com

1   Moore Ruble Yudell

2   Moore Ruble Yudell

Since its foundation in 1977, Moore Ruble Yudell has earned an international reputation based on a commitment to humanistic principles and thoughtful development of unique solutions to an extraordinary range of places and projects. Under the leadership of partners John Ruble, FAIA and Buzz Yudell, FAIA, the firm has built a diverse portfolio that embraces the critical concerns of community, identity, and place.

With the addition of six new principals in 2004, Moore Ruble Yudell continues the legacy of inclusion of a broad community of clients and colleagues, lending vitality and authenticity to the design process, and ultimately enriching the quality and meaning of each work. The firm has received numerous national and international awards for design excellence, and in 1992 was honored by the California Council of the AIA as Firm of the Year.

3   Werner Huthmacher   4   Allan Karchmer   5   Art Gray

1 Chun Sen Bi An Masterplan and Housing, Chongqing, PRC
2 Garden Theater, Glorya Kaufman Hall, University of California, Los Angeles
3 Tango, Bo01 Exhibition Housing, Malmö, Sweden
4 Joseph A Steger Student Life Center, University of Cincinnati, Cincinnati, Ohio
5 Residence, Woodside, California

● 933 Pico Boulevard, Santa Monica, California 90405 USA Tel: +1 310 450 1400 Fax: +1 310 450 1403

MORPHOSIS
studio@morphosis.net   www.morphosis.net

1   Morphosis

2   Morphosis

Morphosis was founded in 1972 to develop an
architecture that would eschew the normal bounds
of traditional forms and materials and surpass the
limiting dualism of modernism and postmodernism.
Growing steadily, the firm is currently comprised
of 40 architects and designers, directed by Thom
Mayne, the 2005 Pritzker Prize Laureate, who
remains committed to the practice of architecture
as a collective enterprise. The firm's objective is to
develop a critical practice where creative output
engages the contemporary discourse of design.

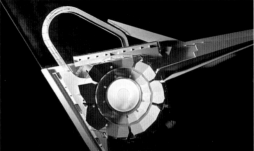
3   Morphosis

4   Farshid Assassi

5   Morphosis

1&2   CALTRANS District 7 Headquarters, Los Angeles, California;
      new headquarters for the California Department of Transportation
3   Palenque at Centro JVC, Guadalajara, Mexico, Consulting Architect:
      Estudio Esteban Cervantes; multiple-use, open-air arena
4   Tsunami, Las Vegas, Nevada; folded walls and angled ceilings define
      Asian grill
5   World Trade Center site proposal, New York, New York; a 1,300-foot
      communication tower and a skyscraper on its side accommodating
      commercial office space

● 2041 Colorado Avenue, Santa Monica, California 90404 USA Tel: +1 310 453 2247 Fax: +1 310 829 3270

MORRIS ARCHITECTS

www.morrisarchitects.com

1   Aker Zvonkovic Photography

2   Raymond Martinot, Martinot Photo Studio

Morris Architects was established in Houston, Texas in 1938. The firm's professional practice is international with projects and registration in 23 US states and work in the Caribbean, Central America, Europe, Mexico, South America, and the Pacific Rim. The firm provides comprehensive architecture and interior design services, masterplanning, programming, landscape architecture, and environmental graphic design services.

Morris Architects is organized into seven design studios, each dedicated to a designated area of focus: Civic, Corporate, Education, Entertainment, Healthcare, Hospitality, and Performing Arts. In addition to Houston, offices are located in Orlando, Florida and Los Angeles, California. During the past five years, over $4 billion worth of projects has been completed worldwide.

4   Hedrich-Blessing

3   Ward Grafton, Morris Architects

5   Aker Zvonkovic Photography

1 Moody Gardens, Galveston, Texas; aerial view

2 Ocean Walk Resort, Daytona Beach, Florida; resort exterior

3 Thornton Park Central, Orlando, Florida; exterior façade of mixed-use facility

4 Denton A. Cooley Building at St. Luke's Episcopal Hospital for The Texas Heart Institute, Houston, Texas; building exterior

5 St. Cyril of Alexandria Church, Houston, Texas; baptismal font and altar

● 3355 W. Alabama, Suite 200, Houston, Texas 77098 USA Tel: +1 713 622 1180 Fax: +1 713 622 7021

MOSHE SAFDIE, FAIA

msafdie@msafdie.com   www.msafdie.com

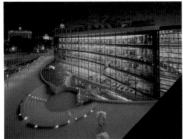

1   Timothy Hursley

Boston-based Moshe Safdie heads Moshe Safdie and Associates, an internationally renowned architecture and urban design firm with branch offices in Toronto and Jerusalem. Beginning with Habitat '67, his seminal experimental housing project for Montreal's Expo, Safdie has contributed meaningfully to almost every building type: museums, libraries, performing arts centers, government buildings, airports, houses, and the realization of entire cities.

Safdie has served as Director of Urban Design and Ian Woodner Professor of Architecture and Urban Design at the Harvard Graduate School of Design, in addition to teaching at various other universities. He is the author of several books on architecture and urban planning, most recently *The City After the Automobile.* Among Safdie's numerous awards and honorary degrees are the Companion Order of Canada and the Gold Medal of the Royal Canadian Institute of Architects.

Significant works include the National Gallery of Canada in Ottawa, the Exploration Place Science Center and Children's Museum in Wichita, Kansas; the Peabody Essex Museum in Salem, Massachusetts; the Salt Lake City Main Public Library in Salt Lake City, Utah; and the Yad Vashem Holocaust Museum in Jerusalem, Israel.

2   Timothy Hursley

3   Timothy Hursley

4   Timothy Hursley

5   Timothy Hursley

Salt Lake City Public Library, Salt Lake City, Utah
1   Library at night
2   Urban Room
Peabody Essex Museum, Salem, Massachusetts
3   Atrium
Yad Vashem Museum, Jerusalem, Israel
4   The triangular spine
5   Aerial view
Portrait credit: Timothy Hursley

● 100 Properzi Way, Somerville, Massachusetts 02143 USA
Tel: +1 617 629 2100 Fax: +1 617 629 2406

MOTOMU UNO + PHASE ASSOCIATES

phase-a@pk.highway.ne.jp http://home10.highway.ne.jp/phase-a/

1   Phase Associates

Motomu Uno has designed urban architecture that considers the relationship between architecture and city in contemporary Japan and Asia since he was a student at the University of Tokyo. In 1985, he established Phase Associates, collaborating with Akihiro Takeuchi, who had previously worked for Tadao Ando. Keizo Ikemura joined the office as a partner in 1999 after returning from New York.

Based in Tokyo, the firm designs residences, office buildings, new township housing, cinema complexes, facilities such as a station plaza at a traffic junction, furniture and interiors. Seeking new technological aesthetics, the firm focuses on urban context and interaction between architecture and landscape.

2   Nobuaki Nakagawa

Futuristic urban architectural projects such as 'Tokyo 2001' and 'Super Arch Structure for Tokyo' by Motomu Uno and others have been very influential in the Japanese architectural scene. Currently on the drawing board is a sustainable and progressive new town project in a special development district in China.

1   Yotsuya Temporary Office, Tokyo, Japan; temporary office with light and transparent structure
2   Villa Fujii, Nagano, Japan; weekend house of light structure for family and friends

● Apt #601, 3-4-29, Motoazabu, Minato-ku, Tokyo 106-0046 Japan
Tel: +81 3 5466 0451 Fax: +81 3 5466 0461

MURAMATSU ARCHITECTS

m-arch@netlaputa.ne.jp www.japan-architects.com/muramatsu-architects/

1

Motoyasu Muramatsu

Motoyasu Muramatsu founded Muramatsu Architects as a design-oriented office in Tokyo in 1993. The firm has completed various public and private works, and has extensive experience in aged-care facilities, residential projects, and furniture design. Other projects include educational, medical, religious, and commercial facilities, offices, museum, and aquariums. Muramutsu Architects establishes a beautiful presence in the environment, and evokes a balmy atmosphere, whether in the city, suburb, or countryside.

The firm aims to penetrate into the relationship between people and environments, to convert those invisible relationships into tangible forms, by creating architectural serial spaces, places, and times that establish these relationships.

2   Nacasa & Partners Inc

3   Nacasa & Partners Inc

1 Residence, Kanagawa, Japan; floating roof
  above the ground
2 MILLION 13th: Pachinko Parlor, Tokyo,
  Japan; luminous glass box rises in dusk
3 Aged-Care Facility, Wakayama, Japan;
  north façade faces the ocean
4 Aged-Care Facility, Wakayama, Japan;
  south façade
5 Aged-Care Facility, Wakayama, Japan;
  west wing extending to south toward ocean

4   Nacasa & Partners Inc

5   Nacasa & Partners Inc

● 5-29-20 Higashinakano Nakano-ku, Tokyo 164-0003 Japan
Tel: +81 3 3362 1915 Fax: +81 3 3362 1921

MURMAN ARKITEKTER

hans@murman.se www.murman.se

1   Hans Murman

2   Åke E-son Lindman

Murman Arkitekter was established in 1985 and today has a staff of 20. The office specializes in the design and planning of offices, retail sites, hotels, restaurants, residential buildings, student dwellings, ski lodges, interiors and furniture design.

In recent years, most of the office's work has been the result of architectural competitions. Projects during 2004 included the new Swedish office for Pfizer, and a residential building and student dwelling in the center of Stockholm.

New head offices for companies such as Scania in Södertälje, Intentia, EF, OM Group, and AP fastigheter in Stockholm, have also recently been refitted by Murman Arkitekter, as was the new press center for the Swedish Government in Stockholm.

3   Åke E-son Lindman

5   Åke E-son Lindman

1 Sturegallerian, Stockholm; shopping mall with a glass atrium over a square
2 The Boston Consulting Group, Stockholm; interior design and refurbishment of a building from 1750
3 Villa in Saltsjöbaden, Stockholm; an L-shaped addition and swimming pool; façade panel of oak
4 VM-huset, Åre, Sweden; administrative office for the 2007 Alpine World Ski Championships
5 Sånga-Säby Courses & Conferences, Ekerö, Stockholm; a low-energy, FCS-certified, wooden building

4   Hans Murman

● Renstiernas Gata 12, Stockholm 116 28 Sweden Tel: +46 8 702 64 50 Fax: +46 8 702 64 99

MURRAY O'LAOIRE ARCHITECTS

mail@dublin.murrayolaoire.com   www.murrayolaoire.com

1   Ros Kavanagh

2   MŌLA

Murray O'Laoire Architects employs more than 190 people in five offices in Ireland, Russia, and Poland. It offers architectural, interior and urban design services, and specialist skills in areas such as healthcare, education, housing, retail, and offices.

MOLA's belief in the art of architecture and urban design as a vital ingredient in all our lives is at the heart of its professional commitment. Client satisfaction is foremost on its agenda and the firm seeks to resolve their needs with creative, appropriate and cost-effective designs, rooted in cultural and social contexts.

The quality of the firm's work is reflected in the many awards it has received over 26 years, including the highest award of the Royal Institute of the Architects of Ireland.

3   Ros Kavanagh

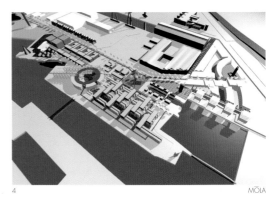

4   MŌLA

1   Galway/Mayo Institute of Technology, Learning Resource Center, Galway, Ireland
2   Cork School of Music, Cork, Ireland; first public-private partnership school for the Department of Education and Sciences in Ireland
3   Belvedere College, Dublin, masterplan for a prestigious 2nd-level institution on a confined inner-city site
4   Titanic Quarter, Harland and Wolff, Belfast, Ireland; masterplan for the redevelopment Harland and Wolff shipyards
5   Irish Pavilion, Expo 2000 Hanover; Irish competition winning entry built for Expo 2000

5   Bitter+bredt

● Fumbally Court, Fumbally Lane, Dublin 8 Ireland Tel: +353 1 453 7300 Fax: +353 1 453 4062

N2DESIGN GROUP ARCHITECTS, LLP

www.n2design.net

1   Philip Ennis

2   Bryan Richter, N2Design Group

3   Bryan Richter, N2Design Group

N2Design Group Architects, LLP grew from the vision of two architects, Harry Nicolaides and Stuart Narofsky, and is dedicated to the creation of original and vibrant designs inspired by its clients. The firm is committed to each client's unique viewpoint, allowing the client's vision to serve as a blueprint upon which its design professionals build, fulfilling the client's needs with creative and exciting solutions. This unique client-focused approach has been nationally recognized, through publications and award-winning designs.

N2Design Group is a full-service design firm that provides integrated architectural, interior and graphic design services. The firm has recently completed the New York headquarters for MCA Records, an award-winning project, and the executive headquarters for Boston University. The range of work extends from projects such as religious buildings to numerous corporate conference centers throughout the United States. N2Design Group also has a well-published portfolio of custom homes and apartments.

4   Philip Ennis

5   Harry Nicolaides

1   Residence, Old Westbury, New York
2   Ronald McDonald House, New Hyde Park, New York
3   Residence, Sand's Point, New York
4   MCA Headquarters, New York, New York
5   Boston University, Boston, Massachusetts

● 30 West 26th Street, 5th Floor, New York, New York 10010 USA
Tel: +1 212 989 7842 Fax: +1 212 989 7843

NAGLE HARTRAY DANKER KAGAN MCKAY ARCHITECTS PLANNERS LTD.

www.nhdkm.com

Nagle Hartray Danker Kagan McKay Architects Planners Ltd. provides a broad range of services related to architecture, interior design, and land planning. Founded on the basis of residential design in 1966, NHDKM now maintains a breadth of experience that includes educational and library facilities, municipal and corporate buildings, communications environments, cultural and religious projects, and historical renovations in addition to single family, multi-family, student, and senior housing.

While the design approach of the firm is grounded in the modernist tradition, it is qualified by location, site topography, building systems, and context. NHDKM is committed to achieving the program and goals of each client—the plan, form, and details of each building must support the client's program at every level. This philosophy has resulted in a consistent body of award-winning work.

1   Hedrich-Blessing

2   Bruce Van Inwegen

3   Hedrich-Blessing

4   Bruce Van Inwegen

5   Bruce Van Inwegen

1 Kinzie Park Tower, Chicago, Illinois; 34-story, 208-unit condominium high-rise
2 The University of Chicago Laboratory Schools Kovler Gymnasium, Chicago, Illinois; 3-story (plus basement) gymnasium complex addition in neo-Gothic style
3 Nathalie Salmon House, Chicago, Illinois; intergenerational residence for families, students, and elderly
4 Spurlock Museum of World Cultures at the University of Illinois Urbana-Champaign, Champaign, Illinois; central core of new 52,000-square-foot museum
5 Ravine House, Highland Park, Illinois; 7,000-square-foot single-family home

● One IBM Plaza, Chicago, Illinois 60611 USA Tel: +1 312 832 6900 Fax: +1 312 832 0004

NAQSH, E, JAHAN-PARS CONSULTING ENGINEERS

info@njp-arch.com www.njp-arch.com

Naqsh, E, Jahan-Pars Consulting was established in 1988 and has since won numerous local and international awards in the fields of architecture and urban planning. Specifically, the firm's projects include offices, residential and commercial buildings, and sports and educational facilities.

The firm's principal, Seyeh Hadi Mirmiran, received his M.A in architecture from the faculty of fine arts at Tehran University in 1968. His personal achievements to date include Architect of the Year, Iran, 2000; a Grand Memar Award for the Rafsanjan sports complex, 2001; and he was selected in 2003 as vanguard architect by the Iranian Construction Engineering Organization (ICEO).

1   M. Asghari

2   H. Nabavi   3   H. Navavi

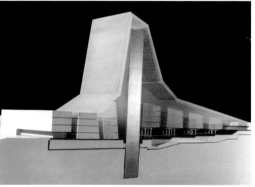

4   NJP Consulting

1 General Consulate of Iran, Frankfurt, Germany; multi-function area
2 Sports Complex, Rafsanjan, Iran; western view
3 National Library of Iran, Tehran, Iran; longitudinal section
4 Exporting Development Bank of Iran, Tehran, Iran; main façade
5 Tehran Bar Association, Tehran, Iran; façade

5   M. Asghari

● No.14. Garmsar East St. Shriraz South St. Mollasadra Ave. Tehran 14358 Iran
Tel: +98 21 880 588 27 Fax: +98 21 880 313 99

NARCHITECTS

n@narchitects.com   www.narchitects.com

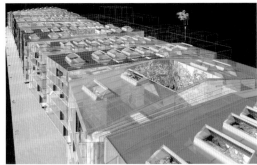

1   nARCHITECTS

nARCHITECTS was formed in 1999 by Eric Bunge and Mimi Hoang. The firm generates new design concepts and techniques for building, and strategies that emphasize the general, systemic, and dynamic over the specific, circumstantial, and fixed. It aims to achieve maximum effect with an economy of conceptual and material means, and a positive impact on the environment.

nARCHITECTS won the 5th annual MoMA/ P.S.1 Young Architects Program 2004, a national competition, for its project "Canopy", a large environment built with freshly cut green bamboo in the P.S.1 courtyard. In 2004, the firm was selected by *Architectural Record Magazine* as one of 11 "design vanguard" architects. Current projects include work with art institutions, interactive installations, and residential lofts and buildings.

2   nARCHITECTS

4   Jorge Pereira

3   nARCHITECTS

5   Frank Oudeman

1   Thermal Bridge, Aomori, Japan; 200-unit housing
2   Dune Terrace, Giza, Egypt; Grand Egyptian Museum competition
3   Party Wall, Artists Space Gallery, New York, New York; robotic wall
4&5 Canopy, New York, New York; 30,000 square-foot environment

● 147 Essex Street, New York, New York 10002 USA Tel: +1 212 253 2853 Fax: +1 212 844 9070

NAYA ARCHITECTS: MANABU+ARATA

m-a.naya@f2.dion.ne.jp www.f2.dion.ne.jp/~m-a.naya/

1 Koui Yaginuma

2 Makoto Yoshida

3 Makoto Yoshida

Manabu Naya and Arata Naya both graduated from the Shibaura Institute of Technology and established NAYA Architects in 1993. To date, they have received many awards for their projects, including prizes in the 5th and 6th Warm Living Design Competition, 2000 and 2001; the Japanese Federation of Architects and Building Engineers Associations Encouragement Award, 2003; and an honorable mention in the Reform, Renewal, and Conversion contest, 2004.

4 NAYA Architects: MANABU+ARATA

1 House in Futakoshinchi, Takatu, Kawasaki, Kanagawa
2 Apartment in Arai, Nakano, Tokyo
3 Teshihouse, Takatsu, Tokyo
4 Ho-chinro, Kawasaki, Kanagawa
5 House in Edogawa, Edogawaku, Tokyo

5 Kozo Takayama

● 2-1376-1F, Kamimarukosannou, Nakahara-ku, Kawasaki, Kanagawa 211-0002 Japan
Tel: +81 4 4411 7934 Fax: +81 4 4411 7935

NELSON CHEN ARCHITECTS LTD.

architects@nca.com.hk www.nca.com.hk

Nelson Chen Architects Ltd. is noted for design excellence and personalized client service in an international practice extending from Hong Kong and China to North America. The firm was established in 1987 as Wong Chen Associates, successor to the former practice of Wong Cho Tong and Clifford Wong, originally founded in 1947. Supported by this legacy of professional achievement, the current firm remains committed to providing its clients with design solutions that are innovative and appropriate.

Under the design direction of Nelson K. Chen, an award-winning architect from the USA, the firm maintains a diversified practice, offering full professional services in architecture, master planning and interior design, including renovations and adaptive reuse of heritage buildings. Recent commissions have ranged in size from 1,000-square-foot interiors to over 5 million-square-foot garden housing developments.

Regardless of size, each project is given the same meticulous attention to achieve the highest standards of design quality and technical performance. The work of Nelson Chen Architects Ltd. has been recognized by numerous publications, exhibitions and international design awards, including the inaugural Architecture Firm Award from the American Institute of Architects Hong Kong Chapter.

1
Stuart Woods

2
Stuart Woods

3
Kerun Ip

4
Li Bun

5
Li Bun

1 Fairview Park Alliance Church, Hong Kong; church and community wing
2 Fairview Park Alliance Church, Hong Kong; sanctuary facing altar
3 Suzhou Garden Villas, PRC; canal-side courtyard housing
4 University of Hong Kong, Hong Kong; office tower above art gallery
5 University of Hong Kong, Hong Kong; atrium gallery with skylight

● 23/F Lippo Leighton Tower, 103 Leighton Road, Hong Kong Tel: +852 2882 8086 Fax: +852 2882 8038

NELSON•TREMAIN PARTNERSHIP, P.A.

fromm@ntp.cc www.ntp.cc

1   Michael Connally

Nelson•Tremain Partnership, P.A. is an architectural and consulting practice dedicated to addressing the design needs of older persons. Gaius Nelson, president of the firm, believes that good design improves quality of life. This firm is committed to working in partnership with care providers to create designs that enhance the dignity and independence of older people.

Facilities for seniors are homes, not transitory places. Environments for seniors should reflect the familiarity and security that the word "home" connotes. The firm combines the talents and expertise of recognized leaders in the field of design for aging, with numerous design citations, articles, professional presentations and successful projects to its credit.

Nelson•Tremain Partnership has worked diligently, for more than 10 years, to advance the art and science of design for aging.

2   Steve Swalwell, Architectural Fotographics

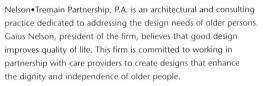
3   Dave Olsen Photography

4   Dave Olsen Photography

1 Freedom House Alzheimer's Care and Research Center, San Antonio, Texas; main entry tower reflects Texas hill country vernacular

2 Village Shalom Continuing Care Retirement Community; Overland Park, Kansas; Children's playground encourages inter-generational activities

3 Creekview, Evergreen Retirement Community, Oshkosh, Wisconsin; aquatic therapy pools

4 Creekview, Evergreen Retirement Community, Oshkosh, Wisconsin; main entrance, nestled between low-slung resident wings, is identified by a tower

5 Keystone Communities Assisted Living Center, Faribault, Minnesota; entry court provides access to assisted living and memory care areas

5   Dave Olsen Photography

● 125 Main Street Southeast, Suite 245, Minneapolis, Minnesota 55414 USA
Tel: +1 612 331 7178 Fax: +1 612 331 8255

NEVZAT SAYIN

nevzatsayin@nsmh.com   www.nsmh.com

1   Nevzat Sayin

Nevzat Sayin was born in Hatay in 1954. In 1978, he graduated from the Aegean University Department of Architecture in Izmir. He completed postgraduate study in architecture, working with Cengiz Bektas, and opened his own architecture studio in 1984.

He has won numerous awards, including the National Architecture Award from the Turkish Chamber of Architects in 1990, 1992, 1996, and 1998; the Turkish Association of Freelance Architects Award in 1998; and a nomination for the Aga Khan Award.

His built works include the Gon1 and Gon2 industrial facilities in Istanbul, Colossus Hotel in Bodrum, and the POAS General Directorate in Istanbul. His work also includes numerous residential and restoration projects in Istanbul and the Aegean coast of Turkey.

2   Nevzat Say

4   Nevzat Say

3   Nevzat Sayin

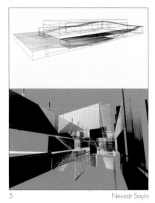

5   Nevzat Sayin

1 Irmak High School,
   Istanbul, Turkey
2 Gon2 Industrial Building,
   Istanbul, Turkey
3 Gorener House,
   Erdek, Turkey
4 Lokman Sahin House,
   Saray, Turkey
5 Umur Industrial Building,
   Gebze, Turkey

● 99 Icadiye Caddesi, Kuzguncuk 81200, Istanbul, Turkey Tel: +90 216 492 9412 Fax: +90 216 310 0870

NEW WORK STUDIO

www.newworkstudio.co.nz

1   Jeff Williams

2   Justin Wright

Justin Wright

3   Justin Wright

New Work Studio is a small New Zealand architectural practice specializing in high quality, innovative architecture. The practice has won 17 Institute of Architects awards since 1999, including the prestigious National Award for Architecture and the New Zealand Award for Architecture.

New Work Studio works in a contemporary style, preferring to use a range of natural materials and textures to produce a timeless quality in its design. The practice explores the nature of construction, the texture of materials and surfaces, spatial dynamics, natural light, energy efficiency and passive solar design in its work.

New Work Studio believes in expressing the nature of New Zealand's position in the Pacific, and its style has been described as 'crafted Pacific abstraction'.

The firm is led by principal architect Tim Nees, with associate Justin Wright and two to three employees.

4   Paul McCredie

5   Paul McCredie

1 Lower Shotover House, Queenstown, New Zealand; large contemporary addition behind historic cottage
2 Northridge House, Queenstown, New Zealand; large rural home in grasslands with mountain views
3 Lake Taupo House, Taupo, New Zealand; lakeside house, view of open living area
4 Seatoun Heights House, Wellington, New Zealand; pavilion house on brow of hill above Wellington
5 Ranger Point House, Breaker Bay, Wellington, New Zealand; seaside house, night view showing translucent cladding

● 147 Cuba Street, PO Box 9853, Wellington, New Zealand Tel: +64 4 801 9880 Fax: +64 4 801 9196

NICHOLAS GIOIA ASSOCIATES PTY LTD

ngioia@bigpond.net.au

1   Trevor Mein

2   Trevor Mein

3   Trevor Mein

The architectural practice of Nicholas Gioia Associates Pty Ltd tends to specialize in small scale projects.

The work of the practice has won many local and international awards and has also been published locally and internationally.

4   Trevor Mein

5   Trevor Mein

1 Arthur's Seat House, Rosebud, Victoria; new two-story holiday house
2 Albert Park House, Melbourne; two-story addition to 19th-century house
3 South Melbourne House, Melbourne; new 100-square-metre infill house
4&5 Richardson Street House, Melbourne; addition to 19th-century house

● 297 Rae Street, North Fitzroy, Victoria 3068 Australia Tel: +61 3 9482 4555 Fax: +61 3 9482 4488

440

NIELS TORP AS ARKITEKTER MNAL

firmapost@ntorp.no www.ntorp.no

1   Runar Kolnes

2   Jiri Havran

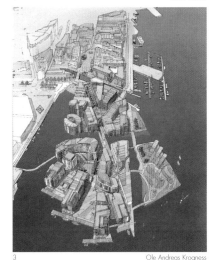
3   Ole Andreas Krogness

Niels Torp Architects designs urban and rural developments, offices, universities, interiors, furniture, stadiums, airports, railway stations, bus terminals, industrial buildings, retail, hotels, hospitals, and housing projects.

The starting point for its projects is the human scale, and the human requirements for warmth, care, and variety in the environment. The firm's designs naturally reflect the clients' thoughts, the significant features of the site, and its view on architecture at that given moment. The conditions applying to one project are unique, resulting in each project always having its own identity.

Niels Torp Architects believes that in a rural setting, the building and the landscape should form a conscious unity. The surrounding landscape is moulded in response to the design of the building. In an urban setting, a dialogue between new buildings and the existing neighbourhood is essential. City buildings should respect and emphasize the urban grid and the urban space it borders upon.

To Niels Torp Architects, even the smallest projects are important and interesting because they always constitute part of a greater whole.

4   Hans Wretling

5   Peter Cook

1   BI Campus Nydalen, Oslo
2   Smestaddammen Park, Oslo
3   Tjuvholmen, Oslo
4   Nils Ericsson Bus Terminal, Gothenburg, Sweden
5   British Airways Headquarters, London, UK

●   Industrigaten 59, PO Box 5387, Majorstuen, 0304 Oslo Norway   Tel: +47 23 36 68 00   Fax: +47 23 36 68 01

NIKKEN SEKKEI

global@nikken.co.jp   www.nikken.co.jp

1   Shinkenchiku-sha

2   Nakaca & Partners Inc

The services of Nikken Sekkei include architectural design, engineering, planning, landscape, interior design, and consulting and management.

The firm is committed to client satisfaction, quality assurance, sustainable design, long life building, communications and networks, and advanced and innovative technology.

"We are ultimately responsible not only for our buildings and users, but also for our society and its natural environment."

3   Nakaca & Partners Inc   4   Shinkenchiku-sha

1 Shanghai Information Tower, Shanghai, PRC; exterior
   view
2 National Museum of Science and Innovation, Tokyo,
   Japan; exterior view
3 National Museum of Science and Innovation, Tokyo,
   Japan; details
4 Shanghai Information Tower, Shanghai, PRC; atrium
   night view
5 National Museum of Science and Innovation, Tokyo,
   Japan; atrium night view

5   Nippon Sheet Glass Co., Ltd

● 2-1-3 Koraku, Bunkyo-ku, Tokyo 112-8565 Japan Tel: +81 3 3818 4095 Fax: +81 3 3814 8567

NORM APPLEBAUM AIA, ARCHITECT

normapplebaumaia@cox.net

1

Kim Brun

2

Norm Applebaum

Norm Applebaum received a Bachelor of Architecture degree in 1968 at Arizona State University, under the late Calvin Straub, FAIA, Architectural Professor of the University of Southern California and Arizona State University Schools of Architecture. Applebaum discovered awareness and sensitivity to the client, the environment, and the importance of clean structural lines from this famous *Arts and Architecture* designer. As a student to architectural visionary Paolo Soleri, he learned about the philosophy of the Mega Structure as a way of living—a new nature and its significance to existence. Michael John Pittas, Dean of the Parsons School of Design, stated that Applebaum is a designer of "masterworks of craftsmanship, detail and drama".

An Applebaum home takes on a sculptural form as cantilevered roof lines, clerestory glass and transparent interiors come together. His eye for detail makes it possible to design more than the structure of the home, but indeed many other elements such as handcrafted furniture, ironwork, leaded glass doors and windows, to flatware, china and rugs.

3

Kim Brun

4

Kim Brun

Matheron Residence, Escondido, California, USA
1   House nestles on a hillside at dusk
2   Leadlight entry doors illustrate a bird in flight
3   Steel beam supports redwood canopy with
    entry trellis beyond
4   Living room ceiling appears to float above,
    separated by clerestory windows

● 9830 Edgelake Drive, La Mesa, California 91941 USA Tel: +1 619 463 1867 Fax: +1 619 465 4102

NORR LIMITED, ARCHITECTS AND ENGINEERS

info@norrlimited.com   www.norrlimited.com

NORR Limited is a fully integrated architecture and engineering firm that was founded in 1938. The company has contributed more than 60 years of innovation and creativity to high-profile, quality commercial and institutional developments.

NORR's project experience includes facilities for office, hotel, residential, sports and recreation, entertainment, health care, corrections, education, research and development, communications, and retail use.

Both NORR and its sister company Giffels, are part of the Ingenium Group of Companies—one of Canada's largest architecture and engineering firms. Its staff of 800 has experience in architecture, engineering, interior design, construction management, and information technology. These expanded capabilities provide NORR clients with the convenience of obtaining complete services from a single source.

As part of NORR's commitment to providing its clients with the highest level of service, projects are placed under the direct supervision of a principal architect and the most competent personnel in each specialty. NORR's clients have come to expect the kind of personal and professional service that yields tailored solutions providing quality, value, cost control, and the ability to meet deadlines.

1   Steven Evans

2   Richard Johnson, Interior Images

3   NORR Limited, Architects & Engineers

5   NORR Limited, Architects & Engineers

4   Hedrich-Blessing

1 Ford Canadian Headquarters, Oakville, Ontario
2 DeGroote Center for Learning and Discovery, McMaster University, Hamilton, Ontario
3 Pierre Elliott Trudeau Judicial Building, Ottawa, Ontario
4 Emirates Towers, Dubai, UAE
5 Canadian Plaza at the Peace Bridge, Fort Erie, Ontario

● 350 Bloor Street East, Toronto, Ontario M4W 3S6 Canada Tel: +1 416 929 0200 Fax: +1 416 929 3635

NEUMANN/SMITH & ASSOCIATES

kneumann@neumannsmith.com   www.neumannsmith.com

1   Justin Maconochie

Neumann/Smith & Associates looks beyond the ordinary for smart design concepts and approaches that give clients more for their money than they ever dreamed possible. Whether designing an office building, museum, fitness center, classroom, library, medical center, place of worship, city hall, parking garage, or custom home, it finds cost-effective ways to create extraordinary facilities. Its architects and interior designers are skilled in master planning, site evaluation, feasibility studies, space planning, architecture, interior design, and project management.

Neumann/Smith & Associates' creativity and unwavering commitment to the highest standards of professional practice have earned the firm more than 125 design awards, the firm of the year Award from AIA Michigan, and numerous features in the international architectural press.

2   Justin Maconochie

3   Justin Maconochie

4   Todd Roberts, Hedrich Blessing

5   Justin Maconochie, Hedrich-Blessing

1   Holocaust Memorial Center, Farmington Hills, Michigan; 50,000-square-foot structure
2   Ford Motor Land Services, Corporate Crossings at Fairlane, Dearborn, Michigan; cost-effective 230,000-square-foot office building
3   The University of Michigan, University Center, Dearborn, Michigan; a glass portal creates a dynamic new entry to the campus
4   Lear Corporation, Ford Interiors & Electronics Division; Dearborn, Michigan; office complements and links existing buildings
5   City of Livonia, community recreation center, Livonia, Michigan; bold geometry identifies entrance

● 400 Galleria Officentre, Suite 555, Southfield, Michigan 48034 USA
Tel: +1 248 352 8310 Fax: +1 248 352 1821

NURMELA-RAIMORANTA-TASA ARCHITECTS

ark.tsto@n-r-t.fi www.n-r-t.fi

1   J. Tiainen

2   A. Luutonen

3   Nurmela-Raimoranta-Tasa

4   K. Raimoranta   5   A. Luutonen

The award-winning firm of Nurmela-Raimoranta-Tasa is based in Helsinki, Finland. Its built projects include: University of Turku, five faculty buildings and refurbishments; Tennis Palace, Helsinki, renovation and refurbishment; Helsinki School of Economics and Business Administration, refurbishment; Municipal services building, Porvoo; Government offices, Snellmaninkatu 6, Helsinki, renovation and annex; and the Mellunkylä Rescue Station, Helsinki.

The firm has won a substantial number of awards, including 21 first prizes in open and invited competitions; the Viljo Rewell Prize, 1973; National Award for Architecture and Planning, 1987; project of the year 1986 for the Malmi Post Office; project of the year 1993 for the Turku University Departments of Chemistry and Biochemistry; and the Finnish Concrete Award 1998.

All partners have taught at the Helsinki University of Technology Department of Architecture. Jyrki Tasa is professor of contemporary architecture at Oulu University.

1 House Into, Espoo, 1998
2 University of Turku, two faculty buildings, 2001, 2002
3 Residential quarter in Lauttasaari, Helsinki
4 Municipal services building, Porvoo, 1993
5 Government offices, Snellmaninkatu 6, Helsinki, 2001

● Kalevankatu 31, 00100 Helsinki, Finland Tel: +358 0 686 6780 Fax: +358 0 685 7588

O'KEEFE ARCHITECTS INC

info@okeefearch.com www.okeefearch.com

Since 1978, O'Keefe Architects inc. has offered expertise in the areas of housing for the elderly, long-term care, and acute care facilities. In addition, the firm's experience covers a wide range of building types, including educational, religious, recreational, commercial and residential projects.

Nationwide, O'Keefe Architects inc. has over 400 projects to its credit, and is recognized for its expertise in the design and development of senior living and healthcare environments.

The firm believes that outstanding quality and functional design creates a facility that will remain financially competitive in today's economic environment. Design solutions address the spiritual, psychological, and social dignity of the elderly residents and encourage independence while performing daily activities. Through exemplary design, facilities created by O'Keefe Architects inc. also provide comfort, security, health, and recreation for the residents without compromising operational efficiencies or initial development cost.

1   George Cott, Chroma Inc

2   George Cott, Chroma Inc

3   George Cott, Chroma Inc

4   George Cott, Chroma Inc

5   George Cott, Chroma Inc

1 Heritage Woods, Agawam, Massachusetts
2 McKeen Towers, West Palm Beach, Florida
3 The Gardens Court, Palm Beach Gardens, Florida
4 Mariner Health of Tampa, Tampa, Florida
5 Wuesthoff Progressive Care Center, Viera, Florida

● 2424 Curlew Road, Palm Harbor, Florida 34683 USA Tel: +1 727 781 5885 Fax: +1 727 781 0255

447

OBM INTERNATIONAL

obmi@obmi.com   www.obmi.com

OBM

OBM

A preferred provider for Leading Hotels of the World's Leading by Design Network and ranked as a top design firm by renowned publications *Hotel Business, World Architecture* and *Interior Design*, OBM International offers expertise in luxury hotel/resort design development, architecture, town planning, and interior design.

For nearly seven decades, OBM has been the premier full-service, design-consulting firm in Bermuda and the Caribbean. Today, OBM continues to develop its reputation as masters of design in the USA, the Caribbean, Europe and Northern Africa. With nine global offices in Antigua, Bath, Bermuda, British Virgin Islands, Cayman Islands, Marbella, Miami, Trinidad and Tobago, and the Turks and Caicos Islands, OBM creates excellence by design.

OBM

OBM

OBM

1 Winsor House, Tucker's Town, Bermuda
2 Peter Island Resort & Spa, Peter Island, British Virgin Islands
3 Ritz-Carlton Coastal Village, St. Thomas, US Virgin Islands
4 Sea Meadow House, Road Town, Tortola, British Virgin Islands
5 Conyers Dill & Pearman, Hamilton, Bermuda

● 2600 Douglas Road, Suite 308, Coral Gables, Florida 33134 USA
Tel: +1 305 441 8767 Fax: +1 305 441 8242

OBRA ARCHITECTS

info@obraarchitects.com   www.obraarchitects.com

1   Adriana Miranda

2   Adriana Miranda

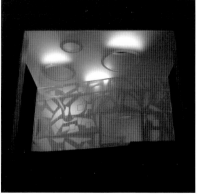

5   Adriana Miranda

Located in New York, OBRA Architects was founded by partners Pablo Castro and Jennifer Lee. Both gained local and international experience working on a variety of public and private works. The firm's projects range from museums, to institutional and educational facilities, and residential works.

Evoking the creative spirit of site and place, the OBRA team welcomes the challenge of large and small projects. An environment of collaboration and maximum effort ensures that all participants are engaged in an active and continuously cultivated design process.

The firm was selected as one of the Emerging Voices of 2005 by the Architectural League of New York, and is publishing its first monograph with the United Asia Art and Design Cooperation in Beijing, PRC. Past projects include the award-winning Freedom Park Museum and Memorial in Pretoria, South Africa, Nine Square Sky Housing in Chile, and Casa en la Finca in San Juan, Argentina.

3   OBRA Architects

4   Adriana Miranda

1   Freedom Park Museum and Memorial, Pretoria, South Africa
2   Freedom Park Memorial, Pretoria, South Africa
3   Tittot Glass Art Museum, Taipei, Taiwan
4   Architettura Povera, Rhode Island School of Design
5   Nine Square Sky, Chile

● 315 Church Street, Fourth Floor, New York, New York 10013 USA
Tel: +1 212 625 3868 Fax: +1 212 625 3874

449

OFFICE FOR METROPOLITAN ARCHITECTURE (OMA)

office@oma.nl www.oma.nl

1   Hans Werlemann

2   Hans Werlemann

3   Hans Werlemann

The Office for Metropolitan Architecture (OMA) is a Rotterdam-based firm concerned with contemporary architecture, urbanism and general cultural issues. The main objective of OMA's design process is to exploit the potential of a particular building type, and to provide the client with a maximum of function as well as intellectual stimulation.

OMA employs approximately 80 architects and designers.

Founded in 1974 by Rem Koolhaas, the office entered a series of major architectural competitions and realized a series of projects, ranging from private residences to public buildings to large-scale urban planning. In 1992, the Kunsthal and its Museum Park in Rotterdam opened and in 1998 the private residence Maison à Bordeaux in France was completed.

At the start of the new century, the office is active in the USA with three projects for the Italian fashion company Prada, the new Seattle Public Library, and the IIT Campus Center in Chicago. Current activities in Europe include the construction of the Porto Concert Hall (Portugal), and the Netherlands Embassy in Berlin (Germany).

The work of Rem Koolhaas and OMA has won several international awards, including the Pritzker Architecture Prize in 2000.

4   OMA

5   Armin Linke

1 Kunsthal, 1992
2 Maison à Bordeaux, 1998
3 Netherlands Embassy, Berlin, 2003
4 Seattle Public Library, 2004
5 Prada Store, New York, 2001

● Heer Bokelweg 149, 3032 AD Rotterdam, Netherlands Tel: +31 10 243 8200 Fax: +31 10 243 8202

OFIS ARHITEKTI

ofis@ofis-a.si   www.ofis-a.si

Led by Rok Oman and Spela Videcnik, Ofis arhitekti's work ranges from small- to large-scale works. The firm has won several local and international awards, including the Piranesi Honours Award (2000) for its housing block in Koseze, Slovenia, the Young Architect of the Year (London, 2001), and was highly commended for its City Museum project in Ljubljana, Slovenia in the 2004 AR+D Awards in London.

1   courtesy Ofis arhitekti

2   courtesy Ofis arhitekti

3   courtesy Ofis arhitekti

4   courtesy Ofis arhitekti

1&4   Villa Bled Extension, Bled, Slovenia

5   courtesy Ofis arhitekti
2,3,5   City Museum Extension, Ljubljana, Slovenia

● Kongresni Trg 3, Ljubljana 1000 Slovenia Tel: +386 1 4260085 / 4260084 Fax: +386 1 4260085

OJMR ARCHITECTS

jay@ojmrarchitects.net   www.ojmrarchitects.net

1   Maria Antonia Viteri

Based in Los Angeles since 1991, OJMR Architects' range of residential, commercial, and industrial architecture and interiors, as well as furniture and urban design, has served such clients as Sanwa Bank, The Children's Book Council, Noble Medical Clinic, Redeemer Lutheran Church, Med Path, and numerous private residential clients. Principal Jay M. Reynolds, AIA, has become pro-active as an architect/developer on several housing and mixed-use projects.

Reynolds' work has been exhibited at the Venice University of Architecture; National Building Museum, Washington, DC; Columbia University, New York; Pacific Design Center, Los Angeles; and Archicenter, Chicago. He attended the University of Oklahoma, Norman campus, earning his Bachelor of Architecture degree while on a baseball scholarship, and received a Master of Science degree in Architecture and Urban Design from Columbia University. In addition to his architectural practice, Reynolds is a studio instructor of interior architecture.

3   OJMR Architects

2   Ciro Coelho

4   Lars Frasier

5   OJMR Architects

1   Defeo House Renovation, Venice, California; indoor/outdoor lifestyle heightened by use of glass for natural light and breezes
2   Desert House, Palm Desert, California; this residence and painting studio represents new-century modernism
3   Townhouses, Palm Springs, California; modernist townhouses co-developed by the architect, under construction
4   Harbor Office Building, Fullerton, California; medical office building as series of geometric volumes
5   Westchester Lutheran School, Los Angeles, California; new school and multi-use spaces added to existing sanctuary

● 501 South Fairfax Avenue, Suite 202, Los Angeles, California 90036 USA
Tel: +1 323 931 1007 Fax: +1 323 931 0109

OKAMOTO SAIJO ARCHITECTURE

paul@os-architecture.com www.os-architecture.com

Okamoto Saijo Architecture focuses on sustainable design, primarily on custom residences and affordable housing developments, but also on community based neighborhood-planning projects. Paul Okamoto and Eric Saijo founded the firm in 1991, receiving their degrees from California Polytechnic State University, San Luis Obispo, California. Okamoto also received his M. Arch from the University of Adelaide, South Australia, and was a Loeb Fellow at Harvard University's Graduate School of Design.

The Johnson-Theis Residence is a second in a series of passive solar residences that uses recycled building materials and incorporates earth thermal walls to mitigate internal temperature swings during the summer and winter seasons. The design is an integration of the site topography, vistas, solar orientation, and surrounding forest vegetation. In contrast, the Chinatown Corps Center is located in the heart of San Francisco's Chinatown, and was remodeled with photovoltaic panels on its roof to produce electricity to this mixed-use community institution.

1   OSA

2   Alan Geller

3   Lewis Watts

4   OSA

Chinatown Corps Center, San Francisco, California
1 Front façade
2 Photovoltaic system
Johnson-Theis Residence, Sebastopol, California
3 South elevation
4 East elevation
5 West elevation

5   OSA

● 18 Bartol Street, San Francisco, California 94133 USA Tel: +1 415 788 2118 Fax: +1 415 986 2815

OLSON SUNDBERG KUNDIG ALLEN ARCHITECTS

www.olsonsundberg.com

1   Olson Sundberg Kundig Allen

2   Olson Sundberg Kundig Allen

3   Eduardo Calderon

Thirty-five years ago, Jim Olson started a firm based on some simple ideas: that buildings can serve as a bridge between nature, culture, and people, and that inspiring surroundings have a positive effect on people's lives. Today the firm has taken those ideas to new and creative levels. The firm's work includes museums, college and university buildings, places of worship, and residences (often for art collectors).

Together the four partners, Jim Olson, Rick Sundberg, Tom Kundig and Scott Allen, have created an office with an international reputation that is extensively recognized in publications and awards. Among the firm's recent design awards are national and regional honors from the American Institute of Architects and an American Architecture Award from The Chicago Athenaeum. The partners, who often lecture on the topic of design, also serve as guest critics for university design studios and as jurors for design award programs.

5   Eduardo Calderon

4   Paul Warchol

1   Seattle University Recreational Center, Seattle, Washington; streetscape rendering of new student recreational center
2   The Bellingham Art Museum and Children's Museum, Bellingham, Washington; rendering of community courtyard with projection wall
3   Lake Washington Residence, Seattle, Washington; lakefront home with sustainable elements
4   Ridge House, Eastern Washington; main living area floats over natural ridgeline
5   Northwest Family Retreat, Western Washington; interior spaces have strong connection to outdoor landscape

● 159 South Jackson Street, 6th Floor, Seattle, Washington 98104 USA
Tel: +1 206 624 5670   Fax: +1 206 624 3730

OMRANIA & ASSOCIATES

omrania@omrania.com.sa   www.omrania.com.sa

1   Paul Kavanagh

2   Paul Kavanagh

4   Ali Al Mubarak

O&A Architecture and Engineering Consultants is a multidisciplinary practice with more than 30 years experience in the Kingdom of Saudi Arabia. It has established a reputation as one of the leading firms in the Kingdom in the fields of town planning, architecture, engineering and project management and is capable of meeting the advanced technological requirements of the 21st century both in Saudi Arabia and worldwide.

O&A offers a range of services covering the full spectrum of building and engineering project management and design, from initial feasibility studies through building program development and engineering design to construction management and supervision. Activities center on architectural and engineering design of building and infrastructure projects, covering residential, commercial, leisure, industrial, medical, educational and mixed-use facilities.

O&A has won a number of national and international competitions, including the prestigious Aga Khan Award for Architecture.

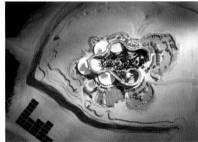

3   Omrania

1   Saudi Research & Publishing Co. Headquarters, Riyadh, Saudi Arabia; internal view, reception area
2   Kingdom Schools, Riyadh, Saudi Arabia; auditorium
3   Towaiq Palace, Riyadh, Saudi Arabia; winner of Aga Khan Award, aerial view (in association with Frei Otto & Buro Happold)
4   King Abdulaziz Library & Auditorium, Riyadh, Saudi Arabia; external view
5   Abraj Atta'Awuneya (N.C.C.I. Headquarters), Riyadh, Saudi Arabia; external view of main entrance elevation (in association with E. Faljaka)

5   Ali Al Mubarak

● P.O. Box 2600, Riyadh 11461, Kingdom of Saudi Arabia
Tel: +966 1 462 2888 Fax: +966 1 462 0354/465 8302

ONL [OOSTERHUIS_LÉNÁRD]

oosterhuis@oosterhuis.nl www.oosterhuis.nl

Kas Oosterhuis was born in 1951, studied in Delft and London, and started his office in 1989 after having lived for one year in the Studio Theo Van Doesburg in Meudon near Paris. He has been a professor at the Technical University in Delft since 2000.

His recent realized works include: multimedia pavilion, Web of North Holland Floriade, 2001; the TT Monument, Assen (with Ilona Lénárd), 2001; 66 houses, 8bit Lelystad, 2001; Florijn-Zuid, 64 houses, Bijlmermeer, Amsterdam, 2003; and the Cockpit Building, an office building integrated into an acoustic barrier on the A2 in Utrecht.

He has written for various publications, and his work has appeared in several books. He has also participated in many architectural exhibitions, including the 2000 Architecture Biennale in Venice.

Awards include a 1999 nomination for the Mies van der Rohe Award, a 1998 *Business Week/Architectural Record* award, a nomination for the 1998 and 2002 National Steel Prize, the 1996 OCÉBNA prize for industrial architecture, and an honorable mention, National Steel Prize, 1996.

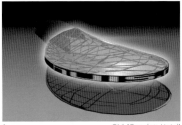

1   ONL [Oosterhuis_Lénárd]

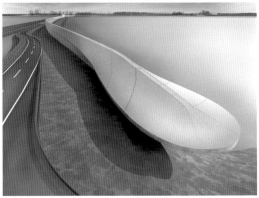

2   ONL [Oosterhuis_Lénárd]

3   ONL [Oosterhuis_Lénárd]

4   ONL [Oosterhuis_Lénárd]

5   ONL [Oosterhuis_Lénárd]

1 Programmable lights in electronic head of Acoustic Barrier
2 Floating head of Acoustic Barrier along A2 highway
3 Acoustic Barrier ending illuminated
4 Acoustic Barrier contains 40,000 different steel nodes and 10,000 different glass plates
5 Acoustic Barrier construction site

● Essenburgsingel 94C, 3022 EG Rotterdam, The Netherlands Tel: +31 10 244 7039 Fax: +31 10 244 7041

OSMOND LANGE ARCHITECTS & PLANNERS

jhb@osmondlange.co.za www.osmondlange.co.za

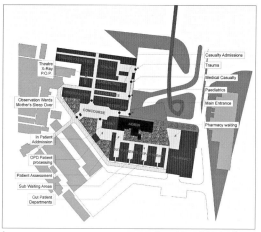

1   Osmond Lange Architects & Planners

Osmond Lange Architects & Planners has been practising in South Africa since 1929 and has offices in Johannesburg, Durban, East London, Cape Town and Umtata and associate offices in Mozambique, Zimbabwe and Botswana. Core staff in South Africa totals 47 persons.

The practice provides architectural and urban planning services and is involved with major office, retail, commercial, industrial, health care and public sector work.

Osmond Lange Architects & Planners has further developed its expertise to also provide a comprehensive project development service.

In today's competitive world, project development demands an encompassing and comprehensive understanding of all its facets to ensure viability and success. This, in brief outline, consists of an understanding and appreciation of the development objective, financial viability, environmental factors, delivery within time and money constraints, and marketing.

2   Osmond Lange Architects & Planners

3   Osmond Lange Architects & Planners

4   Osmond Lange Architects & Planners

5   Osmond Lange Architects & Planners

1 Chris Hani Baragwanath Hospital Redevelopment, Johannesburg
2 Melrose Arch New-Urbanism Project, Johannesburg
3 Nestlé Distribution Centre, Durban
4 DaimlerChrysler Body Plant & Paint Shop, East London
5 Grosvenor Corner Building, Johannesburg

● 199 Oxford Road, Dunkeld, Johannesburg, South Africa Tel: +27 11 788 0965 Fax: +27 11 880 2657

OTIS ARCHITECTURE

otisarch@aol.com otisarchitecture.com

1   Josh White

2   Greg Eisman

Otis Architecture is a southern California-based design firm that captures the artistic quality of architecture. Projects range from custom homes, restaurants, cosmetic dental and medical offices, and office tenant improvement. While the building type may vary from project to project, the strength and unity in design, and the inspired creativity is evident in each instance of Otis' work.

Otis' goal is to create spaces that engage the viewer or visitor—to enhance and deepen their experience. Otis strives to blur the predefined edges between inside and outside, to lessen the distinction between the built and natural environment. There is a keen intent to blend the organic and inorganic, the interior and exterior, the manmade and natural. As Otis states, "this reconnects us to the natural and spiritual world, thus elevating our human experience." Otis Architecture believes in creating architecture with true meaning and timeless spirit.

3   David Heath for Western Exposure Co.

1   Oculus at Entry of Residence, California
2   Living Room and Outdoor Space, California
3&4 Residences, Huntington Harbour, California

4   Karen Otis

● 16871 Sea Witch Lane, Huntington Beach, California 92649 USA
Tel: +1 714 846 0177 Fax: +1 714 846 2817

P&T GROUP

ptaehk@p-t-group.com   www.p-t-group.com

1   P&T Group

The P&T Group, formerly known as Palmer and Turner Hong Kong, is the oldest and largest international architectural and engineering practice in Southeast Asia. With more than 700 staff, working from offices located in Hong Kong, Macau, Bangkok, Malaysia, Taiwan, Singapore, Dubai, Indonesia, Beijing, and Shanghai, projects are undertaken in most Southeast Asian countries.

Palmer and Turner was first established in Hong Kong around 1868, and since its inception, has proved to be a major contributor to the physical development of the region, responsible for many of its old and new architectural landmarks.

The P&T Group offers the full range of architectural, engineering and planning services, with full support from in-house interior and graphic design divisions. Model-making, extensive computer facilities and full administrative support complete this service of total design.

The Group's growth is a reflection of the increasing number of large-scale projects demanding the creativity and expertise of many professional services to clients. The firm's success is demonstrated by the numerous design awards it has received over the years.

2   P&T Group

3   P&T Group

4   P&T Group

5   P&T Group

1   Architecture Gallery, Taipei, Taiwan; luxury apartments
2   All Seasons Place, Bangkok, Thailand; office/residential/hotel development
3   The Harbourside, Kowloon, Hong Kong; three 74-storey tall, prestigious
    residential towers
4   Enterprise Square, Kowloon Bay, Hong Kong; 40-storey office tower
5   No. 1,2 Corporate Avenue, Shanghai, China; grade-A office towers

● 25/F OTB Building, 160 Gloucester Road, Hong Kong Tel: +852 2575 6575 Fax: +852 2891 3834

PAATELA & PAATELA, ARCHITECTS

archimed@paatela-arch.fi www.paatela-arch.fi

The name Paatela has been connected with healthcare architecture in Finland for over 80 years. Founded in 1919 by Professor Jussi Paatela, the firm is now run by the third generation of the same family.

The largest healthcare institutions in Finland have relied on the professional expertise of Paatela Architects throughout the firm's years of practice. Today, the staff consists of several architects with over 20 years of experience and the latest knowledge of modern trends in the functional planning and architectural design of heathcare buildings. Projects have ranged from large new hospital complexes to small-scale renovations; from municipal and district hospitals to private clinics and aged-care facilities.

In addition to hospitals built in Finland, Paatela & Paatela, Architects Oy Ltd has designed projects in several countries worldwide. The firm has special knowledge and long experience of the design and implementation of hospital projects in Russia and other countries of the former Soviet Union. The firm often cooperates with foreign clients and design offices in the implementation of such projects.

1   Render Oy

2   Juhani Annanpalo

3   Paatela & Paatela, Architects Oy Ltd

4   Paatela & Paatela, Architects Oy Ltd

1 Turku University Central Hospital, Turku, Finland; illustration of new hospital complex
2 The Great Saparmyrat Turkmenbashy International Medical Center, Ashgabat, Turkmenistan; west façade
3 Vaasa Central Hospital, Vaasa, Finland; operating theater
4 Helsinki University Central Hospital, Hospital for Dermatological and Allergic Diseases, Helsinki, Finland; aerial view

● Ahertajantie 3, FIN-02100 Finland Tel: +358 9 4520 510 Fax: +358 9 4520 5151

PAI
PARAMITA ABIRAMA ISTASADHYA, PT

tom@paidesign.com   www.paidesign.com

PAI, a 40-person firm, was formed in 1985 with the primary purpose of establishing a local Indonesian company augmented with design and management talent from the USA and other countries. The firm was also purposely structured as a studio-style architectural firm with design and production staff as one group, to ensure continuity of design and coordination from concept through implementation. A partner is in charge of each job and oversees the project's development at each stage.

Services provided by PAI include architecture and interior design.

Types of project experience include masterplanning of residential and resort developments; high-rise residential; multi- and single-family residential; multifaceted resort developments with residential, retail and recreational; themed resorts; restaurants; hospitals; offices and industrial projects.

Current and past clients include developers, corporations, government agencies, banking institutions and private individuals.

1   Ibham Jasin

3   PAI

2   PAI

1 Cityloft, Jakarta, Indonesia
2 Citywalk, Jakarta, Indonesia
3 Citywalk, Jakarta, Indonesia
4 Residence at Kusumaatmaja, Jakarta, Indonesia

4   Ibham Jasin

● Gedung BIKA, Jl. Kemang Raya no. 91, Jakarta 12730 Indonesia
Tel: +62 21 7199 191 Fax: +62 21 7195 447

PARKER DURRANT INTERNATIONAL

dwallace@durrant.com www.durrant.com

1   Don Wong

Founded in 1957, Parker Durrant International has consistently produced award-winning projects for clients worldwide. PDI employs more than 50 architects, interior designers, graphic designers, and graduate professionals.

PDI's merger with Durrant advances the goals of both companies by combining design excellence, engineering expertise, and quality service. With a network of more than 300 professionals in 12 offices located throughout the USA, PDI has a national presence with a global reach. It provides a fully integrated approach to design and engineering that ranges from large, mixed-use facilities to smaller, specialized projects. From planning to occupancy, PDI brings leadership and problem solving skills to meet today's challenges.

PDI's work with a broad range of clients, both domestic and international, has led to the design of museums, corporate headquarters, convention centers, courthouses, libraries, academic buildings, mixed-use facilities, and a variety of cultural and entertainment venues.

PDI emphasizes close working relationships, ingenuity in solving complex design challenges, meeting aggressive schedules, and assisting clients in extraordinary ways.

2   Myung Hwan Cho

3   Michael Ian Shoppen

4   Myung Hwan Cho

5   Myung Hwan Cho

1 Bureau of Criminal Apprehension Headquarters, St. Paul, Minnesota; atrium
2 Busan Convention Center, Busan, Korea; entrance
3 Labor & Industries Building, Tumwater, Washington
4 Daegu Product & Convention Center, Daegu, Korea
5 Minneapolis Convention Center, Minneapolis, Minnesota; auditorium

● 430 Oak Grove, Suite 300, Minneapolis, Minnesota 55403 USA Tel: +1 612 871 6864

PARTNERS IN DESIGN ARCHITECTS

info@pidarch.com www.pidarch.com

1   Arc Photo

2   Barry Rustin

3   Arc Photo

4   Studio B

A commitment to building long-term collaborative relationships with clients, employees, business partners and the communities they serve is fuelled by a passion for exceptional architecture.

Through dedication to high design standards, teamwork and an understanding of programs and budgets, the firm exceeds its clients' expectations, provides professional opportunities to staff, and enhances the built environment.

Founded in 1991, the firm provides quality architectural services from offices located in Deerfield, Illinois and Kenosha, Wisconsin. Its design work is enhanced by the diversity of its project types and the ability to listen and synthesize. An interactive and collaborative design methodology allows clients to play a key role in the design of their unique building solutions.

The firm's continued growth, expanding client base and high number of repeat clients testify to the principle that quality design executed in cost-effective solutions provides clients their best value.

5   Edward Purcell

1   Frank Elementary School, Kenosha, Wisconsin; addition and renovation of 1895 landmark school building
2   LakeView RecPlex, Pleasant Prairie, Wisconsin; community recreation center featuring fitness, aquatics and fieldhouse
3   Greenwich Place, Kenosha, Wisconsin; prominent retail building becomes local landmark
4   Partners in Design Architects, tenant build-out, Kenosha, Wisconsin; dynamic and efficient interiors solutions
5   The Cherry Corporation, Automotive Division, Waukegan, Illinois; nondescript offices transformed into open vibrant environments

●   770 Lake Cook Road, Suite 140, Deerfield, Illinois 60015 USA Tel: +1 847 940 0300 Fax: +1 847 940 1045
600 52nd Street, Suite 220, Kenosha, Wisconsin 53140 USA Tel: +1 262 652 2800 Fax: +1 262 652 2812

PASANELLA + KLEIN STOLZMAN + BERG ARCHITECTS, P.C.

info@pksb.com   www.pksb.com

1   Paul Warchol

PKSB is a strong design practice with an international reputation. The firm has completed a broad portfolio of projects including academic buildings, boutique hotels, places of worship, community centers, and corporate offices. Over the years, PKSB's architectural peers and the professional press have honored the firm's efforts with numerous design awards.

PKSB has drawn its strength from the original studio approach to architectural practice, which encourages an atmosphere of collaboration and respect between the firm's clients and their project teams. Celebrating more than 35 years in practice, PKSB continues to evolve without losing sight of its commitment to modern design that serves the needs of its clients and communities. This constancy of vision sustains the firm as it moves forward to embrace the increasingly powerful confluence of art, architecture, and technology.

The firm's reliance on direct principal involvement that is responsive to each client's needs consistently achieves the highest quality of design.

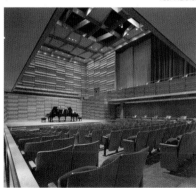

2   Paul Warchol

3   Jock Pottle/ESTO

5   Paul Warchol

1 Congregation Rodeph Sholom, New York, New York
2 Juliet Rosch Recital Hall/Mason Hall Addition and Renovation, Fredonia, New York
3 Education and Development Center, Wise, Virginia; classroom building with laboratories and faculty offices
4 Reed Library Addition and Renovation, Fredonia, New York; 4-story addition to a university library
5 Williamsburg Community Center, New York, New York

4   Paul Warchol

● 330 West 42nd Street, New York, New York 10036 USA Tel: +1 212 594 2010 Fax: +1 212 947 4381

PAUL ANDREU, ARCHITECTE

paul.andreu@paul-andreu.com

1   ADP

2   AXYZ

3   Paul Maurer

Paul Andreu was born in Caudéran, France in 1938. A graduate of two of France's most prestigious engineering schools, l'Ecole Polytechnique and les Ponts et Chaussées, he obtained his certificate as a chartered architect (DPLG) at the Ecole des Beaux-Arts de Paris in 1968.

In addition to his extensive experience with airports, Paul Andreu has designed and realized projects of many different types: Paris' Grand Arche de la Défense (in association with J.O. Spreckelsen); the Olympic ski-jump runway at Saint-Bon Courchevel, France; the French Terminal at the entrance to the Cross-Channel tunnel and the nearby Cité Europe complex at Coquelles; the design concept of the Avenue de France for the Seine Rive Gauche project in Paris; the Osaka Maritime Museum in Japan and the Guangzhou Gymnasium in China. He is the winner of the international design competition for Beijing's National Grand Theatre of China and the Shanghai Oriental Art Centre.

He has won numerous awards for outstanding achievements in architecture, including the Grand Prix National d'Architecture and the Grand Prix de la Fondation Florence Gould.

4   Shinkenshiku-sha

5   ADPi équipe OAC

1   Charles de Gaulle International Airport, Hall 2E, Paris, France
2   China National Grand Theatre, Beijing, PRC
3   Charles de Gaulle International Airport, Hall 2F, Paris, France
4   Osaka Maritime Museum, Japan
5   Oriental Art Centre, Shanghai, PRC

●   15, Rue du Parc Montsouris, Paris 75014 France   Tel: +33 1 5810 0515   Fax: +33 1 5362 0220

PAUL MORGAN ARCHITECTS

office@paulmorganarchitects.com   www.paulmorganarchitects.com

1   Chung Hsiao Hsieh

Paul Morgan Architects produces architecture for the public realm. The firm was established in 2003 following the separation of Morgan McKenna and builds on experience gained in university, library, council, housing, urban design, masterplanning, and commercial projects completed in Melbourne, regional Victoria, and Asia.

Paul Morgan Architects works towards amplifying the brief's functional and expressive potential. In striving for truly innovative buildings and spaces, the practice has developed design strategies in performance envelopes, spatial-acoustic ecology, flexible learning spaces, and university masterplanning. Aesthetic and function are linked in design elements such as a workplace oases, free-plan syndicate rooms, data umbilicals, and sunlight diffusers. Paul Morgan Architects' work in ecological design synthesizes contemporary design with technical and environmental sustainable design principles, which Paul has taught at RMIT University in Melbourne.

Paul Morgan Architects views architecture in a context of cultural production. The success of the practice derives from Paul taking a personal approach from project initiation to completion.

3   Andrius Lipsys

2   Peter Bennetts

1 RMIT University School of Computer Science & IT, Melbourne; oasis interior; Morgan McKenna architects
2 Monash University Faculty of Information Technology, Melbourne; reception desk; Morgan McKenna architects
3 RMIT University Spatial Information Architecture Laboratory (SIAL), Melbourne; sound studios
4 RMIT University School of Computer Science & IT, Melbourne; view of syndicate room past umbilicals toward oasis; Morgan McKenna architects

4   Andrius Lipsys

● Level 10, 221 Queen Street, Melbourne, Victoria 3000 Australia Tel: +61 3 9600 3253 Fax: +61 3 9602 5673

PAUL UHLMANN ARCHITECTS

info@pua.com.au www.pua.com.au

1   David Sandison

2   Matt Kennedy

Paul Uhlmann Architects is an award-winning,
design-based practice, focused on achieving
excellence in architecture by means of responding
to specific environmental and user requirements.
The resultant architecture reflects this through the
creation of ambient and elegant spaces for living
and working. The practice is multidisciplinary,
working on a variety of projects throughout
Queensland, Northern New South Wales,
Australia and the South Pacific.

3   Matt Kennedy

4   David Sandison

5   David Sandison

1 Mt Coot-tha Residence, Mt Coot-tha, Queensland; new urban residential family home
2 Paradisio, Tugun, Queensland; new family beach house
3 The Haven, Brookfield, Queensland; new rural residential retreat
4 Tenzing House, Casuarina Beach, New South Wales; new beach house escape
5 Tugun Towerhouses, Tugun, Queensland; towerhouse development of 4 independent unit dwellings

● 301/87 Griffith Street, Coolangatta, Queensland 4225 Australia
Tel: +61 7 5536 3911 Fax: +61 7 5536 3944

PAYETTE

info@payette.com   www.payette.com

1   Warren Jagger

2   Jeff Goldberg/ESTO

Founded in 1932, Payette provides architecture, masterplanning, programming, landscape architecture, interior design, and graphic design services for complex environments. The practice is focused on buildings for science and technology teaching and research; medical teaching and research; healthcare; and corporate research.

In recent years, Payette has emerged as a leader in the programming, design, and construction of large biomedical facilities to serve as viable scientific communities at major universities.

Current projects include the Biosciences Tower III at the University of Pittsburgh School of Medicine; a new Cancer Institute for Hershey Medical Center of the Pennsylvania State University; the Molecular Cellular and Developmental Biology Building at Yale University; and the Physics Department of Material Science and Engineering, Spectroscopy, and Infrastructure Project at Massachusetts Institute of Technology.

3   Warren Jagger

4   Peter Mauss/ESTO

1 Massachusetts General Hospital, Boston, Massachusetts; patient room
2 Oberlin College, Oberlin, Ohio; new entrance at dusk
3 The Pennsylvania State University, University Park, Pennsylvania (with Bower Lewis Thrower Architects)
4 The Johns Hopkins University, Baltimore, Maryland; exterior
5 University of Iowa, Iowa City; exterior view of MEBRF at night

5   Jeff Goldberg/ESTO

● 285 Summer Street, Boston, Massachusetts 02210 USA Tel: +1 617 895 1000 Fax: +1 617 895 1002

PDT ARCHITECTS PTY LTD

pdt@pdt.com.au   www.pdt.com.au

1

PDT Architects & RTKL

Since its foundation in 1938, PDT has been involved in the architecture and interior design of buildings throughout Australia and New Zealand.

PDT's involvement ranges through every project phase, from pre-design to detailed design and documentation, to interior design and post-contract administration. The firm has an outstanding reputation for its design and documentation expertise, innovative and sustainable designs, and a personal approach to projects, together with an understanding of every client's needs.

PDT provides professional architectural, interior design, master planning and project management services for education, health, and aged-care institutions, office and commercial accommodation, residential and heritage projects, industrial complexes, retail and shopping centers, hospitality and tourism developments, cultural and community facilities, sport and leisure facilities, and transportation facilities.

2

Graham Meltzer Photography

3

Chris Stacey

4

Patrick Bingham-Hall

5

Aaron Tait

1   Queens Plaza, Brisbane, Queensland
2   St Aidan's Anglican Girls School, Brisbane, Queensland
3   UQ Centre, Brisbane, Queensland
4   Suncorp Stadium, Brisbane, Queensland (in association with HOK Sport)
5   Sunsuper, Brisbane, Queensland

● 184 Wharf Street, Spring Hill, Queensland 4000 Australia Tel: +61 7 3232 1300 Fax: +61 7 3232 1350

PECKHAM & WRIGHT ARCHITECTS, INC.

www.pwarchitects.com

Since 1978, Peckham & Wright Architects has delivered architectural and masterplanning services to private businesses, public agencies, and individuals. PWA offers complete project design services, in a high-tech setting, through collaboration of in-house design professionals and outside consultants.

PWA focuses on finding an appropriate design opportunity in every project with attention to color, texture, energy, natural light, and the integration of form and structure. The firm's design aesthetic acknowledges the historical, natural, and built contexts that exist in every project and site.

The success of PWA projects is also the result of careful architectural programming, thoughtful execution of the design, the quality of the construction documents, and the ability to listen and clearly communicate. By developing strong relationships with clients, PWA gains a deeper understanding of client needs, providing timely services and architecture of lasting value.

Since its founding, PWA has focused on sustainability and the relationship between people, the natural environment and the built environment. It has incorporated sustainable design across the entire practice with projects ranging from the Missouri Department of Conservation Campus in Cape Girardeau, Missouri, to town planning in Budapest, Hungary.

1   Deanna Dikeman

2   MU Sports Information

3   Peckham & Wright

4   Peckham & Wright

1   Butterfield Youth Services, Marshall, Missouri
2   Columbia Fire Station 8, Columbia, Missouri
3   University of Missouri NCAA Track, Columbia, Missouri
4   Cape Girardeau Conservation Campus, Cape Girardeau, Missouri

●   15 South 10th Street, Columbia, Missouri 65201 USA   Tel: +1 573 449 2683   Fax: +1 573 442 6213

PERKINS & WILL

www.perkinswill.com

Established in 1935, Perkins+Will is an integrated architecture, interiors, and planning firm recognized for its leadership with clients in corporate, commercial, civic, healthcare, higher education, K-12 education, and science and technology. Sustainable, high-performance and environmentally conscious design are staples of the firm's practice. Nearly 70 percent of Perkins+Will's professional staff is LEED accredited, among the highest percentage of any design firm in North America to achieve this important industry standard. A staff of more than 950 experienced professionals now serves clients out of offices in Atlanta, Beijing, Boston, Calgary, Charlotte, Chicago, Dallas, Glastonbury, Connecticut, Houston, Los Angeles, Miami, Minneapolis, New York, Research Triangle Park, San Francisco, Seattle, Shanghai, Vancouver, Victoria, and Washington, D.C. Perkins+Will routinely ranks among the world's top design firms and has received hundreds of awards, including the coveted American Institute of Architects Firm of the Year Award.

1   Steinkamp-Ballogg

2   Perkins & Will

3   Perkins & Will

1 Peggy Notebaert Nature Museum, Chicago Academy of Science, Chicago, Illinois, USA
2 Qatar Broadcasting Services Complex, Doha, Qatar
3 Universidade Agostinho Neto, Luanda, Angola
4 Los Angeles US Courthouse, Los Angeles, California, USA
5 Washington University School of Medicine, McDonnell Pediatric and Cancer Research Building, St Louis, Missouri, USA

4   Perkins & Will   5   Nick Merrick/Hedrich-Blessing

● 1382 Peachtree Street NE, Atlanta, Georgia 30309 USA Tel: +1 404 873 2300 Fax: +1 404 892 5823

PERKINS EASTMAN

info@perkinseastman.com www.perkinseastman.com

Since 1981, Perkins Eastman has become a leading international architecture, urban, and interior design firm, offering programming, planning, design, strategic planning and consulting, real estate and economic analysis, and program management services. Forging a multi-faceted practice around the interests of its principal designers, the firm has cultivated a diverse portfolio of projects for private- and public-sector clients in several practice areas.

A dual goal of client satisfaction and design excellence has fostered organic growth. Perkins Eastman has expanded from a small office into a service-oriented firm of approximately 550 staff, with offices in New York, Pittsburgh, Los Angeles, Stamford, Charlotte, San Francisco, Chicago, Toronto, and Shanghai.

Recognized for superior design capabilities and client satisfaction, the firm's original principles upon which it was founded continue to lead it in new directions. Through constant efforts to innovate, Perkins Eastman collaborates, researches, and upholds its tradition of excellence.

1   Woodruff/Brown

2   Woodruff/Brown   3   Chuck Choi Architectural Photography

4   Perkins Eastman

5   Chuck Choi Architectural Photography

1 Avalon Riverview, New York, New York
2 Roger Ludlow Middle School, Fairfield, Connecticut
3 University at Albany Fine Arts Sculpture Building, Albany, New York
4 Chongqing Library, Shapingba District, Chongqing, PRC
5 New York University Medical Center Cancer Institute, New York, New York

● 115 Fifth Avenue, New York, New York 10003-1004 USA Tel: +1 212 353 7200 Fax: +1 212 353 7676

472

PERRY DEAN ROGERS | PARTNERS ARCHITECTS

www.perrydean.com

Perry Dean Rogers | Partners' approach to architecture is complex, mature, and provocative. The office's work is the product not of one lead designer, or of self-contained studios under one roof. Rather, multiple talents of different ages collaborate in myriad ways. There is a great deal of borrowing and melding of ideas, which are invented anew and interpreted in refreshing ways. This methodology of practice is what keeps the work both balanced and innovative.

The office approaches each commission with a clear set of convictions: first, analyzing needs and generating solutions by enfranchising the client and users in the design process. Second, remaining open and engaged with clients and their needs—searching for solutions to architectural problems that address and emphasize those client needs. And creating architecture that results in its users seeing the world in a fresh way.

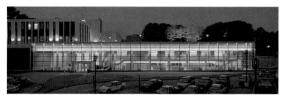

1   Richard Mandelkorn

2   Richard Mandelkorn

3   Richard Mandelkorn

1 Barone Campus Center, Fairfield University, Fairfield, Connecticut; luminous curtainwall reveals student organizations at night
2 Waidner Library, Dickinson College, Carlisle, Pennsylvania; view of library entrance and upper-level study lounge
3 New Town Center and Facilities, Milton Hershey School, Hershey, Pennsylvania; Stacks Visual Arts Center
4 Fontaine Hall, Marist College, Poughkeepsie, New York; entry tower
5 Franklin W. Olin College of Engineering, Needham, Massachusetts; detail of classroom/lab building, new engineering college

4   Richard Mandelkorn   5   Richard Mandelkorn

● 177 Milk Street, Boston, Massachusetts 02109 USA Tel: +1 617 423 0100 Fax: +1 617 426 2274

473

PETER L. GLUCK AND PARTNERS, ARCHITECTS

info@gluckpartners.com www.gluckpartners.com

1   Peter L. Gluck

2   Peter L. Gluck

Since 1972, Peter L. Gluck and Partners has designed buildings throughout the USA, ranging from houses, schools, religious buildings, and community centers to hotels, corporate interiors, university buildings, and historic restorations. Many of these projects have won national and international design awards and have been published in numerous architectural journals and books. Rather than specializing in a particular building type or architectural style, the firm provides appropriate responses to sometimes difficult and conflicting requirements.

In 1992, the firm established AR/CS (Architectural Construction Services), Inc., an integrated system of architectural design and construction management, which provides sophisticated design, quality construction, and unusually low costs in an increasingly difficult building environment. In order to develop these ideas further, Aspen GK, Inc. was established in 1997 as a development partnership, founded to produce well-designed, high-quality housing.

3   Paul Warchol

4   Peter L. Gluck

5   Paul Warchol

1   Bronx Preparatory Charter School, Bronx, New York, polished ceramic tile and corrugated metal façade
2   Crate and Barrel House, New Canaan, Connecticut, view of two forms from pond
3   Farmhouse with Lap Pool and Sunken Garden, Worcester, New York; composition of forms added onto 18th-century farmhouse
4   Lake House with Court, Highland Park, Illinois; zinc roof overlooking curved courtyard
5   Little Sisters of the Assumption Family Health Service, East Harlem, New York; façade composed of operable and fixed panels

● 646 West 131st Street, New York, New York 10027 USA Tel: +1 212 690 4950 Fax: +1 212 690 4961

PETER WALKER AND PARTNERS

www.pwpla.com

1   PWP

2   PWP

3   PWP

4   PWP

The office of Peter Walker and Partners was formed in 1983 for the practice of landscape architecture. The projects, executed worldwide, vary both in scale and program and include urban design and planning, corporate headquarters and university campuses, parks, plazas, and gardens. Exploring the relationships between art, culture, and context, Peter Walker and other members of the firm re-form the landscape—whether urban or natural—and challenge traditional concepts of design.

The office's method of design moves from defining the program to forming the space and experimenting with materials; the tools employed are drawing, model-making, computer graphics, and full-size mock-ups. The decision process reflects the constant exchange occurring with clients, architects and consultants. A knowledge of history and tradition and a deep understanding of contemporary needs and patterns of living, combined with a quest for the appropriate and the particular, allow this firm to produce landscapes that are both timeless and unique.

5   PWP

1 Saitama Sky Forest, Saitama Prefecture, Japan;
   on-structure, urban plaza
2 Jamison Square, Portland, Oregon, USA; public park
3 UCSD Library Walk, San Diego, California, USA;
   university campus promenade
4 Center for Clinical Sciences Research, Stanford
   University, Palo Alto, California, USA; courtyard garden
5 Town Center Park, Costa Mesa, California, USA;
   central open space in a mixed-use development

● 739 Allston Way, Berkeley, California 94710 USA Tel: +1 510 849 9494 Fax: +1 510 849 9333

PFAU ARCHITECTURE LTD.

info@pfauarchitecture.com www.pfauarchitecture.com

Pfau Architecture is a nationally recognized design firm distinguished by its unique projects and environmentally sensitive, leading edge design. Since 1991, it has remained committed to the notion that successful architecture must connect with its users, resulting in the creation of progressive education facilities, humanistic work environments, and inspiring places of worship. The firm strongly believes in promoting stewardship for the world's resources through sustainable design and construction practices, and is a member of the U.S. Green Building Council.

Principals Peter Pfau and Dwight Long lead a staff of 17 highly talented individuals, continuing personal and hands-on involvement with each and every project. This dedication of principal-level involvement provides clients with the highest level of personal service, ensuring their needs are met with a quality product within budget and schedule parameters.

1 Roxanne's

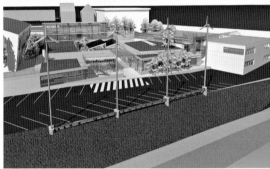

3 Pfau Architecture Ltd

2 J.D. Peterson

4 Matthew Millman

5 Tim Griffi

1 Roxanne's, Larkspur, California; environmentally friendly, gourmet, organic vegetarian 'living foods' restaurant
2 Green Glen, San Francisco, California; commercial office conversion of San Francisco warehouse/factory
3 Lick-Wilmerding High School, San Francisco, California; new technology and design center for college prep high school
4 Outside-In House, San Anselmo, California; transformation of modern Marin County residence
5 350 Rhode Island, San Francisco, California; ground-up, full city block, commercial office complex

● 630 Third Street, Suite 200, San Francisco, California 94107 USA
Tel: +1 415 908 6408 Fax: +1 415 908 6409

PHILIP JOHNSON/ALAN RITCHIE ARCHITECTS

www.pjar.com

1   Philip Johnson/Alan Ritchie Architects

Philip Johnson/Alan Ritchie Architects has been recognized as one of the most creative and innovative architectural firms for more than half a century. Philip Johnson's leadership in the modern movement, and later playing a seminal role in the introduction of post-modernism and deconstructivism, has helped to form new ideas and exciting directions in design and architecture around the world. Now, under the leadership of Alan Ritchie, who worked with Philip Johnson for more than 25 years, the firm continues to explore and present new and cutting-edge designs.

Philip Johnson/Alan Ritchie Architects' emphasis is on quality design and an understanding that input from the client is critical to its process. The firm has won numerous awards and is well known for many distinguished buildings, such as the AT&T Corporate (Sony) Headquarters, Lipstick Building, Penzoil Place, Trump International, Williams Tower, Chrysler Center, The Amon Carter Museum, The Metropolitan, and The Business Center at Drexel University.

2   Philip Johnson/Alan Ritchie Architects

3   Philip Johnson/Alan Ritchie Architects

4   Philip Johnson/Alan Ritchie Architects

1   Fay Showroom, Milan, Italy; interior design for premiere couture retail showroom
2   The Metropolitan, New York, New York; residential/commercial luxury tower which cantilevers over adjoining buildings
3   Marquee Nightclub, New York, New York; signature, arched stainless steel stairway
4   Nanjing Tower, Nanjing, PRC; competition for the proposed tallest tower in Nanjing
5   Urban Glass House, New York, New York; international architecturally inspired luxury high-rise building

5   Philip Johnson/Alan Ritchie Architects

●   4 Columbus Circle, 5th Floor, New York, New York 10019 USA   Tel: +1 212 319 5880   Fax: +1 212 319 5881

PICA CIAMARRA ASSOCIATI

pca@pca-int.com www.pca.int.com

1   PCA archives

2   PCA archives

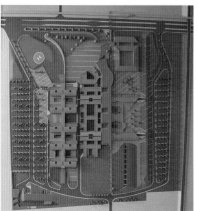

4   PCA archives

The team at PCA is a multidisciplinary partnership, and has worked on projects of international renown such as the multifunctional unit at Arcavacata, University of Calabria.

Its attention to sustainable architecture and environment is clearly visible in many of its projects, including the CNR Technology Centre in Naples (finalist in the International Award for Innovative Technology in Architecture, Sydney, 1988); Fuorigrotta Square; Teuco–Guzzini offices in Recanati (which won the Technology–Environment–Architecture prize, 1998); the University of Caserta; the City of Science (2002) on the coast of Coroglio; the Fair area in Bari; and a project for Beijing Olympic Green.

The work of the firm has been published in international magazines, monographs and books, including *Linguaggi del'architettura contemporanea*, B.Zevi, ETAS 1998; *European Masters – Urban Architecture Barcelona*, 1996; *Piazze e spazi urbani*, Over, Milan 1991; and *Quaternario '88 – Sydney; Architecture of Tall Buildings*, 1995.

3   PCA archives

5   Mimmo Jodice

1 City of Science, Naples, Italy
2 Forteguerriana Library, Pistoia, Italy
3 Ponte Parodi, Genoa, Italy
4 Faculty of Medicine and Surgery, Caserta, Italy
5 Posillipo House, Naples, Italy

● Posillipo,176, Naples 80123, Italy Tel: +39 081 5752 223 Fax: +39 081 575 5952

PIERRE EL KHOURY ARCHITECTS

pelk@dm.net.lb   www.pierreelkhoury.com

Pierre El Khoury's architectural work stands free of the kind of discourse that would either illuminate it or else cover it in a fog of theory. When the production of Pierre El Khoury is examined in search for elements on which to build a discourse, one is confronted by a highly diverse body of work.

Some 200 projects testify to a career that has covered many representative aspects of Lebanese architecture. The firm has a long history of architectural practice, both for public and private organizations. It has provided design services to corporations, individuals, and other sectors in Lebanon and internationally.

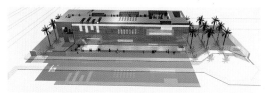

1   Joseph Brakhia

2   Joseph E. Faycal

3   Tony Farjallah

4   Geraldine Brunel

5   Brahim Baddr

1   Qatar Embassy Competition, Beirut, Lebanon
2   Verdun Twins, Verdun, Lebanon
3   ESCWA UN Headquarters, Beirut, Lebanon
4   Opera House Competition, Oslo, Norway
5   BLOM Bank, Verdun, Lebanon

● Port, Derviche Haddad Street, P.O. Box 1142, Beirut, Lebanon
Tel: +961 1 564 222 Fax: +961 1 447 875

PIZZININI, LUXEMBURG, THORSTEINSSON

tryggvi@minarc.com

1   Pizzinini, Luxemburg, Thorsteinsson

2   Pizzinini, Luxemburg, Thorsteinsson

3   Pizzinini, Luxemburg, Thorsteinsson

International architectural practices are common, but the 15-year partnership of Regina Pizzinini, Leon Luxemburg and Tryggvi Thorsteinsson differs from most in the regularity with which these three young mavericks shuttle back and forth between their offices in California and Europe. In their mobility, as in the joyous exuberance of their residential projects, they are true heirs of the late Charles Moore, who inspired them to move from Austria to Los Angeles in 1983, and invited them to study and work with him.

Together, Pizzinini, Luxemburg and Thorsteinsson have designed residences of growing scale and complexity, playing variations on recurring themes: simple geometric forms, interlocking volumes, and primary colors. Like most young architects, they started small, with a guest house and remodels, graduating to residences, and competing for the design of public buildings.

4   Pizzinini, Luxemburg, Thorsteinsson

5   Pizzinini, Luxemburg, Thorsteinsson

1–5   House Hentzig, Luxembourg

● 2324 Michigan Avenue, Santa Monica, California 90405 USA
Tel: +1 310 452 9667   Fax: +1 310 452 9697

PLATT BYARD DOVELL WHITE ARCHITECTS

pbdw@pbdw.com www.pbdw.com

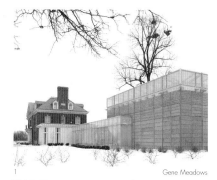

1   Gene Meadows

Platt Byard Dovell White Architects is a 37-person design firm specializing in planning and design for owners of properties in complex contexts. For almost 40 years, the firm has consistently delivered efficient, evocative buildings that enlarge the understanding of their purposes and enrich their neighborhoods.

Among the firm's award-winning designs are new buildings including The New 42nd Street Studios, the Saginaw Art Museum and Chanel's 57th Street retail headquarters, as well as additions to historic districts such as 250 Water Street, 47 East 91st Street, and Equinox. The firm has also restored and won awards for individual landmark buildings such as the Appellate Division courthouse and the Foundation Building of The Cooper Union for the Advancement of Science and Art.

Recent projects for the Andrew W. Mellon Foundation, Columbia, Barnard, Fordham and Sarah Lawrence College have extended the firm's reputation for thoughtful and elegant institutional designs.

2   Elliott Kaufman

3   Matthew Mueller/PBDW

4   David Grinder/PBDW

5   Jonathan Wallen

1 Saginaw Art Museum, Saginaw, Michigan; modern addition to existing historic building (with Wigen Tinknell Meyer)
2 The New 42nd Street Studios, New York, New York; completely modern 11-story creative performing arts "factory"
3 The Reece School, New York, New York; unique new modern building for specialized school
4 Green-Wood Cemetery Mausoleum, Brooklyn, New York; contemporary exploration of neglected building type
5 Equinox Greenwich, New York, New York; contemporary addition to eclectic and historic neighborhood

● 20 West 22nd Street, New York, New York 10010 USA Tel: +1 212 691 2440 Fax: +1 212 633 0144

POWERS BROWN ARCHITECTURE

brown@powersbrown.com www.powersbrown.com

1   Cary Els

2   Baldemar Gonzalez

The binding matrix of Powers Brown Architecture is ethical in nature, with the team members sharing a common attitude regarding the uniqueness of each project and site. This entails a belief that specificity is a condition perhaps unique to architecture as a discipline. The firm works from a belief in the purpose of architecture as a vehicle of cultural meaning, in which architecture separates itself from art in the struggle for objectivity.

Powers Brown Architecture is aware that a building has to be responsible to its circumstances in the city, and it is the great obligation of the architect to consider the project as a piece of the city rather than as a continuation of a body of work, forced to fit to complete the series, as it were. Preferring to work in close collaboration with the context, Powers Brown Architecture eschews blind contextualism as regressive, preferring to work towards the dynamic balance between innovation and appropriateness.

4   Dror Baldinger

3   Dror Baldinger

5   Dror Baldinger

1 St. Paul's Church, Houston, Texas; ceiling detail
2 Westchase District Longrange Planning, Houston, Texas; aerial axonometric view
3 MNP Corporate Headquarters, Houston, Texas; entrance court
4 Metro Light Maintenance Facility, Houston, Texas; lobby
5 Metro Light Maintenance Facility, Houston, Texas; view across train yard

● 1314 Texas Avenue, Suite 401, Houston, Texas 77002 USA Tel: +1 713 224 0456 Fax: +1 713 224 0457

PRINGLE BRANDON

pbmarketing@pringle-brandon.co.uk www.pringle-brandon.co.uk

Pringle Brandon is one of the UK's leading architectural, interior design, and workplace consultancy firms, specializing in office design, fit out, refurbishment, and space planning.

Pringle Brandon understands the need to design workplaces 'inside-out' to be attractive, flexible, and efficient, with a wealth of facilities and work settings to support people performing various functions. At the forefront of the revolution in workplace design over the past decade, Pringle Brandon has worked on many of the UK's high-profile and innovative office projects, adding value to its clients' businesses through informed, imaginative, and effective design solutions.

Projects vary in size and complexity and often include undertaking building feasibility studies, due diligence studies, and pilot projects for new ways of working. Pringle Brandon's recent clients include Allen & Overy, BBC, Bank of America, Banque AIG, Barclays plc, CMS Cameron Mckenna, Diageo, EBRD, HMCE, JPMorgan, Linklaters, London Borough of Ealing, L'Oreal, Mitsubishi, NATS, and Reuters.

1   Zander Olsen

2   David Churchill

3   David Churchill

4   Robert Brown

5   Chris Gascoigne

1   Banque AIG, London, UK; meeting room
2   CMS Cameron McKenna, London, UK; main reception and meeting area
3   CMS Cameron McKenna, London, UK; library and resource center
4   NATS, Southampton, UK; reception and meeting area with LED 'wavy wall'
5   Barclays plc, Canary Wharf, London, UK; staff restaurant

●   10 Bonhill Street, London EC2A 4QJ UK Tel: +44 20 7466 1110 Fax: +44 20 7466 1050

PROVAN BURDETT PTY LTD

architects@provanburdett.com.au

Provan Burdett Pty Ltd Architects was established at the beginning of 1988 by Tania Provan and David Burdett, after studying and working together for 11 years. The result of their long history together has been a shared approach to architecture and design, and to service delivery.

The early years of the firm have seen the focus on residential work diversify to include multi-unit residential, in locations throughout Melbourne, both inner city and suburban, and country Victoria. The scale of projects has ranged from between A$70,000 to A$3 million.

Smaller projects include renovation and addition work to family homes, with the larger projects consisting of new homes in Portsea and Red Hill and 14 apartments in North and West Melbourne and in the alpine resort of Falls Creek.

Provan Burdett's hands-on approach aims to ensure each project has input from both directors while creating a unique solution for each client's brief and site.

1   Peter Bennetts

2   Bozig

3   Provan Burdett

4   Provan Burdett

5   Provan Burdett

1 Frueauf Village, Falls Creek, Victoria
2 Callanans Road, Red Hill, Victoria
3 Franklin Place, West Melbourne, Victoria
4 Leveson Street, North Melbourne, Victoria
5 Hotham Road, Portsea, Victoria

● 22 Franklin Place, West Melbourne, Victoria 3003 Australia Tel: +61 3 9329 3443 Fax: +61 3 9329 3445

484

PTW ARCHITECTS

info@ptw.com.au   www.ptw.com.au

1   Patrick Bingham-Hall

In more than a century of continuous practice PTW Architects has become one of Australia's oldest, largest, and most diverse architectural firms with offices in Australia, China, Vietnam, and the UAE. PTW Architects' approach is to analyze each architectural task and produce a distinctive and specific solution. The firm has developed an established profile in masterplanning and architecture over a diversity of building types including residential, commercial, sporting venues, and buildings for the arts.

Following major involvement in a of range of projects for the Sydney 2000 Olympic Games, PTW has continued its involvement in architecture for sport and major events with work continuing on the Doha 2006 Asian Games and the Beijing 2008 Olympic Games. Recently PTW has achieved notable successes in winning the international competitions for the Olympic athletes' village and also the Beijing National Swimming Centre with its innovative design, known as the Watercube.

2   PTW Architects & CSCEC+Design

3   Rowan Turner

1   The Bond, Sydney, New South Wales, atrium with projecting 'pods' and historic sandstone wall (in collaboration with Lend Lease design)
2   Watercube: National Swimming Centre, Beijing, PRC; rendering showing EFTE cladding and use of projections (in association with CSCEC+Design)
3   Pier Apartments, Sydney, New South Wales; residential apartments with mechanical louver shutters (in association with HPA Architects)
4   Sydney Theatre, Sydney, New South Wales; view of 850-seat drama theater from stage (in association with HPA Architects)

4   Patrick Bingham-Hall

● Level 17, 9 Castlereagh Street, Sydney, New South Wales 2000 Australia
Tel: +61 2 9232 5877 Fax: +61 2 9221 4139

PUGH + SCARPA ARCHITECTS

info@pugh-scarpa.com   www.pugh-scarpa.com

1   Marvin Rand

2   Benny Chan—Photoworks

Pugh + Scarpa is an architecture, engineering, interior design and planning firm founded in Santa Monica in 1991. Pugh + Scarpa has grown to a firm of 43 professionals and is currently working on an assortment of commissions for public, private and institutional clients. Pugh + Scarpa maintains offices in Santa Monica, and San Francisco, California; and Charlotte, North Carolina. Gwynne Pugh AIA, Lawrence Scarpa AIA, and Angela Brooks AIA, are the sole principals.

Pugh + Scarpa approaches each project as the continuation of an ongoing inquiry. The firm encourages a culture of ingenuity and exploration that enables it to maintain a fresh approach to every project undertaken. Ongoing research into materials and technologies as well as a constant re-examination of known conditions, accepted norms and established methods leads to innovative solutions and stimulating new ways of approaching design. This is true regardless of the scale—big or small, whether for public or private use, for rich or for poor. This is an approach that has often led the firm to reinvent established building types.

3   Marvin Rand

4   Marvin Rand

5   Marvin Rand

1   CoOp Editorial; interior remodel of an early Frank Gehry building
2   Bergamot Artist Lofts; north façade facing Bergamot Station Arts Complex
3   Reactor Films; transformation of a shipping container into a
    conference room
4   Absolute Diva; rehabilitation of a retail commercial structure
5   Colorado Court; a 44-unit, energy-efficient, affordable housing project

● 2525 Michigan Avenue, F1, Santa Monica, California 90404 USA
Tel: +1 310 828 0226 Fax: +1 310 453 9606

QUAD3 GROUP

lkarasinski@quad3.com www.quad3.com

Quad3 Group, Inc., a full-service architecture, engineering and environmental services firm, has been providing services to commercial, industrial, government and education clients since 1967. Located in Wilkes-Barre, Philadelphia, and Pittsburgh, the firm maintains a staff of 120 employees. The firm's comprehensive service capabilities provide its clients with a central point of management responsibility, while allowing the firm to assemble a team of in-house specialists that respond to a project's specific needs.

The firm's design philosophy is grounded in the concept of 'forensic design'. "In some ways we see ourselves as much as forensic experts or investigators as we do architects or interior designers," says Leo Karasinski, AIA, Director of Design for Quad3 Group. "In order to achieve the appropriate design solution, we immerse ourselves in the community. This allows us to craft a design that truly reflects the community rather than our own design passions."

1   Chris Barone

3   Bo Parker Photography

2   Jeff Goldberg/Esto

4   Chris Barone   5   Jeff Goldberg/Esto

1 Luzerne County Parking Garage, Wilkes-Barre, Pennsylvania; landmark tower
2 Gerald J. Wycallis Elementary School, Dallas, Pennsylvania; view towards main entry
3 Central Mountain High School, Mill Hall, Pennsylvania; main street looking into central courtyard
4 Pitt Ohio, Hazleton, Pennsylvania; office space terminal entrance
5 Gerald J. Wycallis Elementary School, Dallas, Pennsylvania; entry canopies

● 37 North Washington Street, Wilkes-Barre, Pennsylvania 18701 USA
Tel: +1 570 829 4200 Fax: +1 570 829 0302

R.M.KLIMENT & FRANCES HALSBAND ARCHITECTS

rum@kliment-halsband.com   www.kliment-halsband.com

Robert Kliment FAIA and Frances Halsband FAIA founded R.M.Kliment & Frances Halsband Architects in New York City in 1972. The firm has a staff of 30, including two other partners and two associates.

The work of the firm includes planning and buildings for educational, institutional, commercial and public clients; historic preservation/adaptive reuse; private residences; interiors, furniture and lighting design.

The firm has received more than 50 design awards, including the 1997 Architecture Firm Award from the American Institute of Architects, and the 1998 Medal of Honor from the New York Chapter AIA. It has also received four Honor Awards for Excellence in Architectural Design from the American Institute of Architects.

It has been featured in more than 200 publications, and its work has been given wide exposure in the USA and internationally. A monograph entitled *R.M.Kliment & Frances Halsband Architects: Selected and Current Work* was published by The Images Publishing Group in 1998.

1   Cervin Robinson

2   R.M.Kliment & Frances Halsband Architects

3   Lori Stahl

4   Cervin Robinson

1   Arcadia University Landman Library, Glenside, Pennsylvania
2   United States Post Office and Courthouse, Brooklyn, New York
3   Franklin & Marshall College Roschel Performing Arts Center, Lancaster, Pennsylvania
4   Franklin D. Roosevelt Presidential Library, Henry A. Wallace Visitor and Education Center, Hyde Park, New York
5   Dan M. Russell Jr. United States Courthouse, Gulfport, Mississippi (with Canizaro Cawthon Davis)

5   Cervin Robinson

● 255 West 26th Street, New York, New York 10001 USA Tel: +1 212 243 7400 Fax: +1 212 633 9769

RADAN HUBICKA

hubicka@radanhubicka www.arch.cz/aarh

Radan Hubicka's work focuses on form and place, and a building's relationship with its surroundings. Projects share a common theme—visual and physical contact with nature, both externally and internally. Often the exterior deeply pervades into the interior and vice versa. His architecture is simple yet abstract, with an emphasis on processing the detail in the exact moment of a project's realization.

1   Radan Hubicka

2   Radan Hubicka

3   Jan Maly

4   Jan Maly   5   Jan Maly

1 Residence within National Park, Sumava, Czech Republic
2 Villa, Prague, Czech Republic
3 Block of Flats, Prague, Czech Republic
4 Villa, Prague, Czech Republic; interior
5 Villa, Prague, Czech Republic; exterior

● Wenzigova 17, 120 00 Prague 2, Czech Republic Tel: +420 224 261 076 Fax: +420 224 261 077

RAFAEL VIÑOLY ARCHITECTS PC

info@rvapc.com   www.rvapc.com

1   Brad Feinknopf

2   Brad Feinknopf

Brad Feinknopf

3   Román Viñoly

4   Brad Feinknopf

Rafael Viñoly Architects PC is a critically acclaimed international practice with headquarters in New York and London and site offices across the USA and internationally. Founded in 1982, the 160-person firm provides comprehensive services in building design, urban planning, and interior design. It has successfully completed fast track and design/build projects, as well as conventionally scheduled and organized assignments.

The firm's diversified work encompasses a wide range of building types such as courthouses, cultural facilities, convention centers, educational facilities, and healthcare research facilities. Projects range in scale from intimate interiors and technical laboratory spaces, to high-rise towers, expansive civic spaces, and urban master plans.

Among the firm's most significant projects are the Tokyo International Forum, the Kimmel Center for the Performing Arts, the Carl Icahn Laboratory for the Institute for Integrative Genomics at Princeton University, and the John Edward Porter Neuroscience Research Laboratory for the National Institutes of Health.

1 University of Chicago, Graduate School of Business, Chicago, Illinois
2 National Institutes of Health, Porter Neuroscience Research Center, Bethesda, Maryland
3 Princeton University, The Carl Icahn Laboratory/The Lewis-Sigler Institute for Integrative Genomics, Princeton, New Jersey
4 Jazz at Lincoln Center, New York, New York
5 David L. Lawrence Convention Center, Pittsburgh, Pennsylvania

5   Brad Feinknopf

● 50 Vandam Street, New York, New York 10013 USA Tel: +1 212 924 5060 Fax: +1 212 924 5858

RATIO ARCHITECTS, INC.

info@ratioarchitects.com   www.ratioarchitects.com

1   Craig Dugan/Hedrich-Blessing

2   Bob Haar/Hedrich-Blessing

The guiding philosophy of RATIO Architects can be found in its name. RATIO is based on the Latin word meaning 'to reason' and is the root word of 'rational', meaning proportion, the basis of all good design. The firm believes that successful design is achieved through a clear purpose, logical process and imaginative execution.

This philosophy is the foundation upon which RATIO Architects has operated for more than 20 years. Established in 1982 with two employees and a focus on architectural historic preservation and interior design, RATIO has evolved into an award-winning multidisciplinary design and planning firm offering professional services in:

Architecture
Interior Design
Historic Preservation
Urban Planning
Landscape Architecture

The results of RATIO's interactive design process can be seen in corporate headquarters, educational institutions, government agencies, medical facilities, office buildings, churches, hotels and multi-family housing throughout the Midwest and the United States. While this depth of experience and expertise is applied to each new project, the firm recognizes that every design challenge has its own distinct goals and requires a fresh approach based on its unique purpose.

3   Jeff Goldberg/Esto Photographics

5   Bob Haar/Hedrich-Blessing

1   National FFA Center, Indianapolis, Indiana
2   Art & Journalism Building, Ball State University, Muncie, Indiana
3   Indiana State Museum, Indianapolis, Indiana
4   Hamilton County Courthouse, Noblesville, Indiana
5   Irwin Indoor Practice Facility, University of Illinois, Urbana-Champaign, Illinois

4   George Bond

● 107 South Pennsylvania Street, Suite 100, Indianapolis, Indiana 46204 USA
Tel: +1 317 633 4040 Fax: +1 317 633 4153

RAUH DAMM STILLER PARTNER

rdspartner@t-online.de   www.rdspartner.de

1   RDSP

2   RDSP

Founded in 1950, RDSP has specialized in health-
related institutions for more than 50 years. As well
as hospital design offering hospitality and a healing
atmosphere, RDSP concentrates on the economic
aspects of the healthcare industry. RDSP creates
innovative concepts for patient rooms, operating
theaters and laboratories. The firm has also applied
its understanding of complex healthcare issues to
its numerous completed projects in aged-care
and residences for handicapped people.

3   RDSP

4   RDSP

1 Dortmund Hospital, Dortmund, Germany; main entrance
2 CD Design GmbH, Solingen, Germany; administration
   complex
3 Operations Department, Cologne Hospital, Cologne,
   Germany
4 Office Complex for WKT, Sprockhövel, Germany
5 Psychiatric Unit for Children, Munich, Germany;
   architecture competition

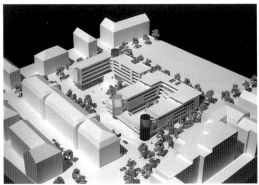

5   RDSP

● Schleusenstraße 5, D–45525 Hattingen, Germany Tel: +49 2324 92 000 Fax: +49 2324 92 0010

RAUL DI PACE ARQUITETURA

rauldipace@rauldipace.com.br www.rauldipace.com.br

1   Raul di Pace

2   Raul di Pace

By concentrating on residential project programs that include apartment buildings, single-family weekend houses, and also the renovation of old homes, the firm has striven, since 1976, to find innovative ways to respond to standard projects.

For a residential condominium project such as the Vila Adriano condominium, the solution provided the clients total freedom of choice with regard to the apartment layout, resulting in unique plans for each household. Owners are also able to redesign the layout of the units if they wish.

The firm's environment-oriented philosophy can be seen in projects like the small chapel in Avare Brazil, located in the middle of a forest park and totally surrounded by nature, which remained untouched for quiet contemplation. This was also a priority in the project for the Kuriuwa Resort Hotel, located on a forest edge and surrounded by mountains in the Brazilian countryside.

Another characteristic of its work is the exploration of the volumes created with tiling (seen in the Private Residence, Avare, Brazil), thus searching for new ways of applying this trait of colonial architecture. For a farmhouse designed some years ago, a new addition was developed to contrast with the older area, thus distinguishing the two styles of architecture.

3   Raul di Pace

4   Raul di Pace

5   Raul di Pace

1 Farmhouse Annex, Ibitinga, Brazil
2 Chapel, Avare Brasil, São Paulo, Brazil
3 Vila Adriano Condominium, São Paulo, Brazil
4 Private Residence, Avare, Brazil
5 Kuriuwa Resort, Minas Gerais, Brazil

● Rua Dr. Clovis de Oliveira 450, CEP 05616-072, São Paulo, Brazil
Tel: +55 11 3721 0800 Fax: +55 11 3721 9306

RDG PLANNING + DESIGN

aoberlander@rdgusa.com   www.rdgusa.com

1   Assassi Production

2   Assassi Production

4   Assassi Production

RDG Planning & Design is a network of planning and design professionals that was officially formed in 1989 as the Renaissance Design Group. The firm uses its own Charette process—a series of interactive meetings to define shared vision, and common objectives with its clients in specific areas of focus: athletic fields and complexes, community and regional planning, corporate, government, healthcare, higher education, historical restoration, K-12 education, museums and cultural centers, parks and recreation, religious, senior living, sports, transportation enhancements, and urban design.

RDG Planning & Design has offices in six locations: Des Moines, Iowa; Coralville, Iowa; Chicago, Illinois; Fort Myers, Florida; Omaha, Nebraska; and Kansas City, Missouri. The firm also operates the two distinct business centers of RDG IA Inc., and RDG SWB Inc. When the service or expertise is unique to one of these centers, RDG internally contracts for these professional services, providing its clients with a centralized point of contact.

3   Assassi Production

5   Assassi Production

1 Des Moines Area Community College, West Campus, West Des Moines, Iowa; entrance elevation
2 Iowa State Capitol Restoration, Des Moines, Iowa; west elevation
3 Des Moines International Airport Canopy System and Entrance Lobby, Des Moines, Iowa; pedestrian canopy and walkway
4 Robert N. Aebersold Student Recreation Center, Slippery Rock University, Slippery Rock, Pennsylvania; main entrance elevation
5 Iowa Association of Municipal Utilities, Office and Training Facility, Des Moines, Iowa; view of building and site development at project completion

● 301 Grand Avenue, Des Moines, Iowa 50309 USA Tel: +1 515 288 3141 Fax: +1 515 288 8631

RÉGIS CÔTÉ AND ASSOCIATES

info_qc@rcaa.ca info@rcaa.ca

1   Régis Côté and Associates

Founded in 1976, Régis Côté and Associates, architects is an alliance of three architects, Régis Côté, Mario LeBlanc and Jocelyn Boilard. RCAA has a permanent team of 68 professionals, technicians, designers, estimators and support staff.

The stable progression of RCAA through the years is directly related to the emergence of a group spirit formed by the firm's recruitment and training practices, always searching for a dynamic, creative and conscientious workforce. The firm applies and integrates, into all of its projects, the most recent technological innovations and uses the most modern management and production methodologies.

2   Régis Côté and Associates

RCAA specializes in educational, institutional, commercial, health and industrial infrastructures and buildings, and more.

The firm has completed more than 2,300 projects, varying in value from $50,000 to $300 million, with a total value of realized projects at more than $1.2 billion.

Régis Côté and Associates has offices in Quebec, Montreal and St-Félicien, Canada, and in Barcelona, Spain. It has partnerships in Edmonton, New York, Los Angeles, Dakar and Vietnam.

3   Régis Côté and Associates

1 Centropolis, Laval, Quebec
2 École de Technologie Supérieure, Montreal
3 Professional Formation Center, Duchesnay, Quebec
4 Price Building, Quebec

4   Régis Côté and Associates

● 115, Abraham-Martin, Suite 500, Quebec G1K 7B5 Canada Tel: +1 418 692 4617 Fax: +1 418 692 1746
430 McGill Street, Suite 600, Montreal H2Y 2G1 Canada Tel: +1 514 871 8595 Fax: +1 514 871 2279

REID ARCHITECTURE

enquiries@ra-lond.com www.reidarchitecture.com

One of the largest practices in the UK with a staff nearing 200, offices in Madrid, and a sister company in Australia, REID architecture has in-depth local and international experience. The firm works across a comprehensive spread of sectors, including mixed-use, retail, offices, leisure, health, education, industrial, and airport schemes.

REID architecture has a knowledge-gathering approach that involves intensive research into new concepts, processes, and materials. Sector specialists are leaders in fields of concept, product, and technical design. By applying the unique knowledge-led architecture process, each project team can benefit from the specialist's understanding, ensuring each design response is inspired. With its reputation for flair and creativity, REID architecture delivers buildings that meet both the aesthetic and commercial aspirations of its clients.

1 REID architecture

3 Andrew Southall

2 REID architecture

4 Hufton & Crow

1 Slough, London, UK; cultural and community building, international design competition winner
2 Castle House, London, UK; 40-story residential tower
3 Farnborough Business Airport Air Traffic Control Tower, London, UK
4 The Gate, Newcastle-upon-Tyne, UK; urban entertainment center

● West End House, 11 Hills Place, London W1F 7SE UK Tel: +44 20 7297 5600 Fax: +44 20 7297 5601

RESOLUTION: 4 ARCHITECTURE

jtanney@re4a.com www.re4a.com

Resolution: 4 Architecture

Based in New York and founded in 1990, Resolution: 4 Architecture is comprised of partners Joseph Tanney and Robert Luntz. Widely published and highly acclaimed, the ten-person office has completed a variety of projects ranging in scale.

Recent recognition includes an AIA Award for an office for a Manhattan-based internet company; a residence for the architect Peter Eisenman and his family; the first place entry in the Dwell Home Design Invitational for a prefabricated home in Pittsboro, North Carolina; and the winning entry in the NCR International Design Competition for an amphitheater in Columbia, South Carolina. Current design preoccupations revolve around pattern making as a means to investigate possible landscapes within the ceiling plane.

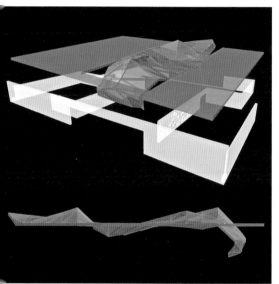

Resolution: 4 Architecture

3   Paul Warchol

Eduard Hueber, ArchPhoto   5   Peter Mauss/Esto

1 Nature's Theater, Columbia, South Carolina
2 Flemington Jewish Community Center
3 Ron's Loft, New York, New York
4 McCann-Erickson Worldwide Offices, New York, New York
5 McCann-Erickson Conference Center, New York, New York

● 150 West 28th Street, Suite 1902, New York, New York 10001 USA
Tel: +1 212 675 9266 Fax: +1 212 206 0944

RGA ARCHITECTS AND PLANNERS

www.rga-arch.com

RGA is dedicated to the premise that to be successful, architecture as an art must provide the highest standards of excellence in planning and design, standards that are discernible and appreciated by human occupants. The firm integrates the operational requirements for each project with all site factors to define planning alternatives. Its approach is to develop these alternatives, leading to the selected option with the most potential for the project's success.

RGA's design process is a deliberate evaluation of these alternatives, allowing solutions to be created, which are economical, operational, and aesthetically sensitive. It brings a level of understanding to its client's needs, interests and visions, and through this understanding, integrates diverse functional requirements, quality standards, and cost considerations to create unique and harmonious architectural solutions for each project.

2   Raymond Gomez

1   Bal Korab

3   Dan Cunningham

4   Dan Cunningham   5   Raymond Gomez

1   LDM Technologies Research Center and Headquarters, Executive Park, Auburn Hills, Michigan; new headquarters for international design/research company
2   Xalapa Museum of Anthropology, Veracruz, Mexico
3   Baan Janelia Farm Corporate Park, Enterprise Software Campus, Ashburn, Virginia
4   Electronic Math and Science Library, State University of New York at Albany, Albany, New York; new 200,000-square-foot electronic library
5   Performing and Creative Arts Center, College of Staten Island, New York; 110,000-square-foot performing arts complex

•   29 Broadway, Suite 1700, New York, New York 10006 USA   Tel: +1 212 201 4450   Fax: +1 212 952 1130

RICHARD PRIEST ARCHITECTS

info@richardpriest.co.nz   www.richardpriest.co.nz

Richard Priest Architects is a dynamic and thriving central-Auckland practice producing contemporary architecture that enhances its clients' lifestyles and workstyles. Its work can be seen throughout New Zealand, Australia and in the South Pacific.

The practice is flexible and conceptual in its approach, with no particular signature Richard Priest style, as each design is created to suit the client and the environs. It prides itself on a highly professional service and attention to both budget and timeframe.

Richard Priest Architects is a founding member of New Zealand Businesses for Social Responsibility and brings an environmentally conscious approach to all of its designs.

Practice principal Richard Priest has won every significant New Zealand architectural award. He has been on the advisory boards for the design degrees at UNITEC and the Auckland University of Technology. His enthusiasm for urban planning has seen him visit and study in cities throughout North and Central America, Southeast Asia, India, Europe and Australia.

1   Alan McFetridge

2   Becky Nunes

3   Becky Nunes

4   Becky Nunes

5   Becky Nunes

1 Tinity Hill Winery, Hawkes Bay,
   New Zealand
2 Tern Point Beach House, Maungawhai,
   New Zealand
3 Epworth Avenue House, Auckland,
   New Zealand
4 Hawera House, Auckland, New Zealand
5 Holy Cross, Auckland, New Zealand

● Private Bag MBE P282, Auckland, New Zealand Tel: +64 9 376 6337 Fax: +64 9 376 6442

RICHARDSON SADEKI

info@rsdnyc.com   www.richardsonsadeki.com

1   Dan Bibb

Founded by Clarissa Richardson and Heidar Sadeki, Richardson
Sadeki is a company that provides architectural, graphic, packaging,
and web design services for companies seeking integrated concept
development and a unique end user experience.

By offering the full array of services necessary to create a company's
visual image, Richardson Sadeki provides a holistic approach to brand
building, ensuring that a cohesive "personality" infuses every element.

To this end, Richardson Sadeki undertakes unique and challenging
projects that combine every aspect of design in the creation of a
visual identity. The studio's current projects cover a wide range of
industries including hotels, restaurants, spas, consumer goods,
beauty, art, and medicine.

2   Andrew Bordwin

3   Andrew Bordwin

4   Andrew Bordwin

1 Skinklinic, New York, New York;
   skin treatment center
2 Boone's Residence, New York,
   New York; private residence
3 Bathhouse, Las Vegas, Nevada;
   20,000-square-foot design
4 Bliss 57, New York, New York;
   7000-square-foot design

● 52 Walker Street Floor 4, New York, New York 10013 USA Tel: +1 212 966 0900 Fax: +1 212 226 3345

500

RIEGLER RIEWE ARCHITECTS PTY LTD

office@rieglerriewe.co.at   www.rieglerriewe.co.at

1   Paul Ott

2   Croce & Wir

Riegler Riewe Architects was founded by Florian Riegler and Roger Riewe in 1987 in Graz, Austria with a branch office in Cologne, Germany. The firm is currently developing projects in Austria, Switzerland, Italy and in the Federal Republic of Germany.

By means of the effective integration of high-quality architecture solutions with professional management logistics Riegler Riewe Architects has been able to gain a considerable national and international reputation.

The firm has received numerous architecture awards, and was nominated for the European architecture prize (6th Mies van der Rohe Award) in 1999, and for the world architecture prize of the UIA in the category 'applied technologies.' Riegler Riewe Architects is a well structured and professionally led enterprise. It has a pool of experts and subcontractors on hand to provide solutions for specific tasks, and specialists are used as project-based consultants.

3   Paul Ott

4   Paul Ott

5   Paul Ott

1   Graz Airport, Graz, Austria; passenger terminal, administration, car park, offices, 1998
2   Railway Station, Innsbruck, Austria; main station, 2001-2003
3   Housing Graz-Straßgang, Graz, Austria; low-cost housing, 1994
4   Technical University, Graz, Austria; computing and electro-technological institutes, 2000
5   Federal Institute for Social Studies, Baden, Austria; educational building, 1998

Portrait credit: Paul Ott

● Griesgasse 10, 8020 Graz, Austria Tel: +43 316 723 253 Fax: +43 316 723 253 4

RIHS ARCHITECTS PTY LTD

gerry@rihs.com.au www.rihs.com.au

Gerry Rihs is fascinated by modernism, aerodynamics, space and light, the future of architecture and its place in society. He launched his own practice, Rihs Architects, in 1979 and now heads up a diversified team committed to the delivery of contemporary, high-quality buildings.

Rihs has a strong belief that the future of architecture will be substantially dependent on the architectural profession's ability to adapt and respond to the rapidly changing demands of building owners and stakeholders. New ideas do not come easily, quickly or cheaply. "The biggest barrier to change is vision lock", to quote James Taylor Ph.D., Futurist.

In order to participate and respond to these changes, Rihs Architects will combine the pursuit of good design and building knowledge in service to its clients. As change is about changing the meaning of value, Rihs will provide ideas and designs, which exceed the expectations of his clients. He would like them to be astonished and, to refer to Louis Kahn, produce architecture which produces a "sense of wonder".

1   Rihs Architects

2   Rihs Architects

3   Rihs Architects

1   Chifley Square, Sydney, New South Wales
2&3   Australia's Animal World, Sydney, New South Wales

● Level 10, 65 York Street, Sydney, New South Wales 2000 Australia
(GPO Box 5230, Sydney 2001) Tel: +61 2 9262 1800 Fax: +61 2 9299 5645

RIOS CLEMENTI HALE STUDIOS

liz@rchstudios.com   www.rchstudios.com

1   Doug Jamieson

Rios Clementi Hale Studios encompasses myriad talents in one firm. Established in 1985, this extraordinary practice has developed an international reputation for its collaborative and multi-disciplinary approach, establishing an award-winning tradition across an unprecedented range of design disciplines. Believing in collaboration, the firm works with other architecture and planning firms throughout the world.

The architecture, landscape architecture, planning, urban, interior, exhibit, graphic, and product designers at Rios Clementi Hale Studios delight in projects as diverse as a new headquarters for The California Endowment, to the Terminator2 3D attraction at Universal City, to the popular retail line of notNeutral home wares, and numerous private residences.

Firm principals Mark Rios, FAIA, ASLA, Frank Clementi, AIA, AIGA, Julie Smith-Clementi, IDSA, and Robert G. Hale, AIA, have won numerous awards, as well as contributed to their professions through teaching and service. Rios Clementi Hale Studios creates buildings, places, and products that are thoughtful, effective, and beautiful.

2   Jennifer Schab

3   Tom Bonner

4   Tom Bonner

5   Derek Rath

1   The California Endowment, Los Angeles, California;
    non-profit headquarters will open in 2006
2   LA Unified School District Primary Center, Los Angeles,
    California; vibrant pictographs guide pre-reading
    students to their classrooms
3   Terminator2 3D, Universal City, California; expressive
    shape and multiple colors
4   Chess Park, Glendale, California; under-used alley is
    transformed into public space
5   notNeutral, Los Angeles, California; retail store
    showcases the firm's own line of home wares

● 6824 Melrose Avenue, Los Angeles, California 90038 USA Tel: +1 323 634 9220 Fax: +1 323 634 9221

RIVER ARCHITECTS

info@riverarchitects.com www.riverarchitects.com

River Architects' objective is to deliver appropriate design solutions that are unique for individual clients. As the firm's name suggests, River Architects aims to be flexible and accommodate the needs of various projects in changing times, hoping to address ecological and social concerns as the practice matures.

Current projects include various loft fitouts at the Greenwich Street Project, bars and restaurants, a restoration of a landmark building in Brooklyn, medical office renovations, a penthouse apartment in Manhattan, and a book on Korean residential architecture.

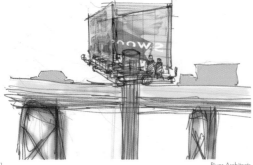

1   River Architects

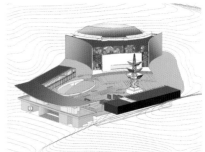

2   River Architects

3   River Architects

4   River Architects

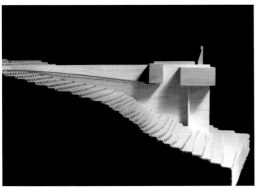

5   River Architects

1   Cathedral in the Sky; Brooklyn-Queens Expressway, New York; exploration of incidental spaces of the urban environment to provide sanctuaries within noisy cities
2   Nam June Paik Museum Competition, Yong-In, Province of Kyonggi, South Korea; traditional Buddhist temple overlaid with a circuit board
3   Melt Restaurant, Brooklyn, NY; fluid lines and warm-to-cool color palette
4   Fusion, New York City, New York; retro-Cuban lounge
5   Artists' Residence at Storm King Art Center, Cornwall, New York; proposal for work studios and residences within sculpture park

● 8 Marion Avenue, Suite 3, Cold Spring, New York 10516 USA Tel: +1 845 265 2254 Fax: +1 845 265 2273

RKD ARCHITECTS

mail@rkd.ie www.rkd.ie

RKD Architects was founded over 90 years ago and in that time it has embraced the many changes which have taken place in Ireland in terms of its culture, economy, and construction industry. At the same time, the firm has maintained its position at the forefront of Irish architecture.

The firm has earned a reputation for its innovative designs across every sector of the economy, producing high-quality buildings in the commercial, industrial, educational, healthcare, and residential categories. It always provides its clients with cutting-edge architectural, interior design, and project management services.

A selection of RKD's key projects include: Independent Newspapers printing facility, Citywest; Guinness Storehouse; Hewlett-Packard, Leixlip; Quinn School of Business, UCD; The Veterinary College, UCD; University College Hospital, Galway; Tallaght Hospital; and AIB BankCentre, Ballsbridge.

1   David Churchill/Arcaid

3   Ros Kavanagh

2   Imagination Limited

5   Ros Kavanagh

4   Gerry O'Leary

1   Independent News & Media Printing Facility, Citywest, Dublin, Ireland; night view of press hall
2   Guinness Storehouse, St James' Gate, Dublin, Ireland; old meets new—refurbishment of original 1904 building
3   University College Hospital, Galway, Ireland; new main entrance at dusk
4   Guinness Storehouse, St James' Gate, Dublin, Ireland; existing storehouse converted into new visitor center
5   Quinn School of Business, University College Dublin, Ireland; main entrance with horizontal brise soliel

●   59 Northumberland Road, Ballsbridge, Dublin 4, Ireland Tel: +353 1 668 1055 Fax: +353 1 668 3699

RNL DESIGN

www.rnldesign.com

1   Joel Eden

RNL Design is an integrated full-service architectural firm with offices in Denver, Los Angeles and Phoenix, serving clients locally, nationally and internationally. Since its inception in 1956, RNL has built its practice providing innovative and inspirational design solutions to clients, surpassing expectations and bringing ideas to life. RNL offers clients a continuum of design services, including architecture, interior design, urban design and planning, landscape architecture, and engineering. It has specialized niche markets in mixed-use urban development, religious work, and transportation projects.

2   Joel Eden

3   Patrick Lim

4   Ron Pollard

5   Joel Eden

1 The Cable Center at the University of Denver, Denver, Colorado
2 The Wellington E. Webb Municipal Office Building, Denver, Colorado
3 The Maplewood Condominiums, Singapore
4 Qwest Solutions Center, Denver, Colorado
5 Cherry Hills Community Church, Highlands Ranch, Colorado

● 1515 Arapahoe Street, Tower 3, Suite 700, Denver, Colorado 80202 USA
Tel: +1 303 295 1717 Fax: +1 303 292 0845
800 Wilshire Boulevard, Suite 400, Los Angeles, California 90017 USA
Tel: +1 213 955 9775 Fax: +1 213 955 9885

ROB WELLINGTON QUIGLEY, FAIA

office@robquigley.com   www.robquigley.com

1   Rob Wellington Quigley, FAIA

Rob Wellington Quigley, FAIA provides architecture and planning services from offices in San Diego and Palo Alto. Founded in 1978, the firm has produced projects throughout the western USA and Japan and received more than 60 awards for design excellence from the AIA.

The firm handles diverse project types and sizes, from large civic, academic, and mixed-use to affordable housing, custom residences and multi-family projects, as well as community planning and urban design. Unusual among nationally known design architects, Rob Quigley is dedicated to an inclusive, participatory design process. The firm is noted for both creative solutions within limited budgets and designs that are sensitive to individual sites and circumstances. Sustainable architecture is a specialty.

Honors and recognitions received include the coveted 1995 Firm Award, presented by the AIA California Council, recognizing "a practice focused around the creative energy and leadership of a dynamic sole practitioner that produces consistently distinguished architecture." Rob is also a recipient of the distinguished Maybeck Award, presented by the AIA California Council in 2005.

2   Brigton Noying

3   Richard Barnes

4   Brigton Noying

5   Marshall Harrington

1   Children's Museum, San Diego, California
2   Gillman Drive Mixed-Use Parking Structure, University of California, La Jolla, California
3   West Valley Branch Library, San Jose, California
4   Downtown Historic Harbor-Front, San Diego, California
5   New Main Library, San Diego, California

● 434 West Cedar 4th Floor, San Diego, California 92101 USA Tel: +1 619 232 0888 Fax: +1 619 232 8966

ROBERT D. HENRY ARCHITECTS

bobhenry@rdh-architects.com   www.rdh-architects.com

1   Dan Bibb

2   Paul Warchol

3   Paul Warchol

4   Robert D. Henry

Robert D. Henry, AIA, is the principal of Robert D. Henry Architects, a New York City-based, full-service design firm offering planning, architecture, and interior design, including specialty lighting and furniture design. The diverse practice includes residential, salon and spa, restaurant, and resort projects, many of which have been recognized with international awards and publications. Henry is a specialist in all aspects of spa design, with projects in Asia, Europe, and North America. Seeking to engage all of the five senses in his architecture, Henry sees himself as "the sensuous architect." He is an active speaker at many spa and hospitality events. Henry received an M.Arch. degree from Columbia University, and teaches at the New Jersey Institute of Technology School of Architecture.

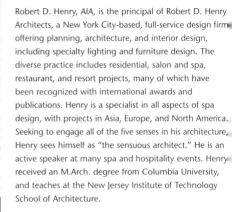

5   Dan Bibb

1 Spa at Amelia Island Plantation, Amelia Island, Florida; vernacular architecture combines with a modern edge
2 Butterfly Studio, New York City, New York; the sleek, contemporary beauty salon has a calming décor
3 Butterfly Studio, New York City, New York; orange "cocoons" are whimsical changing rooms at Butterfly Studio
4 PGA TOUR Spa Laterra, St. Augustine, Florida; massage cabanas "float" on the reflecting pool
5 Ajune Medi-Spa, New York City, New York; clean, clear, and soothing design for retail and spa services in upper Manhattan

● 37 East 18th Street, 10th Floor, New York, New York 10003 USA
Tel: +1 212 533 4145 Fax: +1 212 598 9028

508

ROBERT SIEGEL ARCHITECTS

www.robertsiegelarchitects.com

1   Robert Siegel Architects

Robert Siegel Architects is dedicated to architectural innovation, every day, for every client. It has earned a reputation for original, cross-cultural design, and technical excellence. The firm offers comprehensive expertise in academic and civic buildings, cultural facilities, and commercial and residential interiors.

Based in New York, Robert Siegel Architects is an internationally recognized architecture firm with projects throughout the USA as well as Korea, PRC, and Japan. The mission is to create beautiful and powerful buildings that reinforce the unique strengths of communities.

2   Robert Siegel Architects

4   Robert Siegel Architects

3   Lane Pederson

1 Korean Embassy, Beijing, PRC; under construction
2 Pohang City Hall, PoHang, South Korea; steel and glass suspended atrium space
3 Dixon Loft, New York, New York; sumptuous modern interior design
4 Kawaja Penthouse, New York, New York; glass and stainless steel suspended staircase

● 1001 Avenue of the Americas, New York, New York 10018 USA
Tel: +1 212 921 5600 Fax: +1 212 719 0838

ROBERTO LOEB ARCHITECT

loeb@loebarquitetura.com.br   www.loebarquitetura.com.br

Roberto Loeb is an original presence in Brazilian architecture. His uniqueness lies in the attitude that permeates his very process of creation. Loeb is endowed with an openness to others that transcends the objective functions the programmed space is to fulfill. What guides his design is a keen sensitivity to others and to the environment where the project will be built. A freedom to use and mix languages with no commitment to canons; a freedom unrelated to mannerist formalisms.

The criterion for his choices is their resonance in inventing the form that will materialize the request. What sustains the beauty of the result is his rigor in bringing his creations into being, an aesthetic rigor at the service of his ethical attitude when dealing with life in the spaces created. A wide variety of his work is aimed at all kinds of niches of social life. In Loeb's architecture, forms of existence take shape and assert themselves in their peculiarity, far removed from the perverse power hierarchies that set life into cliched images.

1   Roberto Loeb

2   Guinter Parschalk

4   Guinter Parschalk

3   Roberto Loeb

Jewish Cultural Center, São Paulo, Brazil
1   Façade from Doutor Arnaldo avenue
2   Façade from inner patio
3   Walkway, exhibition and events area
4   Detail
5   Auditorium

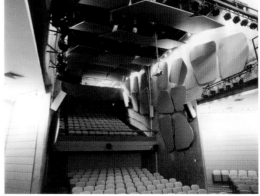

5   Roberto Loeb

● Rua José Maria Lisboa, 1077 Jd. Paulista, São Paulo 01423-001 Brazil
Tel: +55 11 3081 6344 Fax: +55 11 3085 2839

ROCCO DESIGN LIMITED

rdl@roccodesign.com.hk   www.roccodesign.com.hk

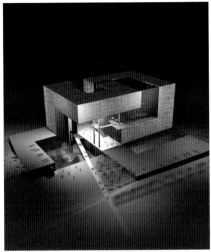

1   Rocco Design

Rocco Design Limited is a Hong Kong-based, multidisciplinary architectural firm which has over its past two productive decades established a solid pool of technical, practical and administrative expertise, but at the same time retained a youthful spirit and prowess for design creativity.

Despite its relatively brief history, the firm has undertaken projects for an impressive range of local and international, private, public and corporate clients, and has won a number of significant design awards, both locally and internationally.

Selected awards include:

2002   Short-listed for stage two of the Duxton Plain Public Housing International Architectural Design Competition, Singapore

2002   HKIA Award for Member's Work Outside of Hong Kong for the Boao Canal Village

2003   HKIA Medal of the year for 1 Peking Road

2003   ARCASIA Gold Medal for Hollywood Terrace

Winner, International Invited Competition for Guangdong Museum

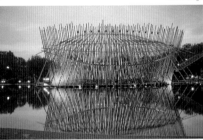

2   Rocco Design

3   Rocco Design

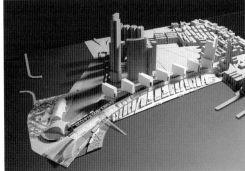

4   Rocco Design

1 Library, Guangzhou, PRC
2 Bamboo Pavilion, Berlin, Germany
3 Boao Canal Village, Hainan, PRC
4 Museum, Guangdong, PRC
5 West Kowloon Cultural District, Kowloon, PRC

5   Rocco Design

● 38/F, AIA Tower, 183 Electric Road, North Point, Hong Kong
Tel: +852 2528 0128 Fax: +852 2529 2135

ROGER HIRSCH ARCHITECT

www.rogerhirsch.com

Roger Hirsch Architect is a design-oriented firm specializing in residential, retail and commercial projects. For the past 12 years its work has focused on client-specific and site-specific projects that are both functional and innovative.

Studying the specific program and site, Roger Hirsch Architect develops a concept that is carried through the entire design process. From broad initial planning to the execution of the finest details, there is a consistency of thought present throughout the firm's work. The resulting projects are imaginative in concept, functional in use, and balanced in form.

Residential work includes house, townhouse and loft designs in many US cities, including New York, Miami and Chicago. Retail and commercial work includes the award-winning IS: INDUSTRIES stationery shops and the LOOP product design showroom and studio in New York. Institutional work includes The Chrysalis Community, a communal living facility for AIDS patients in Vermont.

1   Michael Moran

2   Michael Moran

3   Michael Moran

4   Eddie Mok

5   Eddie Mok

Fire Island House, Fire Island, New York
 1 Front view
2&3 Interior view
IS: INDUSTRIES Stationery Store, SoHo, New York
 4 Interior view
 5 Interior detail, woodstack fixture

● 91 Crosby Street, New York, New York 10012 USA Tel: +1 212 219 2609 Fax: +1 212 219 2767

RONALD FRINK ARCHITECTS, INC.

info@rfa-architects.com   www.rfa-architects.com

Ronald Frink, AIA founded his practice after more than 25 years of experience with such firms as Skidmore, Owings and Merrill as Associate Partner and Senior Designer, and AC Martin Partners as Director of Design. Mr. Frink offers a broad range of experience in the architecture, interior design, programming, planning and execution of significant corporate, institutional, commercial, residential and urban planning projects.

RFA design is fundamentally based in a modernist design esthetic with contemporary applications of dynamic forms, spaces, colors and materials to enhance human scale comforts and delight. RFA determines to bring a sense of celebration and harmony to its designs for a more sustainable and contemporary built environment which includes a sensitive understanding of the project context and the surrounding natural environment.

RFA draws upon the talents and skills of its various team members and endeavors to understand the perception, goals and requirements of its clients and to provide the highest quality design that not only meets, but also exceeds clients' expectations.

1   Benny Chan, fotoworks

2   Foster Karicofe

3   Foster Karicofe

4   RFA

5   Ian Espinosa

1 Purcell Murray Showroom, Huntington Beach, California
2 Pacific BMW, Glendale, California; interior model, showroom view
3 Pacific BMW, Glendale, California; exterior computer model, west elevation
4 The Arbors of Thousand Oaks, Thousand Oaks, California
5 The Geffen Playhouse, Los Angeles, California; rendering of remodeled 1929 theater with new addition

● 2439 W. Silverlake Drive, Los Angeles, California 90039 USA Tel: +1 323 662 0040 Fax: +1 323 662 2955

513

RONALD LU & PARTNERS (HK) LTD.

info@rlphk.com   www.rlphk.com

1   Ronald Lu & Partners

Ronald Lu & Partners is a highly respected architectural, interior, and urban planning practice. Since 1976, the firm has applied innovative ideas and design expertise to hotels, retail centers, high-rise and low-rise residential schemes, offices, service apartments, schools, embassies, and institutional buildings. Its portfolio also includes town planning and railway development planning projects.

Through its 29-year history, Ronald Lu & Partners has served a growing list of local and international clients, and 90 percent of the firm's projects are commissioned by repeat clients.

Since the 1980s, Ronald Lu & Partners has designed many prominent and international projects including the AsiaWorld-Expo, a deluxe hotel at the Hong Kong Disneyland Resort, No. 1 Ho Man Tin Hill and the Peak Tower Revitalisation project, and several commercial and residential development projects in Australia. Recently, the firm was invited to participate in several comprehensive mixed-use projects in the Ukraine and Vietnam.

With its track record and all-round expertise, Ronald Lu & Partners looks forward to delivering its blend of quality design and customer service to clients worldwide.

2   Ronald Lu & Partners   3   Ronald Lu & Partners

4   Ronald Lu & Partners

1 Embassy for the People's Republic of China, Canberra, Australian
   Capital Territory
2 No. 1 Ho Man Tin Hill, Ho Man Tin, Kowloon, Hong Kong, SAR, PRC
3 The Metropolis, Hung Hom Bay, Kowloon, Hong Kong, SAR, PRC
4 Revitalisation of the Peak Tower, The Peak, Hong Kong, SAR, PRC
5 Beijing Normal University – Hong Kong Baptist University United
   International College, Zhuhai, PRC

5   Ronald Lu & Partners

● 22/F Wu Chung House, 213 Queen's Road East, Wanchai, Hong Kong SAR, PRC
Tel: +852 2891 2212 Fax: +852 2834 5442
Room 1006, Jing Guang Center Office Building, Hujialou, Chaoyang District, Beijing 100020 PRC
Tel: +86 10 6597 4405 Fax: +86 10 6597 4340

RONNETTE RILEY ARCHITECT

rr@ronnetteriley.com www.ronnetteriley.com

2   Dub Rogers Photography

1   Dub Rogers Photography

Established in 1987, Ronnette Riley Architect provides architectural services, masterplanning, space programming, and interior design to institutional, corporate, retail, and residential clients. With offices in New York City and Bridgehampton, New York, the firm's portfolio includes a wide range of public and private sector projects from master planning at Columbia University, and corporate offices for American Symphony Orchestra League, to retail store installation for Apple Computer, and renovations of landmark buildings for Restoration Hardware.

While the firm has won numerous awards and is frequently cited for innovation in architecture, the best indicator of its success is the high volume of business it continues to win from repeat clients and referrals.

With its staff of skilled professionals, Ronnette Riley Architect handles a wide variety of assignments. The firm has created a niche for quality design at all scales, from furniture and lighting fixture design to interior design and architecture, and has succeeded in a competitive city.

3   Peter Aaron/Esto Photographics

4   Dub Rogers Photography

1 Emerald Planet Noho, New York, New York; wrap and smoothie parlor service bar
2 Black Residence, New York, New York; view though sliding doors to den/guest room
3 Apple Store Soho, New York, New York; south view from 2nd floor retail (with Bohlin Cywinski Jackson)
4 Friedman Residence, New York, New York; kitchen looking east

● Empire State Building 350 Fifth Avenue, Suite 8001, New York, New York 10118 USA
Tel: +1 212 594 4015 Fax: +1 212 594 2868
PO Box 1462, Bridgehampton, New York 11932 USA Tel: +1 631 537 3397 Fax: +1 501 637 3397

ROSS BARNEY + JANKOWSKI

crossbarney@rbjarchitects.com   www.rbjarchitects.com

1   Steve Hall/Hedrich-Blessing

2   Ross Barney + Jankowski, Inc.

3   Steve Hall/Hedrich-Blessing

5   Ross Barney + Jankowski, Inc.

Ross Barney + Jankowski, Inc. strives to improve the built environment, offering opportunities to people by making better places to live and work. RB+J believes that design should be symbolic of the higher purposes of public building, capturing a contemporary vision of today's society.

The firm has an international reputation for work primarily in the field of institutional design and public buildings such as libraries, public utilities, government, transportation buildings, and elementary schools. Its buildings have received numerous honors and design awards, including four Institute Honor Awards from the American Institute of Architects, the AIA Illinois 2000 Firm Award and 15 awards from the AIA Chicago. Its work has been published in architectural journals such as *Architecture*, *Architectural Record*, and *Architectural Review*, and has been noted in many newspapers. The firm was selected from a national search to design the new US Federal Campus in Oklahoma City after the terrorist bombing of the Alfred P. Murrah Building in 1995.

RB+J's working style is extremely collaborative, with communications structured to allow the maximum creative contribution from individual team members and with its clients being integral parts of the design team. Its design approach begins with a concentrated effort to understand the site and the community in which it is working.

4   Steve Hall/Hedrich-Blessing

1   Levy Senior Center, Evanston, Illinois
2   United States Port of Entry, Sault St. Marie, Michigan
3   Little Village Academy, Chicago, Illinois
4   US Federal Building, Oklahoma City, Oklahoma
5   James I Swenson Science Building, University of Minnesota, Duluth, Minnesota

● 10 West Hubbard Street, Chicago, Illinois 60610 USA Tel: +1 312 832 0600 Fax: +1 312 832 0601

ROSSER INTERNATIONAL, INC.

www.rosser.com

1   William Boyd

2   William Boyd

For six decades, Rosser has provided comprehensive architectural and engineering services to a variety of industries. Rosser International has designed more than one million spectator seats at 100 collegiate and professional sports facilities; provided more than 30 years of design expertise for aviation facilities; planned and designed more than 700 criminal justice projects in 43 states; and provided specialized services to more than 150 military installations worldwide. Other types of facilities designed by Rosser include educational facilities, convention centers, office buildings, and broadcast centers.

Rosser designs:
·Respond to the client's program, schedule, budget, and image goals
·Respond to the context of the site and community
·Express a deliberate relationship between function and form
·Promote sustainable design
·Explore the relationship between people and their living and built environment

3   William Boyd

4   William Boyd

5   William Boyd

John M. and Gertrude E. Petersen Events Center,
University of Pittsburgh, Pittsburgh, Pennsylvania
1   Exterior
2   Exterior corner
3   Lobby
4   Exterior at evening
5   Arena interior

●   524 West Peachtree Street NW, Atlanta, Georgia 30308 USA   Tel: +1 404 876 3800   Fax: +1 404 888 6861

ROTH AND MOORE ARCHITECTS

rm@rothandmoore.com

2   Steve Rosenthal

3   Steve Rosenthal

1   Jeff Goldberg/Esto

Thirty-eight years of practice have established Roth and Moore Architects as a firm deeply committed to excellent architectural design. The work of the firm, encompassing a broad range of building types and scales, is distinguished by its conceptual and compositional rigor, elegant integration of spaces, and sophistication of detail. Most importantly, the designs clearly express the character of specific sites and programs, to produce distinctive and compelling buildings particularly suited to individual circumstances.

Founded in 1965 in New Haven, Connecticut, the firm is headed by Harold Roth, FAIA, and William Moore, AIA. The principals supervise a design and support staff of ten and maintain active involvement with all phases of design, preparation of construction documents, and construction administration. The consistent quality of the firm's work is ensured by the principals' comprehensive management of each project.

Roth and Moore Architects is noted by clients and peers for high levels of service and professionalism, qualities that complement the firm's strength in design. The work of Roth and Moore Architects has been regularly featured in architectural journals and has received a number of national, regional, and local design awards.

4   Robert Benson Photography

5   Peter Aaron/Esto

1   Joseph Slifka Center for Jewish Life at Yale, New Haven, Connecticut; south-facing terrace includes a permanent succah structure
2   Mary Tisko School, Branford, Connecticut; two refectory-shaped pavilions provide the elementary school with a new image
3   Arthur K. Watson Hall, Yale University, New Haven, Connecticut; 2-story common space with load bearing masonry piers
4   Class of 1951 Observatory, Vassar College, Poughkeepsie, New York; two 22-foot diameter domes house reflecting telescopes
5   Fisher Passage, Vassar College, Poughkeepsie, New York; new pedestrian landscaped hillclimb connects two disparate parts of the campus

●   65 Audubon Street, New Haven, Connecticut 06510-1205 USA   Tel: +1 203 787 1166   Fax: +1 203 787 0241

ROTHZEID KAISERMAN THOMSON & BEE

info@rktb.com www.rktb.com

1   Albert Vecerka

2   Peter Aaron/Esto

Since 1963, the New York City firm of Rothzeid Kaiserman Thomson & Bee (RKT&B) has been designing multi- and single-family housing, schools, theaters, libraries, and office buildings, as well as healthcare, sports, and transportation facilities.

The firm's portfolio includes many significant projects, such as the School for the Physical City in Manhattan, High School Redirection in Brooklyn, Cathedral Gardens and 455 Central Park West in Manhattan, City Center Theater in Manhattan, the South Orange Performing Arts Center in New Jersey, and New York Methodist Hospital in Brooklyn.

Projects range from adaptive reuse to new construction. As evidenced by the receipt of over 20 awards, the firm has been widely recognized for its work in the New York metropolitan area. Recent honors include the Andrew J. Thomas Award for Excellence in Housing Design from the New York Chapter of the American Institute of Architects and a Merit Award from DesignShare and *School Construction News* for School for the Physical City.

3   Roy J. Wright

1   Swedish Consulate, New York, New York; restoration of consul's residence, offices, and staff apartments
2   Malsin Room at City Center Theater, New York, New York; conversion of service area into VIP lounge
3   School for the Physical City, New York, New York; alternative middle and high school in converted office space
4   Memphis Downtown, New York, New York; luxury apartment tower in Manhattan's West Village
5   PATH Station, Exchange Place, Jersey City, New Jersey; new station on the Port Authority Trans-Hudson line

4   Peter Mauss/Esto

5   Roy J. Wright

●   150 West 22nd Street, New York, New York 10011 USA Tel: +1 212 807 9500 Fax: +1 212 627 2409

ROWLAND DESIGN, INC.

info@rowlanddesign.biz www.rowlanddesign.biz

The mission of Rowland Design is to provide design solutions which enhance and enrich the clients it serves and reflect their special qualities; and at the same time to recognize and respect the Rowland family of talent for its creativity and dedication.

In its fourth decade, its business is the delivery of architecture, interior design, environmental graphic design, site planning and space planning.

The firm listens to its clients' needs and understands their businesses. It is a service-oriented company with the goal of providing complete customer satisfaction.

Rowland Design's approach to design requirements allows it the flexibility and objectivity necessary to handle a wide variety of successful design projects regardless of their size, location or budget. These services are not simply supplementary, but often the difference between an acceptable project and an exceptional one.

1   Rowland Design

2   Rowland Design

3   Rowland Design

1 Hillcrest Country Club, Indianapolis, Indiana
2 Trippet Hall at Wabash College, Crawfordsville, Indiana
3 Indiana Business College, Indianapolis, Indiana
4 Scholars Inn Gourmet Café & Wine Bar, Indianapolis, Indiana

4   Dan Francis, Mardan Photography

● 701 East New York Street, Indianapolis, Indiana 46202 USA Tel: +1 317 636 3980 Fax: +1 317 263 2065

RRM DESIGN GROUP

www.rrmdesign.com

1
Michael Urbanik

RRM Design Group specializes in the art of the possible. "Creating environments people enjoy" since 1974, the firm infuses environmental awareness and economic viability into community planning and design, public safety, recreation, education, and urban revitalization projects predominantly throughout California, and other western states. From sustainable soccer fields buzzing with kids to revitalized downtowns brimming with farmer's markets, its designs capture form, elevate function, and energize communities.

RRM Design Group has moved thousands of designs off the drawing board and into people's lives. The firm has more than 160 expert professionals employed in offices throughout San Luis Obispo, Oakdale, Healdsburg, and San Juan Capistrano. With cutting-edge technologies, innovative materials, and contemporary forums, RRM Design Group continues to aim higher.

2
Joseph Kasparowitz

3
Michael Urbanik

4
Michael Urbanik

1 Arroyo Grande Fire Station No. 1, Arroyo Grande, California
2 O'Leary Building, San Luis Obispo, California
3 Rabbit Ridge Winery and Tasting Room, Paso Robles, California
4 CSU Stanislaus John Stuart Rogers Faculty Development Center, California
5 Santa Maria Town Center Mall, Santa Maria, California

5
Scott Martin

● 3765 South Higuera Street, Suite 102, San Luis Obispo, California 93401 USA
Tel: +1 805 543 1794 Fax: +1 805 543 9149

521

RTKL ASSOCIATES INC.

www.rtkl.com

Since 1946, RTKL's success has been propelled by an understanding of how people want to live. Among the largest and most comprehensive design firms in the world, the firm's ideas on urban planning and architecture have helped drive significant change in some of the world's best cities. Today, its international staff draws on a broad knowledge base to design for every aspect of people's lives. RTKL provides innovative, customized business solutions and seamless delivery to clients across the commercial, cultural and governmental realms, and around the globe.

RTKL's thought leadership is practiced by its professionals in offices throughout the world, including Baltimore, Chicago, Dallas, Denver, London, Los Angeles, Madrid, Miami, Shanghai, Tokyo, and Washington, DC.

1   RTKL

2   RTKL

3   RTKL

4   RTKL

5   Tim Griffith

1 North Bund, Shanghai, PRC; plan showing renovation of the city's waterfront
2 Digital World Center, Manchester, UK; mixed-use project
3 Principe Pio, Madrid, Spain; renovated historic train station with added retail space
4 DFS Galleria, Singapore; retail environment driven by luxury brands
5 Shanghai Museum of Science and Technology, Shanghai, PRC; award-winning design houses one of the world's largest museum facilities

● 901 S. Bond Street, Baltimore, Maryland 21231-3305 USA Tel: +1 410 537 6000 Fax: +1 410 276 2136

522

RUDY UYTENHAAK ARCHITECTENBUREAU

arch@uytenhaak.nl www.uytenhaak.nl

1   Theo Uytenhaak

2   Luuk Kramer

3   Theo Uytenhaak

4   Luuk Kramer

5   Theo Uytenhaak

1 Hoop, Liefde en Fortuin, Amsterdam, Netherlands;
   project with 369 houses, offices, welfare center
2 Cascade building, Eindhoven, Netherlands; laboratory
   at university campus
3 Tourmaline, Almere, Netherlands; apartment building
4 Cultural Center, Apeldoorn, Netherlands; multifunctional
   center: theater, pop facilities, art education
5 Droogbak, Amsterdam, Netherlands; housing project
   with soundscreen

Portrait credit: Cary Markerink

Rudy Uytenhaak Architectenbureau bv is building a reputation as an exploring and creative practice that develops fitting and innovative buildings for actual and specific commissions. Its projects vary in scale and sort from interior (including alteration), functional architecture, housing, and public spaces, to urban design.

The firm comprises partners with initiative and vision in the processes of research, decision-making and execution.

Solving complexities acts as an incentive and stimulation for the firm. Character, sensitivity and intelligence are the ideal. The architecture can be typified by its context, complexity and scale.

In an ever-increasing, intensively populated and used country, it is important to create space by putting things in order, to define size and coherence and to make clear what is complex.

● Schipluidenlaan 4, 1062 HE Amsterdam, Netherlands Tel: +31 20 305 7777 Fax: +31 20 305 7778

523

SAA ARCHITECTS PTE LTD

saa@saaarchitects.com.sg

SAA Architects was established in 1965 in Kuala Lumpur, Malaysia, under the name of Malaysian Associate Architects. In 1970, the practice expanded to Singapore and in 1995, it became a limited corporation. The SAA group of companies is now represented by a strong regionally based network of associate offices in Singapore, Brunei, Indonesia, Malaysia, Vietnam, and China, with local knowledge of conditions and constraints.

The firm places strong emphasis on excellence of design and detailing, professional integrity, and personal commitment to clients. To achieve a balanced practice based on the highest professional standard, the firm has adopted an international approach to staff recruitment, as well as association with foreign consultants.

The practice provides full architectural services for all types of buildings such as offices, hotel developments, industrial, leisure/recreational, resort masterplanning, institutional, and residential projects. It also has experience in the planning and design of airports, hospitals, marinas, and golf clubhouses.

1   SAA Architects

2   SAA Architects

3   SAA Architects

4   SAA Architects

1   Office Complex at Dhoby–Ghaut Interchange
2   Hillbrooks Condominium
3   SIA Building
4   Plaza Singapura Shopping Centre
5   Hotel Rendezvous

5   SAA Architects

●   78 Shenton Way #24-00, Singapore 079120   Tel: +65 6220 0411   Fax: +65 6224 9929

SALVADEO ASSOCIATES ARCHITECTS

info@salvadeoarchitects.com www.salvadeoarchitects.com

Dedicated to design excellence, Salvadeo Associates Architects, P.C. utilizes the abstraction and representation of geometry, metaphor, and context in their design of modern buildings. The firm's project designs are original, innovative, and inspirational as they connect with everyone entering the building.

Establishing a trusting relationship with its clients, as well as the community is a top priority for this multi-faceted design firm. Guided by the leadership of principal architects David L. Businelli, AIA and Cesare Giaquinto, Salvadeo's design teams are actively involved in consulting, evaluating, and providing advisory support throughout all stages of the design and construction process. Involving their clients in every aspect of the design process allows the firm to identify potential problems and render innovative solutions to their clients' needs.

As an organization that has served the tri-state area for more than 30 years, Salvadeo Associates Architects, P.C. has set the standard for exceptional and invaluable design concepts.

1   Zbig Jedrus

2   Zbig Jedrus

3   Zbig Jedrus

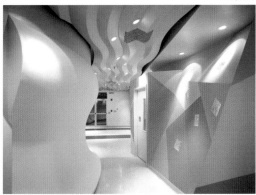

4   Zbig Jedrus

5   Zbig Jedrus

1 Zig-Zag Building, Staten Island, New York; exterior view of retail stores
2 FASTRACKIDS International, Staten Island, New York; view of classroom and waiting area (inside Zig-Zag building)
3 Private Residence, Staten Island, New York; exterior view of residence taken at night
4 St. Clare's Parish Center/Early Childhood Development Center, Staten Island, New York; with Stephen Perrella, AIA; hallway looking toward lobby
5 Marina Café, Staten Island, New York; exterior view of restaurant (on right) at dawn

● 16 Flagg Place, Staten Island, New York 10304 USA Tel: +1 718 667 6340 Fax: +1 718 979 1453

SAMYN AND PARTNERS

sai@samynandpartners.be   www.samynandpartners.be

1   Marie-Françoise Plissart

Samyn and Partners architects & engineers, founded in 1980, is a private company owned by its partners and staff. It is active with its affiliated companies in all fields of architecture and building engineering. Its architectural and engineering design approach is based on questioning, which can be summarised as a 'why' methodology. The firm has an open approach to projects, and listens closely to its clients' demands.

Staff members are involved in architectural and professional organizations, as well as academic and R&D activities including teaching, research, and development.

Samyn and Partners' architectural production has developed in the most diverse sectors: from an opera house to a service station, from a hospital to a bridge, from a research center to an urban masterplan.

2   Marie-Françoise Plissart

4   Samyn and Partners

3   Christian Richters

5   Ch. Bastin et J. Evrard

1 Aula Magna, Louvain-La-Neuve, Belgium; 1200-seat auditorium at university of Louvain
2 Subway Station 'Erasmus', Brussels, Belgium; elevated metro station near Erasmus hospital
3 Totalfinaelf Europe: Service Stations, Orival Area, Highway E 19, Brussels; building which houses catering area spanning motorway
4 Leuven Train Station, Leuven, Belgium; project covers Leuven railway station
5 Radio House Flagey, Brussels, Belgium; renovation of INR (National Institute of Radiobroadcasting) building

● Chée de Waterloo, 1537 B-1180 Brussels, Belgium Tel: +32 2 374 90 60 Fax: +32 2 374 75 50

SANDER ARCHITECTS

whitney@Sander-Architects.com www.Sander-Architects.com

Sander Architects seeks to find a balance between poetry and pragmatics. The design process begins with a consideration of essential elements: environment, program, physical and political site restrictions. Forms are then encouraged to develop which satisfy these basic needs and embrace the possibility of the poetic. In this way, a house for an Orthopedic Surgeon becomes a covert study in anatomy: metaphorical skin and bones. The elements that make up an aerobics studio, its interior architecture and furniture, take on physical tendencies: tension, compression, torsion, sinew. The entry for a Sculptor's house is a 'vessel' whose proportions are based on a large-scale clay jar produced by the owner. These strategies are covert, not obvious, and allow the built environments to resonate thematically with the program and the people who use them. It is a strategy of innuendo, not declaration, a struggle with nuance, an attempt at a quiet fertility. If the work celebrates what it means to inhabit, then in grander terms the work is a celebration of man's rhythms and rituals.

1   Sharon Risendorf

Sharon Risendorf

3   Sharon Risendorf

4   Sharon Risendorf

5   Sharon Risendorf

1   Residence for an Orthopedic Surgeon, San Francisco; this house discusses human anatomy and the activities of the surgeon as much as it does the activities of the architect

2&3   Canal House, Venice, California; divided into separate house and studio, this project embraces aspects of proposed dichotomies: work/live, thought (idea)/ action, ideal/pragmatic, sky/earth

4   Residence for a Sculptor, Breckinridge, Colorado; set below the brow of a hill at 10,000 feet above sea level

5   Aerobics Studio, San Francisco; tensioned expanded metal mesh used as a ceiling light diffuser

● 2413 Grand Canal, Venice, California 90291 USA Tel: +1 310 822 0300 Fax: +1 310 822 0900

SARC ARCHITECTS LTD.

sarc@sarc.fi www.sarc.fi

Established in 1965 and managed by partners Antti-Matti Siikala and Sarlotta Narjus, SARC Architects commissions are wide ranging, encompassing public buildings, offices, housing, renovations, and large-scale planning and development schemes. The office strives to create tranquil spaces for living, and efficient yet stimulating environments for work and commerce.

Several of the firm's projects have won prizes in competitions, and the office continues to participate in competitions both in Finland and internationally. The office is a member of the Association of Finnish Architects' Offices ATL and employs a workforce of 25 architects and architecture students.

1   Jussi Tiainen   2   Jussi Tiainen   3   Jussi Tiainen

4   Jussi Tiainen   5   Jussi Tiainen

1 Sonera Offices, Helsinki, Finland 2000
2 Kone Building, Espoo, Finland
3 Sanoma House, Helsinki, Finland
4 Finnish Pavillion, Expo 2000 Hannover, Germany 2000
5 Metla House, Joensuu, Finland

● Vironkatu 3D, Helsinki 00170 Finland Tel: +358 9622 6180 Fax: +358 9622 61840

SASAKI ASSOCIATES, INC.

info@sasaki.com   www.sasaki.com

1   Sasaki Associates, Inc.

2   Sasaki Associates, Inc.

Sasaki Associates pioneered the concept of interdisciplinary design and planning. All disciplines—planning, landscape architecture, architecture, urban design, civil engineering, and interior design—are represented in the ownership and management of the firm. This structure ensures that each project is led by the discipline or group of disciplines most appropriate to meet the client's needs. The firm's focus is on designing projects that can be built. Its interdisciplinary structure stems from the collaborative spirit that has guided the firm since its inception.

3   Sasaki Associates, Inc.

5   Christopher Lark

1   2008 Beijing Olympic Green Master Plan, Beijing, PRC
2   Jing An Sculpture Park; Shanghai, PRC
3   Thu Thiem Urban Design Plan, Ho Chi Minh City, Vietnam
4   California State Polytechnic University, Pomona, California
5   Detroit Riverfront Civic Center Promenade; Detroit, Michigan

4   Greg Hursley

● 64 Pleasant Street, Watertown, Massachusetts 02472 USA Tel: +1 617 926 3300 Fax: +1 617 924 2748

SATELLITE DESIGN WORKSHOP

mail@satellitedesignworkshop.co.uk   www.satellitedesignworkshop.co.uk

Satellite Design Workshop is an architectural practice that embraces the opportunity to work with other creative fields, encouraging a conceptual discourse within the studio. In conjunction with the body of ideas accumulated through teaching and research, its concerns with site, form and occupation set the framework for a tripartite approach to all its projects.

The relationship of interventions to the existing surroundings and the creation of vibrant internal spaces, enhances and creates one's experience of place. The built environment is viewed as a stimulus for people's enjoyment and awareness of their surroundings, where space is animated and transformed through its occupation.

1   Satellite Design Workshop

2   Thomas Haywood

3   Nicholas Kane

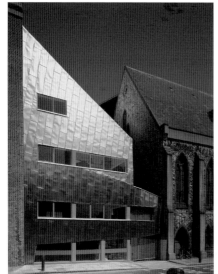

4   Nicholas Kane

1 Jerwood Air Space, London UK;
   proposed rooftop rehearsal space
2 Jerwood Glass House, London UK;
   extension of gallery space
3 The Cross, London, UK; building
   volume and cranked form
4 The Cross, London, UK; stainless-
   steel south façade

● 11-12 Dover Street, London W1S 4LJ UK Tel: +44 20 7629 7776 Fax: +44 20 7629 7779

SATOSHI OKADA ARCHITECTS

mail@okada-archi.com www.okada-archi.com

Satoshi Okada established his architectural practice in 1995. Today, the firm consists of 12 associate architects and three assistants, working on public and private projects. The firm is involved with the design of a variety of projects, from large municipal facilities, landscapes, commercial spaces, and residences, to small pieces of furniture.

Okada has become well known on the international architectural scene, through his relationships with architects and academics. He has lectured extensively, and has been a visiting professor in several countries.

1   Satoshi Okada

2   Satoshi Okada

3   Satoshi Okada

4   Hiroyuki Hirai

5   Hiroyuki Hirai

1   Gallery in Kyosato, Kiyosato, Yamanashi; façade
2   Gallery in Kyosato, Kiyosato, Yamanashi; gallery
3   Residence, Eda, Yokohama; exterior
4   Residence, Minami-Tsuru County, Yamanashi; façade
5   Villa Man-Bow, Atami, Shizuoka; exterior

● 16–12–303 Tomihisa, Shinjuku, Tokyo 162-0067 Japan Tel: +81 3 3355 0646 Fax: +81 3 3355 0658

SAUCIER + PERROTTE ARCHITECTES

spa@saucierperrotte.com   www.saucierperrotte.com

Since its inception in 1988, Saucier + Perrotte has gained an international reputation for its cultural and institutional buildings. Today, the office is involved in institutional, university, and residential projects at national and international levels.

The firm has received more than 30 awards and mentions in Canada and the USA, including the Governor General's Medal in 2002 and the Canadian Architect Award of Excellence in 2001.

Three major projects are currently under construction: the Communications, Culture and Information Technology Building in Mississauga, the Perimeter Institute for Theoretical Physics in Waterloo, and the McGill University Faculty of Music in Montreal. The firm is also a finalist in two prestigious international competitions: the Bank Street Building extension to Parliament in Ottawa and the Canadian Museum for Human Rights in Winnipeg.

1   Marc Cramer

2   Marc Cramer   3   Marc Cramer

4   Marc Cramer

5   Marc Cramer

Perimeter Institute for Theoretical Physics, Waterloo, Ontario
1   South façade showing offices and reflecting pool
2   Detail of south façade
3   Parallel walls with different degrees of transparency in the main hall
4   South façade showing erupting ground plane
5   Main hall on ground floor, garden on mezzanine level

● 110 Jean Talon West, H2R 2X1 Montreal, Quebec, Canada Tel: +1 514 273 1700 Fax: +1 514 273 3501

SAUERBRUCH HUTTON ARCHITECTS

mail@sauerbruchhutton.com   www.sauerbruchhutton.com

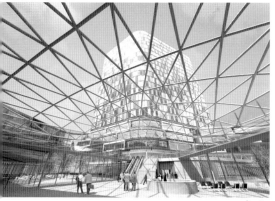

archimation

Matthias Sauerbruch and Louisa Hutton founded their architectural practice in London in the late 1980s, and opened a second office in Berlin in 1993. Today there are approximately 55 people working in the partnership which has been extended by two additional directors.

Through various urban competitions and feasibility studies, sauerbruch hutton has extensively researched the development of the post-industrial city with a particular interest in sustainable building.

With its urban-scale projects completed in Berlin, the practice has started to redefine the current mainstream notion of ecologically aware building. The concern for the economical use of resources—both natural and urban—is juxtaposed and extended into the idiosyncratic treatment of spaces on all scales. The application of up-to-date technology and the employment of passive energy devices coexist with the use of rich bodies of color, materials and textures—designed for the well-being of the individual and his enjoyment of the sensuality of the built (living and working) environment.

Annette Kisling   3   Bitter + Bredt   4

sauerbruch hutton architects

Lepkowski Studios

1 ADAC Headquarters, Munich, Germany; view from lobby
2 GSW Headquarters, Berlin, Germany; view from west
3 Fire and Police Station for the Government District, Berlin, Germany; view from northwest
4 Museum of Contemporary Art, Sydney, Australia (competition 1st prize 2001); harbour view at night
5 Museum for the Brandhorst Collection, Munich, Germany; interior, model

● Lehrter Strasse 57, 10557 Berlin, Germany Tel: +49 30 397 821 0 Fax: +49 30 397 821 30

SB ARCHITECTS

sbarch@sandybabcock.com www.sandybabcock.com

Founded in 1960, SB Architects has earned a reputation for excellence in the planning and design of large-scale resort, hotel, recreational, residential, and mixed-use projects. In its fifth decade, the firm is experiencing a renaissance, with a new name and a new generation of leadership, capitalizing upon its established reputation and exciting new energy.

From its founding office in San Francisco, California and 20-year presence in Miami, Florida, the firm continues to expand its worldwide practice. A mid-sized firm by design, SB Architects combines the close client relationships, hands-on attention, and expertise of a smaller firm with the experience and technological advantages of a large one.

Known for site-sensitive design, the firm's experience with an array of project types, sizes, locations, and architectural styles allows it to plan and design efficiently on the front end, while providing strong leadership through the full development process. More than 185 design awards attest to continued design excellence.

1   courtesy of Thanos Hotels, Ltd.

2   courtesy of Fisher Island Real Estate LLC

3   Tim Street-Porter

4   Dan Forer

5   Jay Graham

1 Anassa Hotel and Spa, Cyprus; award-winning five-star hotel
2 FisherIsland, Miami, Florida; winner of multiple design awards
3 Calistoga Ranch, Calistoga, California; five-star luxury resort
4 The Diplomat Country Club and Spa, Hallendale Beach, Florida; exclusive country club with 60-suite boutique hotel
5 Santana Row, San Jose, California; award-winning urban mixed-use project

● One Beach Street, Suite 301, San Francisco, California 94133 USA
Tel: +1 415 673 8990 Fax: +1 415 275 2003

SCARANO ARCHITECTS, PLLC

info@scaranoarchitects.com   www.scaranoarchitects.com

Founded in 1985 by Robert M Scarano, Jr., AIA, FARA, ALA, award-winning Scarano Architects, PLLC is one of New York City's most prolific architecture firms. With 60 design professionals responsible for an average of 250 projects annually, Scarano Architects is renowned for a broad range of work that includes residential, commercial, institutional, and adaptive re-use projects. In 2004 alone, the firm won five of the prestigious SARA Awards from the New York Council Society of American Registered Architects, a national SARA award, an ALA national Design of Merit award and the Housing Awards of Honor from the Boston Society of Architects AIA division (BSA).

1   Paulo Rivera

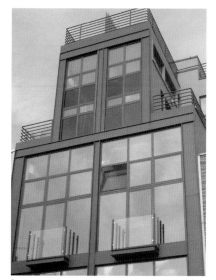

3   David Blaustein

2   Tamar Kisilevitz

1   The Arches at Cobble Hill, Brooklyn, New York; adaptive re-use of landmark church, rectory, and academy
2   171 North 7th Street, Brooklyn, New York; four-story condominium complements architectural vocabulary of area
3   110 York Street, Brooklyn, New York; glass and steel roof extension near Manhattan Bridge
4   The Toy Factory, Brooklyn, New York; 1920's toy factory converted into 56 luxury lofts.
5   234 West 20th Street, New York, New York; sixth and penthouse floors added to Chelsea building

4   Jack Deutsch   5   Eugene Drubetskoy

● 110 York Street Brooklyn, New York 11201 USA Tel: +1 212 222 0322 Fax: +1 212 222 4486

535

SCDA ARCHITECTS PTE LTD

scda@starhub.net.sg   www.scdarchitects.com

SCDA is a multidisciplinary architectural practice established in 1995. The design principal is a graduate of Yale University and has extensive professional and academic experience, having taught in universities in the USA and Singapore. The office currently employs a staff of 32, including 21 architects, three interior designers and a graphic designer. Its holistic approach to architecture includes full interior design and planning services. The practice has extensive experience with private residences, resort hotels, apartments, commercial buildings, masterplans, and product design.

SCDA's design strives for tranquility and calmness, qualified by space, light and structural order. Architectural expressions are distilled to capture the spiritual essence of 'place'. Its architecture and interiors are inspired by the cultural and climatic nuances of context, integrating landscape, water features and blurring the distinction between interior and exterior. Spaces are often enhanced by lush gardens, water courts and air wells, engendering sensuous engagement with the elements. Projects display sensitivity to the inherent beauty of natural materials expressed through clarity in construction details and elemental architectural expression.

1   Albert Lim K.S   2   Harshan Thomson

3   Visual Mediaworks

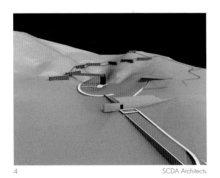

4   SCDA Architects

1 BLVD, Singapore
2 Heeren Street Shophouse, Malacca
3 Andrew Road House, Singapore
4 Columbarium, Guangzhou, PRC
5 Cassia Drive House, Singapore

5   Albert Lim K.S

● 10 Teck Lim Road, Singapore 088386 Tel: +65 6324 5458 Fax: +65 6324 5450

SCHMIDT, HAMMER & LASSEN

info@shl.dk www.shl.dk

1   Jørgen True

2   Roberto Fortuna

"The driving force of our work is the pleasure of designing—the pleasure of creating architecture and design with human aspect."

Arkitekterne maa Schmidt, Hammer & Lassen K/S is of the opinion that, above all, architecture is created for the people living and working in and around it, providing the sensation of the pleasant and the comfortable and at the same time touching the outstanding, the extraordinary and the unexpected—all through the very same essential architectural means: functional design, appropriate materials, form and light.

Deeply rooted in the Scandinavian tradition, Schmidt, Hammer & Lassen wishes to create an architecture that brings man in focus and is dominated by simplicity, precision and the highest standards of quality and finish.

The architectural office Schmidt, Hammer & Lassen was established in 1986 and is run by architects Morten Schmidt, Bjarne Hammer, John F. Lassen, Kim Holst Jensen, and Morten Holm.

3   Schmidt, Hammer & Lassen

4   Jørgen True

5   Schmidt, Hammer & Lassen

1   Nykredit New Headquarters, Copenhagen, Denmark; suspended 'meeting boxes' create dynamics in bright atrium
2   Installation for the Danish Federation of Architects, Copenhagen, Denmark; finely balanced correlation between architecture and choreography
3   ARoS, new Aarhus Art Museum, Aarhus, Denmark; sweeping interior public street unfolds
4   Extension of the Royal Danish Library, Copenhagen, Denmark; body of atrium cuts into building, designed as an organic room in motion
5   Culture Centre, Greenland, Katuaq, Nuuk, Greenland; inspired by the dramatic arctic nature it is also an image of the northern lights
Portrait credit: Alberto Serejo

●   Aaboulevarden 37.5, Clemensborg, Aarhus 8000 Denmark Tel: +45 86 20 1900 Fax: +45 86 18 4513

SCHNEIDER+SCHUMACHER

office@schneider-schumacher.de www.schneider-schumacher.de

Simplicity and perfection, discipline and esprit, optimal functionality and striking images: undogmatic designs that stand out for their lightness and elegance emphasize that these opposites or contradictions are nothing than assumed antagonisms that can in fact be combined to create stunning buildings that people like to use.

schneider+schumacher describes its approach to architecture as 'poetic pragmatism'. "There may be several technical solutions to solve the same problem, but maybe only one that has also got a certain poetic aspect, flair or unexpected point of view. It is this one aspect that we are trying to find."

After developing such projects as the Info-Box at the Potsdamer Platz in Berlin, the J. Walter Thompson advertising agency in Frankfurt, and KPMG in Leipzig, bigger projects are coming their way, such as Eurohypo near Frankfurt and the development of international projects. In 2002, the Westhafen-Tower and surrounding buildings added a new landmark to the Frankfurt skyline.

1   Jörg Hempel

2   Jörg Hempel

3   Jörg Hempel

4   Jörg Hempel

5   Jörg Hempel

1 ERCO Automated Warehouse, Luedenscheid, Germany
2 Info-Box, Potsdamer Platz, Berlin, Germany
3 Westhafen-Pier, Frankfurt, Germany; offices and parking
4 Westhafen-Tower and Westhafen-Brückengebäude, Frankfurt, Germany; offices
5 Memorial Soviet Special Camp Nr.7/ Nr.1 1945-1950, Sachsenhausen, Oranienburg, Germany

● Niddastrasse 91, Frankfurt am Main D-60329 Germany Tel: +49 69 2562 6262 Fax: +49 69 2562 6299

SCHWARTZ/SILVER ARCHITECTS

rsilver@schwartzsilver.com   www.schwartzsilver.com

Schwartz/Silver's focus is on projects with needs that are often more particular than they are general. The firm's talent is in finding design solutions that emerge from the specific circumstances of projects: a strong identity, a delicate context, a constrained site, or a complex client or user group. A consequence of its dialogue-driven, site-specific approach is a predominance of buildings for cultural and educational institutions—museums, libraries, arts and learning centers. Current projects are for Princeton University, the University of Virginia, and a joint initiative between the City of Baton Rouge and Louisiana State University.

1   Schwartz/Silver Architects

3   Matt Wargo

2   Steven Traficonte

5   Peter Aaron/Esto

1 The Arts Block, Baton Rouge, Louisiana; art museum, art school and performing arts complex
2 The Abbe Museum, Bar Harbor, Maine; museum of native American culture and heritage
3 New England Aquarium West Wing, Boston, Massachusetts; entry pavilion, visitor amenities and changing exhibit gallery
4 MIT Rotch Library, Cambridge, Massachusetts; library of architecture, art and planning
5 Lazarus House, Copake, New York; country house

4   Richard Mandelkorn

● 530 Atlantic Avenue, Boston, Massachusetts 02210 USA   Tel: +1 617 542 6650   Fax: +1 617 951 0779

SEAN GODSELL ARCHITECTS

godsell@netspace.net.au

"Architects are primarily charged with interpreting the physical needs and emotional aspirations of society through the medium of building. To remain relevant we must be conscientious observers of society rather than of our own navels—architecture for its own sake has no real meaning to me."

Sean Godsell is a first-class honors graduate from the University of Melbourne who has received numerous national and international design awards. The defining principle in his work is simplicity. His designs emerge from an innate desire for order. Coupled to this desire is his interest in the complexities of people and the societies they attempt to construct. Over the last year, the office has been involved in a diverse range of projects. It has completed a photographic laboratory and gallery, an arts and craft gallery, and a beach house. The firm's first large-scale building, a science faculty building for Woodleigh School, was completed in 2002.

1   Trevor Mein

2   Earl Carter

3   Earl Carter

1 Kew House
2 Peninsula House
3 Carter/Tucker House
4 Woodleigh School
     Science Building
5 Lab X

4   Hayley Franklin   5   Trevor Mein   Portrait credit: M. Wee

● 45 Flinders Lane, Melbourne, Victoria 3000 Australia Tel: +61 3 9654 2677 Fax: +61 3 9654 3877

SEVKI PEKIN

sevkipekin@superonline.com www.sevkipekin.com

Sevki Pekin

Sevki Pekin

Sevki Pekin

Sevki Pekin

Sevki Pekin was born in 1946 and graduated from Robert College in Istanbul. He studied at the Faculty of Architecture of Vienna Technical University and received his diploma in 1973 from the School of Architecture of the Vienna Fine Arts Academy. He worked with Peichl and Boysan, in various offices in London, Vienna and Istanbul.

In 1975, he founded Sevki Pekin Architecture and Construction Company. He received the Prof. Baravelle Award from the Vienna Fine Arts Academy in 1973, and the Josef Frank Award from the Austrian Architectural Society in 1974. He also received awards from the Chamber of Architects of Turkey's National Exhibitions, in 1996, 2000 and 2002. He has lectured and worked as a jury member in various universities in Turkey, and his work has been published in Turkish and international periodicals.

1 Summer Residence, Bademli, Turkey
2 Summer Residence, Bodrum, Turkey
3 Kocaeli Chamber of Industry Social Facilities, Izmit, Turkey
4 Six Houses, Sapanca, Turkey

● BJK Plaza A/1G S. Seba Caddesi, Besiktas 80680 Istanbul, Turkey
Tel: +90 212 258 3588 Fax: +90 212 258 3533

SEVKI VANLI

sevkivanli@hotmail.com

Since his graduation from the Florence Faculty of Architecture in the 1950s Sevki Vanli has been responsible for 100 buildings, four books, and numerous articles.

Vanli is strongly influenced by both architectural history and Mediterranean tradition, for which his architecture shows an enthusiasm. The architect is of the view that details are central in a design's plan and cross section, with each visual characteristic a reflection of the other

courtesy Sevki Vanli

courtesy Sevki Vanli

courtesy Sevki Vanli

courtesy Sevki Vanli

courtesy Sevki Vanli

1 Erkeksu Country Complex Golf Club, Ankara, Turkey, 1990
2 World Trade Centre, Ankara, Turkey, 1987
3 Tandogan Dormitory, Ankara, Turkey, 1967
4 Turkish Embassy, Tripoli, Libya, 1981
5 Exporters Union Country Club, Ankara, Turkey, 1988

● Rafet Canitez Cad. Elif Naci Sok. No: 7/2, Or-An, Ankara Turkey
Tel: +90 312 490 3255-56 Fax: +90 312 490 5490

SFCS

sfcs@sfcs.com www.sfcs.com

For SFCS, careful listening and respect has led to enduring client relationships—some dating back to the 1940s. SFCS provides professional services in the fields of architecture, engineering, planning, and interior design from its offices in Roanoke, Virginia and Charlotte, North Carolina.

At SFCS, the concept of partnering is paramount. Teams form across design and engineering disciplines to work with the client, relying on the client's expressed goals to develop creative, cost-effective designs. The design focus mirrors client objectives, whether operational, budgetary, scheduling, or of the built environment.

SFCS maintains a strong commitment to designing environments for its clients that adhere to the highest functional and aesthetic standards, while enhancing the productivity and quality of life of those who will live, work, or learn there.

Current projects include senior living communities, colleges and universities, training and conference centers, hospitals and clinics, corporate offices, and government facilities.

1   Tim Schoon

2   Tim Schoon

3   Tim Schoon

4   Tim Schoon

5   Rick Alexander

1 Westminster Canterbury on Chesapeake Bay, Virginia Beach, Virginia; serpentine form enhances views for senior living residents
2 The Highlands at Wyomissing, Wyomissing, Pennsylvania; sunlit living room in the memory support center
3 Torgersen Hall, Virginia Tech, Blacksburg, Virginia; bridge connects technology center to library, creating gateway
4 Lakeview Village, Lenexa, Kansas; apartment building lounge in senior living community
5 Carilion Health System Riverwalk Parking Garage, Roanoke, Virginia; covered walkway connects hospital to parking garage (with Carl Walker Inc.)

● 305 South Jefferson Street, Roanoke, Virginia 24011-2003 USA Tel: +1 540 344 6664 Fax: +1 540 343 6925

543

SHEEHAN VAN WOERT BIGOTTI ARCHITECTS

draw@svwbarchitects.com   www.svwbarchitects.com

1   Danielle Grabarz

2   Angela Bigotti

Sheehan Van Woert Bigotti Architecture (SVWB) is an award-winning firm with offices in Reno, Nevada and Folsom, California. Established in 1975, SVWB has performed architectural services on various private and public projects.

A diverse portfolio of educational, institutional, religious and government projects has earned it a reputation for controlling time and cost constraints while maintaining innovative design. SVWB's commitment to making a difference involves a sincere interest in the success of others. The firm is dedicated to creating a better quality of life through the relationships it builds, services it provides, and designs it creates.

Viewing architecture as art, as well as a profession, SVWB focuses on creative thought from pragmatics to aesthetics. The firm's approach to design lets emotion, analysis, and instinct combine to allow originality to emerge. Through careful study of site, form, function, and material, the personality of each project evolves into a meaningful and memorable environment.

3   Valerie Clark Photography

4   Danielle Grabarz   5   Danielle Grabarz

1 Holy Cross Catholic Community, Sparks, Nevada; a place to gather and unify the community
2 Sierra Nevada Job Corps Maintenance Building, Stead, Nevada; a modular design utilizing metal structure and panels
3 Southern Wine and Spirits, Las Vegas, Nevada; a design build remodel of an existing warehouse
4 University of Nevada Reno, Student Services Building, Reno, Nevada; a balance between progressive and conservative university architecture
5 Sisters of Our Lady of Mount Carmel, Reno, Nevada; a private monastery with a public worship space

● 300 South Wells Avenue, Suite One, Reno, Nevada 89502 USA
Tel: +1 775 328 1010 Fax: +1 775 328 1020

SHEPLEY BULFINCH RICHARDSON AND ABBOTT

Oegleston@sbra.com   www.sbra.com

1   Peter Aaron/Esto

Shepley Bulfinch Richardson and Abbott is a national design practice serving the education, healthcare, and research markets. The firm's clients include Dartmouth–Hitchcock Medical Center, Harvard University, MIT, and Children's Hospital Boston. Founded in 1874 by Henry Hobson Richardson, SBRA is the oldest architectural firm in Boston and one of the oldest in the country. The firm provides architecture, planning and interior design services and is widely recognized for the diversity of its practice and expertise. The firm was named one of America's best-managed firms in a survey by *Architectural Record* magazine, as well as one of America's top 100 design firms in a survey by *Interior Design* magazine. SBRA employs approximately 200 professionals and serves clients worldwide from its headquarters in Boston, Massachusetts.

2   Jean M. Smith

3   Richard Mandelkorn   4   Peter Mauss/ESTO   5   Jean M. Smith

1 Irving S. Gilmore Music Library, Yale University, New Haven, Connecticut; reference reading area
2 Hasbro Children's Hospital, Providence, Rhode Island; patient and family waiting room
3 Higgins Hall, Boston College, Chestnut Hill, Massachusetts; sun-filled atrium
4 Bronson Methodist Hospital, Kalamazoo, Michigan; the Healing Garden
5 Dartmouth–Hitchcock Medical Center, Lebanon, New Hampshire; skylit mall

● 40 Broad Street, Boston, Massachusetts 02109-4306 USA Tel: +1 617 423 1700 Fax: +1 617 451 2420

SHIM-SUTCLIFFE ARCHITECTS

studio@shimsut.com   www.shim-sutcliffe.com

Shim-Sutcliffe Architects is a Canadian architectural practice committed to the full integration of architecture and landscape. Each of its design projects explores the link between a strong conceptual idea and its fullest realization through construction details. The firm's interest in the construction and fabrication of buildings, sites and their intersections has forced it to question fundamental relationships between object and ground, building and landscape, man and nature. Shim-Sutcliffe's built work ranges from public projects for universities and local municipalities to private residences. The use of water as a link between building and landscape is explored through the seasons in many award-winning projects. The studio works in an intense and probing manner, sharing ideas with clients through the development of many drawings and numerous models at many scales.

1   Michael Awad

2   Michael Awad

3   James Dow

4   James Dow

1 Weathering Steel House, Toronto, Canada; view from interior looking at reflecting pool in winter
2 Moorelands Camp Dining Hall, Lake Kawagama, Ontario, Canada; view of dining hall with linear skylight above
3 Island House, St Lawrence River, Canada; view of reflecting pond with house beyond
4 Ledbury Park, Toronto, Canada; view looking under Cor-ten steel pedestrian bridge with reflecting pool/skating canal in foreground and skate change pavilion beyond

● 441 Queen Street East, Toronto, Ontario M5A 1T5 Canada Tel: +1 416 368 3892 Fax: +1 416 368 9468

SHINICHI OGAWA

info@shinichiogawa.com www.shinichiogawa.com

1   Shinichi Ogawa

Shinichi Ogawa is the principal architect of Shinichi Ogawa & Associates. He is also a professor of the Kinki University School of Engineering, Japan, and a visiting professor at Edinburgh College of Art, School of Architecture, UK.

Exhibitions include:
1996: The 19th International Exposition Milano Triennale Japan Pavilion, Palazzo dell'Arte, Milano
1996: UIA Barcelona '96, XIX Congress International Union of Architecture, Barcelona
2001: Japan 2001 London, 4x4 Japanese Avant-Garde Exhibition – 16 Japanese Architects, London
2002: Gwangju Biennale 2002, Gwangju, Korea

2   Shinichi Ogawa

3   Shinkenchiku-sha

4   Shinkenchiku-sha

5   Shinkenchiku-sha

1 Abstract House, Hiroshima, Japan
2 104X, Yamaguchi, Japan
3 Cubist House, Yamaguchi, Japan
4 Isobe Studio and Residence, Yamaguchi, Japan
5 K House, Tokyo, Japan

● 5-33-18 Inokuchi Nishi-ku, Hiroshima 733-0842 Japan Tel: +81 82 278 7099 Fax: +81 82 278 7107

SHUBIN + DONALDSON ARCHITECTS

russell@sandarc.com www.shubinanddonaldson.com

Architects Russell Shubin, AIA, and Robin Donaldson, AIA, instil human, group, and organizational dynamics into architecture on the cutting edge of high design in the places they create for people to live, work, gather, sell, dream, and collaborate.

When Shubin + Donaldson Architects takes on a project for an ad agency, entertainment studio, retail store, community center, or custom residential client, it undertakes a commitment to ensure that its designs fully express strategic ideas, thus achieving the client's objectives. This innovative firm achieves those objectives through a process of working with the client from conception to construction. The architects bring vision and technological sophistication to this process, resulting in projects that are as complex and varied in scope as they are responsive to their contexts.

Established in 1990, the firm's work—ranging from ground-up construction to adaptive reuse—has won 18 architectural awards since 1995.

1   Shubin + Donaldson Architects

2   Tom Bonner   3   Ciro Coelho

4   Ciro Coelho   5   Tom Bonner

1   Vandenberg Village, Santa Barbara, California; multi-tenant housing is part of mixed-use plan
2   Ground Zero Advertising, Marina del Rey, California; uniform workstations, dramatic ramp, and scrim projections define ad agency
3   Hope Ranch Residence, Santa Barbara, California; monumental minimalism mixes with Mexican modernism
4   Guest House, Carpinteria, California; glass-enclosed house connects with nature
5   Ogilvy Advertising, Culver City, California; dramatic "Tube" entry defines progressive feeling of ad agency interior

●   3834 Willat Avenue, Culver City, California 90232 USA Tel: +1 310 204 0688 Fax: +1 310 204 0219

SHUHEI ENDO ARCHITECT INSTITUTE

endo@tk.airnet.ne.jp   www2c.airnet.ne.jp/endo/

Shuhei Endo, a young Japanese architect based in Osaka, attracted international attention when he won the Andrea Palladio Prize in 1993. Shuhei Endo's architecture situates itself at the intersection of two paths: on the one hand, his experimentation with non-Euclidean geometries, an essentially three-dimensional undertaking, and on the other, his researches into the use of a particular material, galvanized sheet metal. The resulting spaces are fluid, dynamic, mobile, ambiguous, incomplete and even indeterminate. Shuhei Endo curves, doubles, folds and twists a series of metal sheets to the point of dissolving the limits between interior and exterior, between surface and volume, between floor and roof, achieving dramatic effect with a great economy of means.

1
Yoshiharu Matsumura

2
Yoshiharu Matsumura

3
Toshiharu Kitajima

5
Yoshiharu Matsumura

4
Shuhei Endo Architect Institute

1   Springtecture H, Shingu-cho, Hyogo prefecture, Japan; managers room
2   Rooftecture C, Taishi-cho, Hyogo prefecture, Japan; crematorium
3   Springtecture B, Biwa-cho, Shiga prefecture, Japan; Atelier + House
4   Bubbletecture M, Maihara-cho, Shiga prefecture, Japan; kindergarten
5   Rooftecture K, Nishinomiya, Hyogo prefecture, Japan; office building

● 5-15-11, Nishitenma, Kita-ku, Osaka 530-0047 Japan Tel: +81 6 6312 7455 Fax: +81 6 6312 7456

SILVANO FARESIN

studiofaresin@faresin.it www.faresin.it

Silvano Faresin was born in Vicenza in 1943. He studied locally, completing his education at the Fine Arts Academy in Venice, and from an early age worked for local architect Gianfranco Papesso. He later attended the I.U.A.V. in Venice to study under Carlo Scarpa and Giuseppe Mazzariol, graduating in 1971 with a thesis on the regional administation offices at Padua with Ignazio Gardella, which was published in the *Controspazio* architecture magazine.

He set up his own practice in Vicenza, at first designing small houses, later expanding with industry and sport projects, multi-family housing, auditoriums, theaters, and schools. He has also completed numerous restorations in Vincenza's historic city center.

From 1985 to 1993, he taught at the University of Florida, Gainsville USA. Between 1987 and 2002 he was part of the scientific committee of the Andrea Palladio study centre in Vicenza (C.I.S.A) with a teaching role from 1989 to 1991, and as vice-president from 1987 to 1991. Numerous publications feature his work.

1   Paolo Mazzo, Famiglia 38

2   Paolo Mazzo, Famiglia 38

3   Paolo Mazzo, Famiglia 38

4   Paolo Mazzo, Famiglia 38

5   Paolo Mazzo, Famiglia 38

1 Caoduro House, Monticello Conte Otto, Italy
2 Nursery and Kindergarten, Bassano del Grappa, Italy
3 Viale Crispi Housing, Vicenza, Italy
4 Linear Housing, Vicenza, Italy
5 Multifunctional Building, Vicenza, Italy

● Contrà Misericordia, 40, Vicenza 36100 Italy Tel: +39 0444 922 484 Fax: +39 0444 923 211

SINGERARCHITECTS

singer@singerarchitects.com   www.singerarchitects.com

The goals of SingerArchitects range from bringing order to an entire community through patterns of city-use planned in a functionally thoughtful and visually exhilarating way, to the celebration of the life of a single family by the integration of that life into the nature of the surrounding community through an architecture of today.

SingerArchitects has established a national reputation for innovative and qualitative architectural design. Beginning with City Park, the one-million-square-foot urban plaza and parking structure, which was the cornerstone for the resurgence of the urban core of Fort Lauderdale in Broward County, SingerArchitects has produced signature buildings in the areas of public education, private and public institutions, and commercial enterprise.

Since 1964, the firm has received more than 50 awards for design excellence and has been published in all major US architectural journals as well as in Japan and Belgium. The firm was recognized in 1997 as the Firm Of The Year by the Florida/Caribbean American Institute of Architects, for outstanding achievement in design, community involvement, education and service to the profession.

1   Esto Photographics

Ed Zealy

3   Ed Zealy

1 City Park Municipal Garage, Fort Lauderdale, Florida; carpark designed for people plus accommodation of automobiles
2 Fire Prevention Bureau, Fort Lauderdale, Florida; municipal offices built in a lake to conserve land
3 Lawrence Brody Residence, Star Island, Miami Beach, Florida; bayside house framing views of city skyline
4 Boca Raton Museum of Art, Boca Raton, Florida; a contemporary art museum as urban redevelopment
5 Florida Atlantic University/Broward Community College Higher Education Complex, Fort Lauderdale, Florida; higher education building placed in an urban setting

Ed Zealy   5   Robert Bogdal

● 13 West Las Olas Boulevard, Fort Lauderdale, Florida 33301 USA Tel: +1 954 463 5672 Fax: +1 954 463 5677

SITE ENVIRONMENTAL DESIGN INC.

info@siteenvirodesign.com   www.siteenvirodesign.com

1   Peter Mauss/Esto

SITE is an internationally recognized architecture and environmental design firm, composed of architects, artists, and designers. The firm was founded in 1970 to serve clients worldwide, with offices located in the heart of New York City.

Under the direction of Denise MC Lee and James Wines, the mission of SITE is to unite building design with visual art, landscape, green technology, and the surrounding context as part of an integrative vision. This approach provides the clients with a personalized and memorable architectural identity, as well as widespread public appreciation for their commitment to environmental responsibility and enhancement of community life.

2   SITE

In response to the current age of information and ecology, SITE believes that a truly sustainable architecture for the future must be based on an expanded definition of green design, and a heightened level of communication with the public. This commitment includes social, psychological, ecological, and contextual information as the basis for a new architectural language.

3   SITE

1 Shake Shack in Madison Square Park, New York, New York; food kiosk in an urban historic park
2 Annmarie Garden on St. John, Solomons, Maryland; formal garden as exhibition gallery extension
3 Annmarie Garden on St. John, Solomons, Maryland; visitor and exhibition center

● 25 Maiden Lane, New York, New York 10038 USA Tel: +1 212 285 0120 Fax: +1 212 285 0125

SIX DEGREES PTY LTD

6deg@sixdegrees.com.au www.sixdegrees.com.au

1   John Gollings

Six Degrees adds value with:
- Clear and concise planning and project delivery
- Durable design and materials selections
- Innovative construction methods
- Design that connects with the landscape and urban environment
- Socially and environmentally responsible solutions
- A humane approach, which is inclusive and promotes richness, stories and surprises

2   John Gollings

4   Shania Shegedyn

3   John Gollings

5   Trevor Mein

1 Kooyong Lawn Tennis Club, Melbourne, Australia; view from courts
2 Kooyong Lawn Tennis Club, Melbourne, Australia; west façade
3 Kooyong Lawn Tennis Club, Melbourne, Australia; glazing detail: Azez Glass
4 Pelican Restaurant–Bar, Melbourne, Australia
5 Townhouses, Melbourne, Australia

● PO Box 14003, Melbourne, Victoria 8001 Australia Tel: +61 3 9321 6565 Fax: +61 3 9328 4088

SJB ARCHITECTS

architects@sjb.com.au www.sjb.com.au

1   Tony Miller, Arcphoto

2   Tony Miller, Arcphoto

3   Tony Miller, Arcphoto

4   SJB

SJB is a firm of architects, interior designers and planners.

A large, multidisciplinary team means that SJB can offer a comprehensive range of services in design and planning. A variety of locations allows a national focus. Years of experience and accumulated knowledge, and the application of this expertise to every project undertaken, means that significant value is added to the firm's built products.

SJB prides itself on its professionalism, service orientation, and business acumen, the sum of which allows the delivery of built projects which are both practical and progressive.

Into the future, SJB intends to build on this record of achievement, and continue to create humanistic architecture that responds to the many ways in which people live. In doing so, SJB aims to positively influence the world, creating connections and communities as well as buildings.

Through its contribution to the built environment, SJB strives to inspire and challenge, delight and intrigue. This challenge drives it forward.

1 NewQuay at Melbourne Docklands; SJB/FKA Architects
2 Railway Air Rights Development, South Yarra, Victoria
3 Medina Grand Adelaide Treasury, Adelaide, South Australia; SJB Architects and Danvers Schulz Holland Architects in association
4 BMW ZQ Import Centre, Australian Headquarters, Mulgrave, Victoria
5 Probuild Offices, South Melbourne, Victoria

5   Tony Miller, Arcphoto

● 25 Coventry Street, Southbank, Victoria 3006 Australia Tel: +61 3 9699 6688 Fax: +61 3 9696 6234
The Cannery, 28 Richards Avenue, Surry Hills, New South Wales 2010 Australia
Tel: +61 2 9380 9911 Fax: +61 2 9380 9922

554

SKIDMORE, OWINGS & MERRILL LLP

www.som.com

1   Steinkamp/Ballogg Chicago

2   Timothy Hursley

3   Peter Aaron/Esto

4   Nick Merrick/Hedrich-Blessing

Skidmore, Owings & Merrill LLP (SOM) is one of the leading architecture, urban design and planning, engineering, and interior architecture firms in the USA. Since its founding in 1936, SOM has completed more than 10,000 projects located in more than 50 countries around the world. The firm has received more than 800 awards including the first Firm of the Year Award, awarded in 1961 by the American Institute of Architects for design excellence. Honored again in 1996, SOM is the first firm to win this award twice.

SOM's work ranges from the architectural design and engineering of individual buildings to the masterplanning and design of entire communities. SOM has conceived, designed, and built projects for both public and private clients that include corporate offices, banking, and financial institutions; government buildings; healthcare facilities; religious buildings; airports; recreational and sports facilities; university buildings; and residential developments.

Currently, the firm maintains offices in Chicago, New York, San Francisco, Washington DC, Los Angeles, London, Hong Kong, and Shanghai.

5   Tim Griffith

1 Hong Kong Convention and Exhibition Centre Extension, Hong Kong; symbol for the new era in Hong Kong
2 San Francisco International Airport, San Francisco, California; a striking symbol of San Francisco, premier gateway to the Pacific Rim
3 New York Stock Exchange • 30 Broad Street, New York, New York; a living workshop that integrates technology and information for the 21st century
4 Jin Mao Tower, Shanghai, PRC; the third tallest building in the world and centerpiece of Shanghai
5 Changi Airport Train Station, Singapore; a grand welcome to Singapore

● 14 Wall Street, New York, New York 10005 USA Tel: +1 212 298 9300 Fax: +1 212 298 9500

SLCE ARCHITECTS

www.slcearch.com

1   SLCE

2   Tom Sobolik

3   SLCE

SLCE is an 80-person architectural firm, established in 1941. Through its 65-year history, the firm has developed a broad style menu, based on sound architectural practice and building experience. In the residential arena, SLCE Architects is truly expert—the firm has designed over 10,000 residential units in recent years alone. SLCE's work includes everything from award-winning low-rise/low-density/low-income public housing to high-rise, luxury residential buildings. Additionally, SLCE has completed design work on over $250 million of healthcare construction, including planning and phased development of multiple, special-use facilities as diverse as laboratories, libraries and staff residences.

SLCE's educational facility design projects include alteration and new construction of a wide variety of uses: classrooms, libraries, dormitories, recreation, and theaters, for users ranging in age from pre-school to post-graduate.

SLCE Architects has earned the respect of the development community for providing sophisticated designs within budget and time constraints. SLCE's recent and current projects are a testament to its ability to perform successfully in complicated urban contexts such as New York City.

4   Addison Thompson

1   The Milan, New York, New York
2   101 West End Avenue, New York, New York; 33-story building comprises 507 luxury apartments, health club, parking, and prime retail space
3   The Atlas, New York, New York; 46-story apartment building comprises 374 units, health club, with 4-story retail and office base
4   German Mission to the U.N.

●   841 Broadway, New York, New York 10001 USA   Tel: +1 212 979 8400   Fax: +1 212 979 8387

SLHO & ASSOCIATES LTD.

slho@slho.com.hk www.slho.com.hk

SLHO & Associates Limited is an architectural firm with over 30 years of experience and unrelenting enthusiasm towards design, always aiming to provide design solutions that are appropriate, innovative yet cost effective and non-conforming to mediocrity.

Architecture, interior design and urban planning are treated as part problem solving, part anticipating the psychological perception that will be experienced, part questioning, re-evaluating the generally accepted norm, and part pushing the envelope of what architecture is about, providing a design that will evolve through time.

Over the years, a wide selection of projects has been completed, including: domestic houses, high-rise residential towers, high-rise commercial buildings, multi-story sports complex with indoor swimming pool, home for the aged, religious institution, school, master planning for large scale commercial planning in China, integrated social service centre, retail shops, show flats, and a clinic.

1   Virgile Simon Bertrand

2   Chan Yiu Hung

3   Ho Chuen Tak

4   Chan Yiu Hung

1 Manhattan Heights, Kennedy Town, Hong Kong
2 HKYWCA Jockey Club Tuen Mun Integrated
   Social Service Centre, Tuen Mun, Hong Kong
3 South China Athletic Association Multipurpose
   Sports Complex, Causeway Bay, Hong Kong
4 HKYWCA Jockey Club Shatin Integrated Social
   Service Centre, Shatin, Hong Kong

● 15/F, Iuki Tower, 5 O'Brien Road, Wan Chai, Hong Kong Tel: +852 2832 9832 Fax: +852 2834 0430

557

SLOBODAN DANKO SELINKIC

slobodan@tiscali.it www.geocities.com/danko_selinkic

Slobodan Danko Selinkic is a strong believer in the importance of the written word in architecture. He strives to accompany and define his projects, which are created primarily through sketch, with words. He has written significant architectural critiques and engaged in didactic work, including *Architecture on the Soil of Yugoslavia From 1918-1990 and The Specificity of Italian Architecture Vis-à-vis European Modern Architecture.*

He defines "small as beautiful" using Montenegro as an example, to remind us that the megalomania of present-day architecture is not the only path to follow, especially for the smaller and poorer countries of the world. Ongoing projects include a small business and residential building in Serbia, *The Influence of the Post-Modern on Architecture in Serbia, and Stone in the Architecture of Mrs. Svetlana Kana Radevic.*

| 1 | Courtesy Slobodan Danko Selinkic | 2 | Courtesy Slobodan Danko Selinkic | 3 | L Pejovic |

4   Courtesy Slobodan Danko Selinkic

1 Reconstruction of Historical Apartment, Rome, Italy; uncovering a wall
2 Marble Lamp "The Ice Tower", Rome, Italy; for the exhibition Roman Architects for the Via Giulia
3 Eco-Logic Lab Collective Exhibition, Venice, Italy; detail from staging
4 Family Home, Stanici, Croatia
5 Serbia & Montenegro Pavilion, Venice, Italy; Venice Biennale 2004

5   Courtesy Slobodan Danko Selinkic

● Largo Vassalletto 6 Rome 00196 Italy Tel: +390 6321 0248 Fax: +390 6321 0248
Bul.Avnoja 110 Novi Beograd 11000 Serbia and Montenegro Tel: +381 601 217 Fax: +381 112 1414 68

SMALLWOOD, REYNOLDS, STEWART, STEWART & ASSOCIATES, INC.

marketing@srssa.com www.srssa.com

Smallwood, Reynolds, Stewart, Stewart is an international design firm dedicated to providing its clients innovative, professional services in the areas of planning, architecture, interior architecture and design, landscape architecture and graphic design.

The more than 165 talented professionals comprising the firm's staff have extensive experience with a broad range of corporate, commercial, hospitality, residential, industrial, government and educational clients, designing a variety of project types including offices, high-rise residential, hospitality, retail, educational and athletic facilities, correctional institutions, industrial and manufacturing facilities and warehouses. Over 120 of its projects have been recognized for design excellence by the design and development community.

The firm established a regional design consultancy office for Asia in Singapore in 1991, and representative offices in Beijing and Shanghai in 2002. With a significant regional presence and experienced multinational professional staff, SRSS offers a full range of design services on current large-scale projects throughout Asia and the Middle East.

1   Ng Hwee Yong

Robert Miller

3   John Edward Linden

4   John Nye

5   Robert Miller

1   Castle Green Condominiums, Singapore; 831,614-square-foot project is located in northeastern Singapore
2   The Four Seasons Hotel, Cairo, Egypt; a 275-key, 430,600-square-foot luxury business hotel
3   IBM Corporation, Dusseldorf, Germany; a 6-story, 161,000-square-foot office building
4   Corporate Square, Beijing, PRC; a 17-story, 968,000-square-foot office tower
5   The Ritz-Carlton Rose Hall, Montego Bay, Jamaica; a 430-key, 5-story luxury resort hotel near historic Rose Hall Plantation

●   3565 Piedmont Road, Building One, Suite 303, Atlanta, Georgia 30305 USA
Tel: +1 404 233 5453   Fax: +1 404 264 0929
83 Clemenceau Avenue, #14-03 UE Square, Singapore 239920   Tel: +65 6835 4355   Fax: +65 6835 4322

559

SMITH-MILLER + HAWKINSON ARCHITECTS

contact@smharch.com www.smharch.com

1   Paul Warchol

2   Erieta Attali

Smith-Miller + Hawkinson Architects is a New York City-based architecture and urban planning firm founded in 1983. The firm has conceived public and private projects across the United States, ranging from residential commissions and parks to corporate buildings, public transportation terminals, theaters and museums. Henry Smith-Miller and Laurie Hawkinson's work derives from an ongoing investigation into the general culture of architecture—its history, as well as its complex and changing relationship to society and contemporary ideas—and from an effort to transform that culture by reinterpreting basic programs through a negotiation of traditional craft and vanguard techniques. *The New York Times* describes the firm's work as "proof that craftsmanship, technology and cutting-edge architecture can live happily under one roof."

3   Michael Moran

4   Robert Polidori

5   Paul Warchol

1–3 Corning Museum of Glass, Corning, New York
4   Wall Street Ferry Terminal at Pier 11, New York, New York
5   North Carolina Museum of Art, Master Plan and Amphitheater, Raleigh, North Carolina

● 305 Canal Street, New York, New York 10013 USA Tel: +1 212 966 3875 Fax: +1 212 966 3877

SOLOMON E.T.C
A WRT COMPANY

info@solomonetc-wrt.com   www.solomonetc-wrt.com

1   Christoper Irion

2   Christoper Irion

3   Russell Abraham

4   Grant Mudford

The main focus of Solomon E.T.C's work has been residential architecture and the interaction between housing and urban design. From this base the firm's work has expanded in several directions including large-scale urban planning; regulatory structures that govern urban design; and residential, commercial and institutional architecture. The firm maintains a staff of 15–20 people and frequently works in collaboration with other offices with complementary skills.

The firm's work has been widely exhibited and published in leading architectural journals in the US and abroad. The work has received 71 design awards including four Progressive Architecture Awards, national awards from the American Institute of Architects, the American Institute of Planners, the Housing and Urban Development Secretary's Platinum Award of Excellence, and three Charter Awards from the Congress of New Urbanism.

In April 2002, Solomon E.T.C. merged with Wallace Roberts & Todd, a planning and design firm widely recognized for its interdisciplinary approach and environmental ethos, to become Solomon E.T.C., a WRT Company.

5   Russell Abraham

1 Ornstein–Schatz Residence, Fairfax, California; south-facing porch with trellis
2 Ornstein–Schatz Residence, Fairfax, California; passively heated and cooled indoor pool
3 101 San Fernando, San Jose, California; midblock courtyard
4 Vermont Village Plaza, Los Angeles, California; streetscape
5 101 San Fernando, San Jose, California; streetscape

● 1328 Mission Street, 4th Floor, San Francisco, California 94103 USA
Tel: +1 415 575 4722 Fax: +1 415 436 9837

SQUIRE AND PARTNERS

pr@squireandpartners.com   www.squireandpartners.com

1   Smoothe

2   Peter Cook/VIEW

3   Peter Cook/VIEW

4   Peter Cook/VIEW

Squire and Partners was established in 1976 and has over 25 years experience in designing and managing the construction of new buildings and renovations in key central London locations.

The services the practice is able to offer include: masterplanning, planning, architecture, interior design, space planning, project management and construction design management.

Squire and Partners is a design-led practice that understands the complicated constraints involved in commercial development.

The practice utilizes the talents of its design teams to enhance the value of the projects it undertakes.

The practice's conceptual work is based on contemporary ideas of planning and sustainability, while the details express current technology and manufacturing processes. The architecture is derived from classical rules of scale, rhythm and proportion.

Squire and Partners currently employs around 95 staff, and has a strategy for the future based on the development of young talent and the constant reinvestment of its resources into the business.

5   Squire and Partners

1 199 Knightsbridge, London; new luxury residential building in prestigious Knightsbridge location
2 4 Bouverie Street, London; new Portland stone office building located off Fleet Street
3 West India Quay, London; masterplan, cinema, health club, residential and landscaping
4 Limehouse Youth Club, London; new community youth club building for Limehouse district
5 1 Millharbour; mixed-use tower on prominent site in Millenium Quarter

● 77 Wicklow Street, London WC1X 9JY UK Tel: +44 20 7278 5555 Fax: +44 20 7239 0495

STANLEY SAITOWITZ /
NATOMA ARCHITECTS INC.

stanley@saitowitz.com

Stanley Saitowitz / Natoma Architects Inc. is a firm committed to design excellence. The theoretical position establishes a particular concept for each project, giving unique measure to the specific program and site. The approach to design is considered 'human geography', and is especially cognizant of the relation of building and setting.

Completed projects include the California Museum of Photography in Riverside; Yerba Buena Lofts, a 200-unit residential building in San Francisco; 1022 Natoma Street, a live/work building in San Francisco; the Potrero Lofts; and residences at Stinson Beach, Los Gatos, Napa, Almaden, Oakland, Berkeley, San Francisco, Tiburon, Napa and Davis.

Current projects include the Visual Arts Library at the University of California, Berkeley; the Energy Efficiency and Electricity Reliability Laboratory at Lawrence Berkeley Laboratories; Beth El Synagogue in La Jolla; and Beth Sholom Synagogue and Community Hall in San Francisco.

Awards include The American Institute of Architects 1998 Henry Bacon Medal for Memorial Architecture, and The Boston Society of Architects 1997 Harleston Parker Award. The book, *Stanley Saitowitz - Architecture at Rice 33*, received a 1998 AIA International Architecture Book Award for Monographs. The Transvaal House was declared a National Monument by the National Monuments Council of South Africa in 1997.

1 Stanley Saitowitz / Natoma Architects Inc.

2 Tim Griffith

3 Tim Griffith

4 Tim Griffith

5 Steve Rosenthal

1 Beth Sholom Synagogue, San Francisco, California
2 Yerba Buena Lofts, San Francisco, California
3 Oxbow School, Napa, California
4 Lieff House, Napa, California
5 New England Holocaust Memorial, Boston, Massachusetts

● 1022 Natoma Street #3, San Francisco, California 94103 USA
Tel: +1 415 626 8977 Fax: +1 415 626 8978

563

STAUCH VORSTER ARCHITECTS

durban@svarchitects.com   www.svarchitects.com

Established in 1943 by Helmut Stauch, a leading modernist working within a regionally derived vernacular, the practice has evolved into one of the largest and most established practices in southern Africa.

In recent surveys of international practices, Stauch Vorster Architects has been rated for the past three years in the top 200 practices globally, and the largest in Africa. The practice operates from offices within South Africa, with associate offices in Mozambique and Namibia. The practice has considerable experience in the design of retail centers, educational buildings, hospitals, corporate offices and urban design projects.

The practice has won many awards; among the more important are the ISAA Award of Excellence 2000 (ICC Durban), ISAA Merit Award, and SAPOA Merit Awards.

The Stauch Vorster Architects philosophy is to provide 'design' delivery within a framework process, in which contract, program, budget and timing develops an appropriate and unique solution for each project.

2   SVA

1   SVA

4   SVA

3   SVA

5   SVA

1 Airways Park, South African Airways
   Headquarters, Johannesburg
2 PRD2 Office Tower, Umtata
3 Kingsmead Office Park Gatehouse,
   Durban
4 Mangosuthu Technikon, Lecture Theaters,
   Durban
5 International Convention Centre, Durban;
   SAIA Award of Excellence 2000

● PO Box 3720, Durban 4000 South Africa Tel: +27 31 263 1350 Fax: +27 31 263 1976

STEED HAMMOND PAUL

info@shp.com www.shp.com

Steed Hammond Paul, an over 100-year-old architecture firm, offers a complete line of planning, architecture, interior design, and construction administration services. The firm has offices in Hamilton, Columbus, and Cincinnati, Ohio. Throughout its history, the firm has undertaken a variety of projects in both the public and private sectors. Its work experience ranges from small improvements to multi-million-dollar building designs and award-winning historic renovations. During the past five years, approximately 90 percent of its work has been for repeat clients.

Steed Hammond Paul's organization is defined by its customers and its vision is 'Architecture Inspired by the Community'. The firm specializes in consensus management, value-added design, and responsiveness for the markets it serves: places of education, places for the public, places of recreation, places of business, and places of healthcare.

1 Greg Matulionis

2 Greg Matulionis

3 Greg Matulionis

4 Greg Matulionis

5 Miles Wolf

1 Donovan Arts Center, Cincinnati, Ohio; distinct angles of the interior entice creativity
2 Donovan Arts Center, Cincinnati, Ohio; softer-scaled entrance in keeping with surrounding campus architecture
3 Fairfield Lane Public Library, Fairfield, Ohio; classic clock tower provides a picturesque symbol
4 Fairfield Lane Public Library, Fairfield, Ohio; warm library interior promotes a user-friendly environment
5 Highlands Middle School, Ft. Thomas, Kentucky; dramatic exterior blends with surrounding civic architecture

● 1014 Vine Street, Suite 2100, Cincinnati, Ohio 45202 USA Tel: +1 513 381 2112 Fax: +1 513 381 5121

565

STEFFIAN BRADLEY ARCHITECTS

inquiries_us@steffian.com www.steffian.com

1   Robert Benson Photography

2   Steffian Bradley Architects

3   Steffian Bradley Architects

4   Peter Vanderwarker

Steffian Bradley Architects (SBA) is an award-winning, international architecture, planning, interior, lighting, and urban design firm with offices in Boston and London. Established in 1932, SBA specializes in design and planning for healthcare, academic, residential, and corporate/commercial clients, with current projects in the USA, United Kingdom, and PRC. The firm's diverse practice balances vision and creativity with a dedication to meeting the needs of its clients and the community. SBA's design and planning experience displays aesthetic and functional excellence, incorporating environmental considerations and sustainable design solutions. The firm has significant experience reconciling complex zoning requirements, and resolving the concerns of neighborhood and community groups. In partnership with its clients, SBA endeavors to improve and enhance the lives of the people who live and work in the environments created.

5   Bruce T. Martin

1 Baystate Health System D'Amour Center for Cancer Care, Springfield, Massachusetts; 64,000-square-foot patient-focused healing environment
2 Tianjin Gateway, Cambridge, Massachusetts; urban plan for cultural and entertainment destination
3 Children's Activity Center, Guangzhou, PRC; urban cultural and educational 'place for discovery'
4 The Devonshire, Boston, Massachusetts; high-rise mixed-use luxury apartments
5 Massachusetts Institute of Technology, Graduate Dormitory, Cambridge, Massachusetts; 740-bed urban residence hall that promotes community

● 100 Summer Street, Boston, Massachusetts 02110-2106 USA Tel: +1 617 305 7100 Fax: +1 617 305 7199

STELLE ARCHITECTS

info@stelleco.com   www.stelleco.com

Stelle Architects is an award-winning architecture, planning, and interior design firm that specializes in the design of educational, cultural and institutional buildings, as well as coastal residences. Founded by Frederick Stelle, AIA, in 1984, Stelle Architects is equally adept in the design of new buildings, adaptive re-use, and the expansion of historic structures. With every project, the firm strives to produce architecture of formal and functional simplicity, aesthetic integrity, and vision.

Stelle Architects strives to achieve a balance between conservation, the context of the site, and representing our time. Each project has its own style, sharing the common commitment to optimism and originality. Historical references are recognized in spirit only. Every project is a new beginning and no two are alike.

1   Jeff Heatley

3   Mancia Bodmer

2   Jeff Heatley

5   Jeff Heatley

4   Jeff Heatley

1 Beach House, Fire Island, New York
2 Island Residence, Shelter Island, New York
3 Swiss House, Zurich, Switzerland
4 Ranch House, East Hampton, New York
5 Mecox Pavilion, Bridgehampton, New York

Portrait credit: Bettina Stelle

● 48 Foster Ave, PO Box 3002, Bridgehampton, New York 11932 USA
Tel: +1 631 537 0019 Fax: +1 631 537 5116

STEPHEN ALTON ARCHITECT, P.C.

info@stephenalton.com www.stephenalton.com

Stephen Alton, AIA is the founder and principal of Stephen Alton Architect, P.C., established in 1993 in New York. The firm designs retail, residential, and hotel projects worldwide.

Alton's projects include multi-unit residential developments in NYC, Brooklyn, and New Jersey for developers such as Archstone Smith, Avalon Bay Communities, and CSFB Private Equity Group. Hotel projects include masterplanning and a new restaurant for the Ritz Carlton San Juan, the redesign of typical suites for Ian Schrager's Hudson Hotel, lobby and suites for Hotel Wales, and design leadership for the Hotel Adagio in San Francisco.

The firm's portfolio also includes numerous residential projects, restaurants, and store and prototype designs for such prestigious retail outlets as Chaps Ralph Lauren, Sacco Shoes, Ligne Roset Furniture, Genesco, and Donna Karan.

1   Stephen Alton Architect, P.C.

2   Stephen Alton Architect, P.C.

3   Arch Photo / Eduard Hueber   4   Arch Photo / Eduard Hueber

1 Cooper Square II, New York, New York; interior public spaces for multi-unit residential building
2 Nicole, New York, New York
3 Apartment 22, New York, New York
4 Mare, New York, New York; shoe store
5 West End Avenue, New York, New York; exterior façade for multi-unit residential building

5   Stephen Alton Architect, P.C.

● 416 West 13th Street, Suite 206, New York, New York 10014 USA
Tel: +1 212 243 3315 Fax: +1 212 243 3320

STEVE LEUNG ARCHITECTS LTD

sla@steveleung.com.hk www.steveleung.com

1   Ulso Tsang

Steve Leung Architects Ltd. and Steve Leung Designers Ltd. were restructured and established in 1997 by the award-winning registered architect and interior designer, Steve Leung. The firm's main office is located in Hong Kong, and manages large-scale projects in key cities including Guangzhou, Shenzhen, Shanghai, Beijing, Hangzhou, Zhuhai, Ningbo, Chongqing, and Chengdu.

The firm specializes in leading architectural and interior design projects including office buildings, high-rise and low-rise residential buildings, club houses, residential units, show flats, offices, shopping malls, hotels, restaurants, and bars, many of which are regarded highly in the Chinese and international markets.

The firm's work reflects a strong and unique character of minimalism, placing people's needs as its top priority, ensuring that the designs are always acclaimed for successfully bringing space to life with a guarantee of harmony and ambience.

2   Ulso Tsang

3   Steve Mok

4   Ulso Tsang

5   Ulso Tsang

1 The Colonnade, Hong Kong
2 18 Farm Road Club House, Kowloon, Hong Kong
3 Fairwood Café, Hong Kong
4 56 Repulse Bay Road, Hong Kong
5 Dong Lai Shun Chinese Restaurant, Kowloon, Hong Kong

● 9/F, Block C, Sea View Estate, North Point, Hong Kong SAR PRC
Tel: +852 2527 1600 Fax: +852 2527 2071

STEVEN EHRLICH ARCHITECTS

inquire@s-ehrlich.com   www.s-ehrlich.com

1   Milroy & McAleer

2   Craig Schwartz

Steven Ehrlich Architects is a nationally recognized design firm, known for extending Los Angeles' tradition of architectural innovation through the fusion of technology with cultural and environmental sensitivity, in residential, commercial, and institutional projects. Praised by clients and users of its buildings, the firm's work has consistently shown sensitivity to program, budget, context, and quality of space.

Steven Ehrlich's "multicultural modernism" design aesthetic recognizes and embraces the dynamic moment of the present, even while responding to and incorporating resonant elements of the cultural context. The firm has distinguished itself with seven national American Institute of Architects design awards, and was named 2003 California Architectural Firm of the Year by the AIA.

3   Peter Vanderwarker

4   Peter Vanderwarker

5   Julius Shulman & Juergen Nogai

1   San Bernardino Valley College, Learning Resource Center, San Bernardino, California
2   Kirk Douglas Theater, Culver City, California
3&4 Kendall Square Biotech Research Laboratory, Cambridge, Massachusetts
5   700 Palms Residence, Venice, California
Portrait credit: Elon Schoenholz

● 10865 Washington Boulevard, Culver City, California 90232 USA Tel: +1 310 838 9700 Fax: +1 310 838 9737

STEVEN HOLL

mail@stevenholl.com www.stevenholl.com

Steven Holl founded Steven Holl Architects in New York in 1976. The firm has gained an international reputation for excellence in design in a variety of project types including museums, educational facilities, and housing.

Time Magazine named Steven Holl as America's best architect, for "buildings that satisfy the spirit as well as the eye." His honors include National AIA Design Awards, the Grande Medailles d'Or and the Alvar Aalto Medal. He was recently honored by the Smithsonian Institution with the Cooper Hewitt National Design Award in Architecture.

He is best known for the Kiasma Museum of Contemporary Art in Helsinki; the Chapel of St. Ignatius in Seattle, and Simmons Hall at the Massachusetts Institute of Technology.

His current work includes the Nelson Atkins Museum of Art in Kansas City; a seven-tower hybrid housing project in Beijing; a water treatment facility in Hamden, Connecticut; a new marina development in Beirut, Lebanon; and a new building for the School of Art and Art History at the University of Iowa.

1   Paul Warchol

1 Kiasma Museum of Contemporary Art, Helsinki, Finland
Portrait credit: Mark Heitoff

● 450 West 31st Street, 11th Floor, New York, New York 10001 USA
Tel: +1 212 629 7262 Fax: +1 212 629 7312

STUDIO 63 ARCHITECTURE AND DESIGN

info@studio63.it www.studio63.it

1   Yael Pincus

2   Yael Pincus

Studio 63 Architecture and Design was founded in 1998 by Piero Angelo Orecchioni and Massimo Dei and is situated in the historical center of Florence, Italy. In 2003 a New York office was established, followed by an office in Hong Kong in 2005.

The firm specializes in interior architecture and design. Projects are characterized by their strong relationship between different art forms such as architecture, design, graphics, and plastic arts.

Major clients include the Sixty Group Spa. for which over the last three years, Studio 63 Architecture and Design created the concept and retail design of all flagship stores for Miss Sixty, Energie, and Killah around the world.

3   Yael Pincus

4   Yael Pincus

5   Yael Pincus

1&2 Miss Sixty Retail Design Store, New York, New York
  3 Energie Retail Design Store, London, UK
4&5 Energie Café, Catania Italy

● Piazza Santa Maria Sopr'Arno 1, Florence 50124 Italy Tel: +39 0552001448
601 West 26 St. Suite 1510, New York, New York 10001 USA Tel: +1 2126759784

STUDIO ATKINSON

sa@studioatkinson.com www.studioatkinson.com

1   Studio Atkinson

2   Studio Atkinson

Studio Atkinson is an architecture practice committed to the production of beautiful and meaningful contemporary architecture. An architecture that is reductive in nature—that is, composed of very few parts, but which when combined result in a greater whole. These designs may be reflections on a geographic area, prevailing building type, or simply an object's use. Invariably, they are restrained and timeless, and convey a dignity and sense of history without affectation or self-consciousness.

Stephen Atkinson, design principal, was born in 1967 in Baton Rouge, Louisiana. He finished at the Harvard Graduate School of Design with distinction in 1992. After apprenticing for six years at the firm of Machado and Silvetti in Boston, he founded Studio Atkinson and moved to New York City. The firm has received a Progressive Architecture Award, an ar+d award from *The Architectural Review*, and several awards from the Boston Society of Architects.

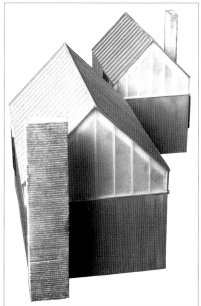

3   Studio Atkinson

4   Studio Atkinson

5   Studio Atkinson

1 Chapel, Alamogordo, New Mexico
2 Chapel, Alamogordo, New Mexico; interior view
3 Project for an art studio, Grafton, Massachusetts
4 House, Zachary, Louisiana
5 House, Zachary, Louisiana; interior view

● 546 Guinda Street, Palo Alto, California 94301 USA Tel: +1 650 321 6118 Fax: +1 650 321 0620

STUDIO BAU:TON—NONZERO\ARCHITECTURE

info@bauton.com   www.bauton.com   www.nonzeroarch.com

studio bau:ton-nonzero\architecture is an architecture, design, planning, and project management organization with a comprehensive approach to the challenges of today's built environment. Committed to creating lasting and outstanding buildings, its designs are functional, sustainable, and socially conscious, in their exploration of space, materials, and technology.

Specializing in the design of buildings, with unique requirements for acoustic and visual performance, and media technology, studio bau:ton is bridging architecture, art, and technology. Its projects for music, film, broadcasting, and new media include production and performance facilities for professional and personal uses worldwide.

nonzero\architecture's focus is architecture and its potential to enrich and enhance people's lives, including projects for public, residential, institutional, and commercial clients.

1   studio bau:ton-nonzero\architecture

2   studio bau:ton-nonzero\architecture

3   Edward Colver

4   John Ellis

5   Kazumi Kurigami / Camel

1 Center for the Recording Arts, North Hollywood, California; entry plaza and student lounge pavilion
2 Queens Museum of Art Competition, New York, New York; competition entry for museum expansion and renovation
3 Studio Atlantis, Hollywood, California; recording studio facility, main lounge area
4 Via de la Paz Residence, Pacific Palisades, California; addition and renovation of original Richard Neutra house
5 Sony Music Studios, Nogizaka, Tokyo; main recording space with adjacent sound isolation booths

● 3780 Wilshire Boulevard, Suite 202, Los Angeles, California 90010 USA
Tel: +1 213 251 9791 Fax: +1 213 251 9795

STUDIO DANIEL LIBESKIND

info@daniel-libeskind.com   www.daniel-libeskind.com

1   Archimation

The office of Daniel Libeskind began by winning the competition for the Jewish Museum in Berlin. In the last 14 years, the practice has designed and realized major museum projects and other public cultural projects around the world. Studio Libeskind's projects range from small- to-large scale, publicly financed to privately funded, object-based to IT installations, or a combination of both, and from free-standing sites to placement in sensitive historic environments.

Since 1990, the office has been fortunate to be involved in a diverse array of urban, architectural, and cultural projects. The office has won competitions for major cultural buildings and significant urban projects in Germany, England, Ireland, USA, Japan, Spain, Israel, Mexico, Korea, and PRC. Daniel Libeskind's architecture continues to reflect a profound interest and involvement in philosophy, art, music, literature, theater and film, and a continuing commitment to expanding the horizons of architecture and urbanism.

It is fundamental to Daniel Libeskind's thinking and motivation that buildings and urban projects are crafted with perceptible human energy, and that they speak to the larger cultural community in which they are built.

2   Bitter & Bredt

4   Bitter & Bredt

3   Bitter & Bredt

1 World Trade Center, New York, New York
2 London Metropolitan University, Graduate Centre, London, UK
3 Studio Weil, Mallorca, Spain
4 Imperial War Museum North, Trafford, Manchester, UK
5 Jewish Museum, Berlin, Germany

5   Bitter & Bredt

● 2 Rector Street, 19th Floor, New York, New York 10006 USA Tel: +1 212 497 9100 Fax: +1 646 452 6198

STUDIO DOWNIE ARCHITECTS

info@studiodownie.com   www.studiodownie.com

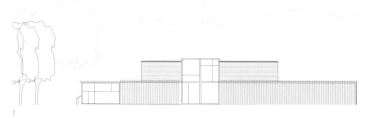

1
Studio Downie Architects

Studio Downie was established in 1993. The firm's projects include the £9.2m masterplan for the headquarters of the Royal Geographical Society, offices for BAA-Lynton, a library, archives, and visitor display for Corpus Christi College, Cambridge, cafés for the Royal Parks, and offices for the French Treasury.

Many projects have involved carefully considered insertions of contemporary designs within listed historic townscapes or sensitive protected landscapes.

Current projects include a new education center and gallery for the Cass Sculpture Foundation, the library for the Royal College of Surgeons, a concrete pool house in West Sussex, a central-London mixed-use commercial building, interiors for St Thomas' Hospital, London, and an extension to the Lyme Regis Museum.

2
James Morris / Axiom

3
James Morris / Axiom

5
Studio Downie Architects

4
Katsuhisa Kida

1 New Education Centre, Cass Sculpture Foundation, West Sussex
2 Display pavilion and reading room viewed from garden, Royal Geographical Society, London, UK
3 Public entrance from Exhibition Road, Royal Geographical Society, London, UK
4 Visitor Gallery & Display Pavilion, Cass Sculpture Foundation, West Sussex, UK
5 Concrete Pool House, Binderton, West Sussex, UK

● 146 New Cavendish Street, London W1W 6YQ UK Tel: +44 20 7255 1599 Fax: +44 20 7636 7883

STUDIO GAIA

contact@studiogaia.com www.studiogaia.com

1   Nagamitsu Endo

Studio Gaia is unique for its non-conventional approach to design, and outstanding capacity to transform spaces into enclaves of minimalist elegance. Its founder, Ilan Waisbrod, developed the firm's focus on creating harmony between interior and exterior architectural forms, while eschewing the purely ornamental.

Studio Gaia has artfully blended chic design and theatrical flair to create a succession of fashionable institutions, such as Republic, Cafeteria, Bond St, and Kenneth Cole. The firm's influence is now being felt internationally owing to the design of dramatic new W Hotels in Mexico City and Seoul. Forthcoming projects include Tokyo's Disneyland Hotel Restaurant and the exclusive GAIA furniture line.

2   Jaime Navarro

3   Studio Gaia

4   Ilan Waisbrod

5   Jae Youn Kim nad Seung Hoon Yum

1 Republic Restaurant, New York, New York
2 W Mexico City, Mexico City, Mexico
3 Private Residence, Jalisco, Mexico
4 Cafeteria Restaurant Miami, Miami Beach, Florida
5 W Seoul, Seoul, Korea

● 401 Washington Street, 4th floor, New York, New York 10013 USA
Tel: +1 212 680 3500 Fax: +1 212 680 3535

STUDIO GRANDA

studiogranda@studiogranda.is   www.studiogranda.is

Studio Granda was established in Reykjavik, Iceland in 1987 by Margrét Hardardóttir and Steve Christer.

The practice has undertaken commissions for public and private clients as well as infrastructure, planning, product design, and collaborations with artists. This range of experience has reinforced the belief that design philosophy grows from the issues specific to each project, rather than from a universal design theory. Each scheme is developed according to its own unique needs, and frequently, the final product is the result of a long process of listening, testing, reconsideration, and invention.

The practice is small and all team members are involved at every step of the design process. Consequently, conceptual thought and management are not isolated from the day-to-day task of information production and site supervision; they are considered as an integral part of the transformation of a vision into a built entity.

The process of creation may be complex but the final result should appear effortless and natural.

1   Sigurgeir Sigurjónsson

2   Sigurgeir Sigurjónsson   3   Sigurgeir Sigurjónsson

4   Sigurgeir Sigurjónsson

Skrudas Residence, Gardabaer, Iceland
1 View from northwest
2 Garden court
3 Living room with Atlantic Ocean view
4 Terrace shared by dining room and living room
5 Family room

5   Sigurgeir Sigurjónsson

● Smidjustigur 11b, Reykjavik IS-101 Iceland Tel: +354 562 2661 Fax: +354 552 6626

STUDIOS ARCHITECTURE

info@studiosarch.com   www.studiosarch.com

STUDIOS Architecture is an international architecture, interiors, and planning practice with a staff of 150 and offices in San Francisco, Los Angeles, New York, Washington, DC, and Paris. Founded in 1985, STUDIOS is active in the programming, master planning, design, and construction of corporate campus, academic, civic, and commercial office building design, including strategic consulting and design of interior architecture. STUDIOS was recently voted by its peers as one of the 10 best design firms in the USA in *Contract* magazine, and is listed as one of the top 200 architecture firms worldwide by *World Architecture*, one of the top 500 design firms by *ENR*, and a top 40 interiors firm in the USA by *Interior Design* magazine. Its work has won more than 135 national, regional, and local design awards and has been featured in more than 100 publications.

STUDIOS is known for innovative design built with limited construction budgets. Flexible spaces that can be used for multiple purposes are a common feature of its work. The firm is also dedicated to creating people-oriented architecture, buildings and interiors that promote collegiality and interaction. STUDIOS maintains several LEED certified staff in all U.S. offices.

1   Tim Griffith

2   Tim Griffith   3   Eric Laignel   4   Tim Griffith

1   Orrick Herrington & Sutcliffe, LLP, San Francisco,
2   Milpitas City Hall, Milpitas, California
3   Bloomberg L.P. Headquarters; Paris, France
4   Foundry Square, Building Two, San Francisco, California
5   Levi Strauss & Co.; New York, New York

5   Andrew Bordwin

● 99 Green Street, San Francisco, California 94111 USA Tel: +1 415 398 7575 Fax: +1 415 398 7763

STUDYO 14 LTD
ARCHITECTS AND URBAN DESIGNERS

studio14arch@yahoo.com www.studio14.com.tr

1   Studyo 14 Ltd.

Studyo 14 Ltd. was established in 1965 by M. Doruk Pamir as an architectural firm which developed into a limited company in 1992.

Since then the group has received seven international and 27 national design prizes, as well as two special achievement awards. More than 700,000 square meters of buildings have been realised, ranging from elaborate urban complexes to single residential units.

2   Studyo 14 Ltd. 3   Studyo 14 Ltd.

5   Studyo 14 Ltd.

4   Studyo 14 Ltd.

1&2   Islamic Center for Technical Vocational Training
       and Research, Tongi, Bangladesh
  3   Süzer Plaza, Istanbul, Turkey
4&5   Atakol Residence, Krynia, Northern Cyprus

● 277/8 Bağdat Caddesi, Göztepe, Istanbul 34728 Turkey
Tel: +90 216 360 2459 / 358 1571 Fax: +90 216 385 8838

STUTCHBURY + PAPE

snpala@ozemail.com.au

1   Julie Cook

2   Julie Cook

4   Julie Cook

Established in 1981, the practice has been known as Stutchbury and Pape Architecture Landscape Architecture since 1991 when landscape architect Phoebe Pape joined architect Peter Stutchbury as director and partner of the practice.

The practice has received 17 Royal Australian Institute of Architecture Awards since 1995 and has received in total 49 local, state and national architectural and environmental awards. In 2001 Stutchbury and Pape (in association with Suters Architects) was awarded the NSW Royal Australian Institute of Architects' highest award for Public Buildings, the Sir John Sulman Award.

The work of Stutchbury and Pape has featured in numerous publications both in Australia and internationally. A Peter Stutchbury monograph was released in 2000, and recent projects were featured in *New Directions in Australian Architecture* the following year. The firm's work has been exhibited in London, New York, Stuttgart, Sydney, Adelaide and Melbourne.

The practice was founded on environmentally sustainable design principles. Stutchbury and Pape is widely recognized for this commitment, receiving the TAS/ Francis Greenway Green Buildings Gold Medal, and the Prime Minister's Banksia Award in 2001.

Peter Stutchbury is currently a Conjoint Professor in Architecture at the University of Newcastle.

3   Julie Cook

5   Julie Cook

1–5 Wedge House, Whale Beach, Sydney, Australia; Wedge House is situated on a steep site overlooking the ocean and rocky coastline of Sydney's northern beaches

● 4/364 Barrenjoey Rd, Newport, New South Wales 2106 Australia
Tel: +61 2 9979 5030 Fax: +61 2 9979 5367

SUMET JUMSAI

architects@sja3d.com   www.sja3d.com

Sumet Jumsai's practice dates back to 1969 and for some time the firm was known as Sumet Jumsai Associates Co. (SJA). It became SJA 3D Co. in 1989 when young partners were brought in to assume operation. To date, the firm has covered all types of work, from urban and mass transit planning, tourism and cultural conservation masterplans, to large scale complexes—commercial, industrial, institutional, sports and health, as well as individual buildings.

While overseeing the firm's projects, Sumet Jumsai continues to undertake specific design works. He also paints and occasionally lectures at Cambridge University where he was a faculty member of the Department of Architecture, and at Melbourne University where he is a Professorial Fellow. His other affiliations include being an Honorary Fellow of the American Institute of Architects, Thai National Artist, and member of the French Académie d'Architecture.

1

Sky Line Studio

2

Sky Line Studio

3

Sky Line Studio

Privy Council Chambers, Bangkok, Thailand
1 Main lobby
2 Front view
3 Main lobby detail
4 View from public park at rear
5 Building detail

4   Sky Line Studio   5   Sky Line Studio

●   106/1 Sukhumvit 53, Bangkok 10110, Thailand Tel: +66 2 259 0035 Fax: +66 2 259 2376

SUSAN MAXMAN & PARTNERS, ARCHITECTS

smp@maxmanpartners.com   www.maxmanpartners.com

Susan Maxman & Partners (SMP) is a 20-person firm offering a full range of design services while stressing on listening to clients, building consensus, and emphasizing innovative design solutions. Recognizing the tremendous impact of buildings and development on the natural environment, SMP designs projects that look beyond the immediate needs of the program to the needs of future generations. This approach to planning and design takes into consideration the broader issues of one's relationship to the natural environment and ecological order recalling the Native American adage, "We do not inherit the land from our ancestors, we borrow it from future generations." Governed by this attitude, SMP aims to design in a way that conserves rather than consumes, supports rather than destroys, and mitigates rather than exacerbates the condition of man on the natural environment.

3   Tom Bernard

2   Susan Maxman & Partners, Architects

4   Peter Olson

3   Barry Halkin

5   Catherine Tighe

1 Camp Tweedale, Oxford, Pennsylvania; exterior of multipurpose activity building
2 Cusano Environmental Education Center at the John Heinz National Wildlife Refuge, Philadelphia, Pennsylvania; fall exterior
3 Younkin Success Center for the Ohio State University, Columbus, Ohio; evening view
4 Julia de Burgos Bilingual Elementary School, Philadelphia, Pennsylvania; courtyard view
5 Vacation Residence, Harvey Cedars, New Jersey; exterior

● 1600 Walnut Street, 2nd Floor, Philadelphia, Pennsylvania 19103 USA
   Tel: +1 215 985 4410 Fax: +1 215 985 4430

SUSSNA+MATZ ARCHITECTS

info@sussna-matz.com www.sussna-matz.com

1   Norman McGrath

2   Hope Wurmfeld

3   Barry Halkin

Design at Sussna+Matz Architects PA strives to achieve variety of form, leaps of imagination in images and organization, elegance of craft and composition, and mind-sparking ideas.

The clients' dreams and aspirations are always the program. And the prospect of creating spaces for people that delight, satisfy, and challenge them possesses the possibility of making a place for them to thrive in, and which will shape their lives.

4   Massimo Gammacurta

1   Award-Winning New Residence, Rosemont, New Jersey
2   DeWitt Stern Group, New York, New York; renovation of corporate headquarters, executive conference center
3   Rockwood Specialties, Princeton, New Jersey; new global headquarters, executive offices area
4   Princeton University, Dillon Gym Complex Renovations, Stephens Fitness Center, Princeton, New Jersey

●   53 State Road, Princeton, New Jersey 08540-1318 USA Tel: +1 609 924 6611 Fax: +1 609 924 5230

SUTERS ARCHITECTS

newcastle@sutersarchitects.com.au   www.sutersarchitects.com.au

1   Greg Callan

Suters Architects is a multidisciplinary architectural practice that strives for architectural excellence and creative leadership in all aspects of its professional services. The practice commenced in 1958 and has evolved into a dynamic architecture firm of national significance. Operating from Sydney, Melbourne, Newcastle, and Brisbane, the firm is also affiliated with architectural practices in the UK, USA, and Malaysia. Suters Architects has successfully demonstrated its ability and capacity to service projects at local, national and international levels.

3   Tim Williams

2   Bart Maiorana

1   Lindemans Ben Ean Winery, Pokolbin, New South
    Wales; refurbishment of historic winery
2   BAE Systems, Lead-in Fighter Facility, Williamtown,
    New South Wales; aircraft hangar space, workshops,
    stores and offices
3   Etage, City Quarter Project; adaptive re-use of 4-story
    former hospital building
4   Broken Hill Hospital, Broken Hill, New South Wales;
    new 80-bed hospital
5   Life Sciences Building, The University of Newcastle,
    New South Wales

4   Roger Hanley   5   Alan Chawner

● 16 Telford Street, Newcastle, New South Wales 2300 Australia Tel: +61 2 4926 5222 Fax: +61 2 4926 5251

585

SVPA ARCHITECTS INC.

design@SVPA-architects.com   www.SVPA-architects.com

1   Archigraphica, Johnathon Clayton

SVPA Architects Inc. was established in 1953, and is a privately owned, subchapter 'S' corporation. Its areas of expertise include architecture, planning, landscape architecture, and interior design services. It has received over 3,000 commissions and 80 percent of its work is repeat business from satisfied clients.

With a staff of 21 experienced professionals, there is direct principal involvement on every project, ensuring the delivery of successful, within-budget and on-time projects. SVPA has a proven ability to listen to its clients' special needs.

2   Dale Photographics

3   Cameron Campbell

1   Pomerantz Center, The University of Iowa, Iowa City, Iowa; 5 stories, containing approximately 72,000 gross square feet
2   Pella Corporation Headquarters, Pella, Iowa; 81,325-square-foot, 3-story office facility and 565-square-foot signature entry plaza.
3   Rain and Hail Insurance Service, Inc., Urbandale, Iowa; 3-story, 90,900-square-foot corporate headquarters building
4   Wells Fargo Home Mortgage, West Des Moines, Iowa; 6-story, 435,000-square-foot office building
5   SVPA Architects Inc., West Des Moines, Iowa; SVPA's offices received the First Place Iowa Blue Flame Gas Award

4   Cameron Campbell

5   Russ Ver Ploeg, AIA

● 1466 28th Street, Suite 200, West Des Moines, Iowa 50266 USA
Tel: +1 515 327 5990 Fax: +1 515 327 5991

SWABACK PARTNERS

vswaback@swabackpartners.com www.swabackpartners.com

Swaback Partners is a 45-person, multidisciplinary team of architects, planners, and interior designers with honors and awards for the design of commercial and institutional buildings, custom residences, and the planning of entire communities.

The partners of the firm hold architectural registrations in California, Arizona, Colorado, New Mexico, Texas, Missouri, Michigan, Wisconsin, Illinois, Indiana, Kentucky, North Carolina, South Carolina and Florida. Work in other countries has taken the partners to Russia, Japan, Mexico, and Saudi Arabia.

Public and private sector planning includes everything from neighborhood design to new communities, ranging in size from 1,000 to 96,000 acres and located in Wisconsin, Arizona, Utah, California, Hawaii, and Mexico. Commercial and institutional work includes galleries, hotels and resorts, visitor centers, recreation facilities, and country clubs.

The firm's partners are Vernon D. Swaback, FAIA, FAICP, John E. Sather, AIA, AICP, and Jon C. Bernhard, AIA.

1   Swaback Partners

2   Swaback Partners

4   Swaback Partners

3   Swaback Partners

5   Swaback Partners

1 Corporate Headquarters
2 Custom Residence
3 Arizona Biltmore Hotel
4 Church
5 DC Ranch Masterplan

● 7550 East McDonald Drive, Suite A, Scottsdale, Arizona 85250 USA
Tel: +1 480 367 2100 Fax: +1 480 367 2101

SWANKE HAYDEN CONNELL ARCHITECTS

gursel.a@shca.com   www.shca.com

Swanke Hayden Connell Architects (SHCA) is an international, award-winning firm with offices in New York, London, Sheffield, Paris, Istanbul, and Moscow, as well as Miami, Florida; Washington, DC; Newark, New Jersey; and Stamford, Connecticut. Recognized for its enduring design quality, from large multi-million dollar projects to small on-call assignments, SHCA provides the management skills, design talent, necessary resources, and appropriate expertise in the following range of services: architecture and masterplanning, interior design and space planning, historic preservation, and graphic design.

Founded in 1906 in New York as the firm of Walker and Gillette, SHCA has a proud legacy of remaining in the forefront of design excellence. Its clients include international corporations, banking and financial institutions, insurance companies, law firms, communication and publishing trades, developers, educational institutions, government, non-profit entities, and leading healthcare facilities.

1   Swanke Hayden Connell Architects

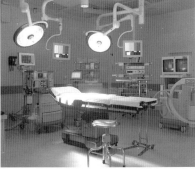

2   Grey Crawford

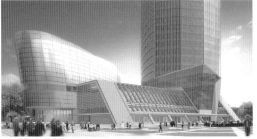

3   Swanke Hayden Connell Architects

4   Paul Warchol   5   Swanke Hayden Connell Architects

1 Radius Holdings, Kent, UK
2 Short Hills Surgical Center, Short Hills, New Jersey
3 Moscow International Business Center, Moscow, Russia
4 Brown Brothers Harriman, Corporate Headquarters, New York, New York
5 Merrill Lynch Headquarters London, UK

● 295 Lafayette Street, New York, New York 10012-2701 USA Tel: +1 212 226 9696 Fax: +1 212 219 0488

SWATT ARCHITECTS

www.swattarchitects.com

Founded in 1975, Swatt Architects is an award-winning architectural firm recognized for design excellence in architecture, planning, and interior design.

The firm provides diverse services to a very diverse clientele on a wide variety of building projects, ranging from the adaptive re-use of the largest pair of masonry buildings in San Francisco, to unique and highly crafted individual residences.

The firm believes that the most successful architectural projects respond first to client and user needs, and then combine the most appropriate technology and materials, along with sensitive design to achieve architecture of lasting value.

1   Richard Barnes

2   Cesar Rubio

3   Russell Abraham

4   Cesar Rubio   5   Cesar Rubio

1 Kohavi Residence, Portola Valley, California;
   entry elevation
2 Private Residence, Palo Alto, California; entry
   and living room elevation
3 Swatt Residence, Lafayette, California; living room
   and terrace
4 Private Residence, Palo Alto, California; gallery
   and stair from courtyard
5 Private Residence, Palo Alto, California; dining room
   with library above

● 5845 Doyle Street, Suite 104, Emeryville, California 94608 USA Tel: +1 510 985 9779 Fax: +1 510 985 0116

SYDNESS ARCHITECTS, P.C.

info@sydnessarchitects.com www.sydnessarchitects.com

Sydness Architects is a full-service architectural firm offering unparalleled design experience in commercial office buildings, hotels, residential complexes, master-planned communities and mixed-use developments. The firm provides services to corporate and developer clients in the USA and abroad, with major completed projects located across the country and in Asia.

Whether the project is a high-rise office building, a residential development, or luxury hotel, Sydness Architects listens closely to client needs, while responding to the community and architectural context so that the project is both a sound investment and a good neighbor.

Committed to design excellence, Sydness Architects offers management and technical expertise to meet project objectives at any scale. All of the firm's architects are adept in every aspect of building design, working under the direction of Jeff Sydness who, during his 25-year architectural career, has created or upgraded facilities for such companies as J.P. Morgan, Hines, JMC Communities, Starwood Hotels and Resorts, and the USAA Realty Company.

2   Jock Pottle

1   Sydness Architects

3   Jaime Ardiles-Arce

1 Song Jiang Development, Shanghai, PRC; residential, retail, hotel, office
2 Shanghai United Bank Tower, Shanghai, PRC; 50-story, 1-million-square-foot mixed-use project
3 St. Regis Hotel, Shanghai, PRC; 42-story five-star hotel, interior
4 St. Regis Hotel, Shanghai, PRC; 42-story five-star hotel, exterior
5 250 East 49th Street, New York, New York; 22-story luxury residential tower

4   Mr. Miao Zhi Jiang

5   Sydness Architects

● 1150 Avenue of the Americas, New York, New York 10036 USA Tel: +1 212 719 4777 Fax: +1 212 719 4433

T.R. HAMZAH & YEANG

trhy@trhamzahyeang.com   www.trhamzahyeang.com

T.R. Hamzah & Yeang Sdn. Bhd. is a signature architecture and planning firm recognized for its work on ecologically responsive design and planning. The firm carries out projects in Europe, Asia, and the USA. Projects include the National Library Board Building in Singapore, the 15-story Mesiniaga Building (IBM franchise) in Malaysia, and the Palomas Tower in Mexico City.

Led by the principals, Dr Ken Yeang and Tengku Robert Hamzah, the firm's work has been published extensively in the international press. Dr. Yeang is also the author of several authoritative books on ecological design, including *Bioclimatic Skyscrapers* (Ellipsis, 1998), and *The Skyscraper Bioclimatically Considered* (John Wiley & Sons, 1996)

The firm has received many awards for its extensive range of built works, including the RAIA (Royal Australian Institute of Architects) International Awards in 1997 and 1999, the Aga Khan Award for Architecture (1995) for the Mesiniaga Building, and many others.

1   K.L. Ng Photography

2   K.L. Ng Photography

3   K.L. Ng Photography

4   K.L. Ng Photography

5   K.L. Ng Photography

1   Beijing WTSC
2   National Library Board building, Singapore
3   UMNO
4   Mewah Oils
5   Mesiniaga building, Malaysia

● 8, Jalan 1. Taman Sri Ukay, 68000 Ampang, Selangor, West Malaysia
Tel: +60 3 4257 1966 Fax: +60 3 4256 1005

TABANLIOGLU

info@tabanlioglu.com.tr www.tabanlioglu.com.tr

1   Enis Ozbank

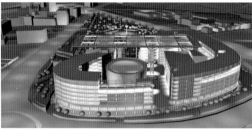

2   Tabanlioglu Architecture

3   Tabanlioglu Architecture

The firm was established in 1956 by Dr Hayati Tabanlioglu and since then has been responsible for many major state buildings in Turkey, including Erzurum Ataturk University, Ataturk Cultural Centre in Istanbul and Istanbul Ataturk Airport.

Atakoy Tourism Centre in Istanbul is another of the firm's earlier works. It contained the Galleria Shopping Centre, which was awarded the ICSC European Design first prize in 1989. In 1990, Murat Tabanlioglu returned to Turkey, having completed his study and international activities in Vienna, and began to work with Dr Hayati Tabanlioglu. The joint projects, until the death of Dr Hayati Tabanlioglu in 1994, include Dogan Media Centre and Carousel Shopping Centre and Hospital, both in Istanbul. Melkan Gursel Tabanlioglu joined the group in 1995.

Since then, the firm has completed many media centers, office buildings, shopping centers, hospitals, airport projects, congress centers, factories, and interior design projects, on a national and worldwide scale.

5   Manoel Nunes

4   Cemal Emden

1 Dogan Printing Centre, Ankara, Turkey
2 Istanbul Metropolitan Municipality Building and City
   Hall, Istanbul, Turkey; competition project (1st prize)
3 Salipazari Maritime and Tourism Complex Project,
   Istanbul, Turkey
4 Dogan Media Town, Istanbul, Turkey
5 Expo 2000 Turkish Pavilion, Hanover, Germany

● 145-147/4-5 Mesrutiyet Caddesi Tepebasi, 80050 Istanbul Turkey
Tel: +90 212 251 2111 Fax: +90 212 251 2332

TAKASHI YAMAGUCHI

ya@yamaguchi-a.jp   www.yamaguchi-a.jp

Takashi Yamaguchi was born in Kyoto in 1953. After graduating from Kyoto University, he worked with Tadao Ando Architect & Associates. In 1988, he became a founding member of ARX, an international research group for architectural theory. In 1996, he founded Takashi Yamaguchi & Associates. Since 2002, he has held a position at Waseda University, and is a Fellow of IMDC, Japan.

He has received several awards, including finalist in the Spreebogen International Competition for a new German Capital in Berlin, 1992; the Asakura Prize of the 18th SD Review, 1999; and first place, Benedictus Awards (AIA, UIA), 2001.

Takashi Yamaguchi has held teaching and lecturing positions at Eindhoven University of Technology, Netherlands (2000); Kyoto University, Japan (2000–2003); Massachusetts Institute of Technology and Harvard University, USA (2001); and Tsinghua University, China (2002).

1   Takashi Yamaguchi & Associates

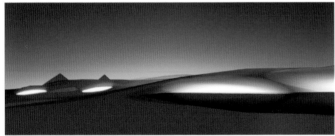

2   Takashi Yamaguchi & Associates

1 Racing Fluid Forms
2 Egyptian Museum, Giza, Egypt
3   Takashi Yamaguchi & Associates   3 Glass Temple, Kyoto, Japan

● Fusui Building, 1-3-4 Ebisunishi Naniwa-ku, Osaka 556003 Japan
Tel: +81 6 6633 3773 Fax: +81 6 6633 5175

TANGE ASSOCIATES URBANISTS–ARCHITECTS

www.tangeweb.com

Founded on the philosophy and vision of Kenzo Tange, a pioneer in the world of urban and architectural design, Tange Associates was established by his son Paul Noritaka Tange to mark the start of a new era. With extensive experience in architectural design, urban planning, and various schemes for regional development, the firm takes pride in each and every one of its projects— government projects, public facilities, commercial buildings, and other prominent works around the globe—to satisfy the varied values and individual needs of today.

Tange Associates continues to explore new possibilities in societal and environmental issues, and provides professional expertise to create exciting and dynamic architectures and master planning of the highest quality and commitment to client satisfaction, while showing that all of this can be done with a very human approach.

1   Tange Associates Urbanists–Architects

2   Tange Associates Urbanists–Architects

4   Tange Associates Urbanists–Architects

3   Tange Associates Urbanists–Architects

5   Tange Associates Urbanists–Architects

  1   Tokyo Prince Hotel Park Tower, Tokyo, Japan
2&3   West Kowloon Cultural District, Hong Kong
  4   Salvatore Ferragamo Headquarters, Tokyo, Japan
  5   President Group Headquaters Building, Taipei, Taiwan

●   24 Daikyo-cho Shinjuku-ku, Tokyo, Japan   Tel: +81 3 3357 1888   Fax: +81 3 3357 3388

TAPPÉ ASSOCIATES, INCORPORATED

www.tappe.com

1   Sam Sweezy

Tappé Associates Inc., is an award-winning, full-service architectural firm offering highly responsive design services to clients who share its desire to create buildings and spaces that impact the lives of the individuals that work in and visit the buildings.

Tappé Associates Inc., was founded in 1979, continuing a practice established by Tony Tappé in 1962. Currently, the staff consists of 40 professionals, including 11 registered architects. The firm offers complete programming, planning and design services to fully coordinate all aspects of a project.

Tappé's experience encompasses many building types, with expertise and focus on educational, institutional, and municipal facilities. Since 1992, the firm has obtained approvals for 27 public projects, representing more than $600 million in project costs, and has provided design services on 19 municipal facilities.

The firm is comfortable working in a variety of architectural vocabularies, settings and contexts. Its approach is to actively involve those who will use and occupy the building in the exploration and evaluation of design ideas.

2   Peter Vanderwarker   3   Sam Sweezy

5   Greg Dysart   4   Meliti D. Dikeos

1   Nevins Memorial Library, Methuen, Massachusetts; renovated Great Hall
2   Berlin Memorial School, Berlin, Massachusetts; main hall near administration
3   Worcester Public Library, Worcester, Massachusetts; arcade to entry
4   The Carroll Center for the Blind, Newton, Massachusetts; exterior detail of entry vestibule
5   MIT Hayden Library, Cambridge, Massachusetts; 24-hour study space

●   Six Edgerly Place, Boston, Massachusetts 02116 USA   Tel: +1 617 451 0200   Fax: +1 617 451 3899

TED WELLS LIVING SIMPLE

ted@tedwwells.com   www.tedwwells.com

Everything Ted Wells designs—homes, gardens, interiors, monasteries—has a common theme: simplicity. He divides his time between studios in California and Spain. His television show, *America's Homestyles*, can still be seen on the Home and Garden network in the US. He believes in quiet simplicity and creates honest, meaningful and fulfilling spaces. For his clients, it's not about impressing others, it's about expressing oneself.

1   Anton Getty

2   Anton Getty   3   Anton Getty

4   Anton Getty   5   Anton Getty

1 Muñoz House, Laguna Beach, California; structural Cor-ten steel panels and glass
2 Muñoz House, Laguna Beach, California; garden porch, interior view
3 Simon House Conservatory, Laguna Niguel, California; wood studs, slate roof, glass, copper and zinc
4 Westgreen Private Chapel, Laguna Niguel, California; boulders, frameless glass, Cor-ten steel frame
5 Double R Ranch House, Orange Park Acres, California; courtyard entrance gate in plaster

● 30942 Westgreen Drive, Laguna Niguel, California 92677 USA Tel: +1 949 495 6009 Fax: +1 949 495 6149

TEEPLE ARCHITECTS INC.

info@teeplearch.com   www.teeplearch.com

1   Michael Awad

2   Tom Arban

From its inception in 1989, Teeple Architects Inc. has built a reputation for innovative design and exceptional service. The firm established this reputation through a broad range of institutional, commercial and residential projects including community and recreation centers, libraries, schools and university buildings. The firm has become known for designing projects of exceptional material and spatial quality, with a strong conceptual basis derived from the specific needs and aspirations of each client.

3   Tom Arban

The goal of Teeple Architects is to create innovative design projects in which the architectural concept is intimately linked to the day-to-day use and inhabitation of the building. An ability to respond creatively to the dictates of the site, context, budget and client requirements has characterized the work of the office. In this era of specialization, the firm believes in the continuing value of the general architectural practice and to this end, has pursued work in the commercial, institutional and residential fields, ranging in scope from broad planning, major institutional projects, and urban design studies, to highly detailed interiors.

4   Tom Arban

The firm has explored themes such as architecture as site, the space of landscape, diverse space and translucent space. These themes have been expressed through subtle compositions of material and texture, and careful attention to detail.

5   Tom Arban

1   Ajax Main Central Library, Ajax, Ontario
2   Eatonville Public Library, Etobicoke, Ontario
3   Graduate Residence, University of Toronto, Toronto, Ontario; joint venture
    with Morphosis, Inc.
4   York University Honour Court and Welcome Centre, Toronto, Ontario
5   Pickering West Branch Library and Community Centre, Pickering, Ontario

● 5 Camden Street, Toronto M5V 1V2 Canada Tel: +1 416 598 0554 Fax: +1 416 598 1705

TEGET ARCHITECTURAL OFFICE

mk@teget.com   eu@teget.com   www.teget.com

Founded by architects Mehmet Kutukcuoglu and Kerem Yazgan in 1996 following a first prize in a national architectural competition, Teget Architectural Office offered architectural services during its first four years in Ankara, capital city of Turkey. By the year 2000, Ertug Ucar replaced Kerem Yazgan as a partner, and the firm moved to its current office in Istanbul.

Since the firm's establishment, the architects of Teget have worked on a wide variety of architectural programs. From airports to single-family houses, some of these projects have been built and some are under construction. The firm is known for its innovative solutions to challenging problems and experiments with building materials. The partners have received a number of prizes from both national and international architectural and planning competitions.

Teget has recently developed the ability to systematically construct mid-size buildings in order to acquire a better control of its design work. Parallel to their professional architectural business, the partners are also involved in academic and artistic activities.

1   Teget

2   Teget

3   Teget

4   Teget

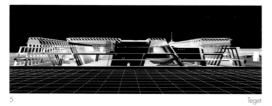

5   Teget

1&2   House, Ankara, Turkey, 1998
  3   Izmir Port District Planning Competition Project, Izmir, Turkey, 2001
  4   Opel Building, Ankara, Turkey, 1998
  5   Dalaman International Airport Competition Project, Turkey, 1999

● 1/9 Kiblelizade Sokak, Beyoglu 34430 Istanbul, Turkey Tel: +90 212 244 2243 Fax: +90 212 244 2273

TEH JOO HENG ARCHITECTS

tjhas@magix.com.sg

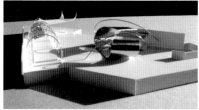

1   Teh Joo Heng Architects

2   Teh Joo Heng Architects

Teh Joo Heng Architects was established in April, 2000 by Teh Joo Heng, an architect with 12 years prior practice experience.

Teh Joo Heng Architects is a design-oriented firm that focuses on creating imaginative and innovative design solutions to conventional design problems, thereby bringing a fresh perspective to all design projects commissioned.

The design philosophy demands thorough inquiry into design issues in a rigorous search for innovative design solutions. The design process respects the traditional built environment and regional culture as heritage while embracing new technological possibilities. The design solution is expressed in strong and clear architectural forms and spaces to meet the aspiration of the client, while adding to the body of knowledge in architecture and the built environment.

The principal is a hands-on architect with extensive professional and academic experience.

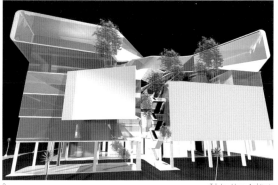

3   Teh Joo Heng Architects

4   Teh Joo Heng Architects   5   Teh Joo Heng Architects

1   Public Amenities, Singapore; inserting dynamic space within rigid public housing context
2   25 Bin Tong Park, Singapore; form and space articulation through solid/void expression
3   EISB Corporate Headquarters, Kuala Lumpur, Malaysia; hybridized corporate space with integrated vertical landscaping
4   NTUC Headquarters Competition (3rd Prize); high-rise office typology re-examined
5   63/65 Emerald Hill, Singapore; sculptured volume contrasting with rectilinear conservation house interior

●   140 Robinson Road #05-09 Chow House, 068907 Singapore   Tel: +65 6372 1110   Fax: +65 6372 1398

TEK
THANHAUSER ESTERSON KAPELL ARCHITECTS, PC

info@tek-arch.com www.tek-arch.com

1   Brian Rose

2   Brian Rose

TEK's fundamental view is that architecture is an agent of change. When approached with rigorous inquiry and artistry, architecture can enhance and redefine the relationship between individuals and their environment. TEK operates based on the belief that everyone is entitled to buildings and spaces that support their activities, inspire their actions and delight their senses.

Founded in 2002, the firm is a new collaboration of veteran New York City architects Charles Thanhauser, Jack Esterson and Martin Kapell. The trio's diverse portfolios include projects for performing arts groups, major non-profit organizations, retailers, and universities. They have designed private luxury residences, housing for the homeless, corporate offices, and community healthcare centers. TEK's efforts have been recognized in major US and international design publications, and with numerous awards. As a means of grounding and expanding the context of their design ideas, the principals all teach, write on architecture and design and serve on the boards of not-for-profit organizations.

3   Brian Rose

4   TEK

5   Chun Y Lai

1 Brooklyn College Computer Center, Brooklyn, New York; new entry pavilion at Brooklyn College
2 Maurice Villency Flagship Store, New York, New York; block-long Manhattan flagship for high-end contemporary furniture retailer
3 Brooklyn College Computer Center, Brooklyn, New York; 24-hour-access computer study facility in lounge setting
4 Throgg's Neck Community Center, Bronx, New York; public housing community center: gymnasium, classrooms & computer facilities
5 M & C Saatchi, New York, New York; dynamic loft office interior for major advertising firm

● 19 Union Square West, New York, New York 10003 USA Tel: +1 212 929 3699 Fax: +1 212 929 9718

TH & IDIL

thidil@ttnet.net.tr

TH & IDIL Architecture, Planning and Consulting Ltd. was established in 1987 by Tamer Basbug, Hasan Ozbay and Baran Idil. The practice is based in Ankara and also has a branch in Izmir. Most of the work completed to date has been in area of public buildings and town planning, which have generally been commissioned as the result of competitions. The practice has an excellent record in architectural competitions, winning 12 and collecting over 70 prizes in total.

Some of the firm's best-known works include: Ministry of Foreign Affairs and Annex Building, Ankara; Gaziosmanpasa Government Center, Istanbul; City Hall, Gaziantep; Fatih Government Center, Istanbul; Urla City Hall, Izmir; Ostim Business Center, Ankara; Harran University Campus, Urfa; Turkish Embassy, Islamabad, Pakistan; Baliktasi Hotel, Ordu; Urla Housing Development, Izmir; Hatipoglu Residence, Ankara; Congress Center and Fair, EGS Park, Denizli; Planning of Kalekapisi District, Antalya; City Plan, Elazig; and City Plan, Tokat.

1   TH & IDIL

2   TH & IDIL

3   TH & IDIL

4   TH & IDIL

5   TH & IDIL

1   Gaziantep City Hall, Gaziantep, Turkey
2   Harran University Campus, Urfa, Turkey
3   Ministry of Foreign Affairs, Ankara, Turkey
4   Turkish Embassy, Islamabad, Pakistan
5   Fatih Government Center, Istanbul, Turkey

●   10/6 Piyade Sokak, Cankaya, 06540 Ankara, Turkey   Tel: +90 312 439 5943   Fax: +90 312 439 6236

THE ARCHITEKTENGRUPPE N+M GMBH

offenbach@n-plus-m.de www.n-plus-m.de

The Architektengruppe N+M GmbH is an emerging architectural office with its headquarters in Offenbach/Main and an office in Berlin. The business activities cover all services in architecture, interior design and urban development, building management, project development, and consulting.

Its founders and staff are experienced in constructing, refurbishing, renovating, and reconstructing high-rise and administration buildings, major hospitals, retail, and entertainment centers. As a service provider, N+M ensures the greatest possible financial result for the client through the continuous examination of architecture, technical feasibility, and functional connections.

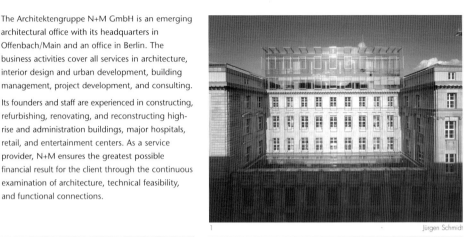

1   Jürgen Schmidt

2   B. C. Horvath

4   Johannes Vogt

3   HTP

5   N+M

1   Deutsche Bank, Berlin, Germany; refurbishment of bank and
    Guggenheim-Museum
2   Main Triangel, Frankfurt, Germany; office building
3   City Tower, Offenbach/Main, Germany; high-rise office building
4   Siemens Power Generation Office, Offenbach/Main, Germany
5   Children's Hospital, Fuerth, Germany; new 82-bed children's hospital

●   Berliner Strasse 77, D-63065 Offenbach am Main, Germany   Tel: +49 069 8203 0   Fax: +49 069 8203 200

THE BUCHAN GROUP

tbg@melbourne.buchan.com.au   tbg@brisbane.buchan.com.au   www.buchan.com.au

1   Murray Hedwig

2   Tim Griffith

3   Michael Nicholson

4   Tim Griffith

The Buchan Group has designed some of the most significant Australian and New Zealand projects of the last decade including the redevelopment of the historic GPO in Sydney, the redevelopment of Finger Wharf, the Channel 7 headquarters at Melbourne's Docklands, Christchurch Art Gallery in New Zealand, and Harbour Town Shopping Centre on Queensland's Gold Coast. The group has offices in Brisbane, Gold Coast, Melbourne, Perth, Sydney, and New Zealand, and more than 300 staff.

The Buchan Group is active in China, Taiwan, Japan, and the Middle East, where it is currently designing a number of large-scale mixed use, retail, residential, health, and education developments.

The Buchan Group's buildings are characterized by a strong sense of design innovation, enduring aesthetic quality, and relationship to context. The group strives to create quality built forms that are fit for purpose. It embraces the philosophy that good design is not compromised by economics; but rather, it is another challenge for the designer to resolve.

1 The Palms Shopping Centre, Christchurch, New Zealand
2 No.1 Martin Place, Sydney, New South Wales;
   redevelopment of Sydney's historic general post office
   includes a hotel and office tower
3 The Wharf at Woolloomooloo, Sydney, New South Wales;
   mixed-use redevelopment of historic Finger Wharf
4 The Grandstand, Victoria Racing Club, Flemington, Victoria
5 Christchurch Art Gallery, Christchurch, New Zealand

5   Murray Hedwig

● GPO Box 4584, Melbourne, Victoria 3001 Australia Tel: +61 3 9329 1077
PO Box 341, Fortitude Valley, Queensland 4006 Australia Tel: +61 7 3859 9222

THE NEXT ENTERPRISE – ARCHITECTS

office@thenextenterprise.at   www.thenextenterprise.at

1   Lucas Schaller

Provoking the random and unpredictable is the next ENTERprise – architect's strategy for producing spatial and functional architecture. Ernst J. Fuchs and Marie Therese Harnoncourt established the firm in 2000 in Vienna. They have worked together in different constellations since the early 1990s.

As authors of urban interventions including Hirnsegel No.7 1995, Stadtwind 2000, and Tinkbrunnen 2003; experimental installations Blindgänger 2000, and Audiolounge 2002; and urban concepts (how to start a city 2003), these two Vienna-based architects single out the importance of form, for which they eschew any kind of preconception, solely by validating the complex processes of which it is the product.

3   the next ENTERprise – architects

4   Lucas Schaller

2   Lucas Schaller

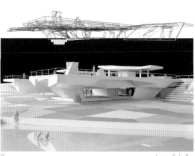

1 audiolounge, 9th International Architecture Exhibition
   entry, Venice, Italy
2 Outdoor Pool, Caldero, Italy
3 Durchblick Observation Tower, Vienna, Austria;
   competition entry 2002 MUQUA
4 Nam June Paik Museum, Kiheung, South Korea;
   competition entry 2003,
5 Underground Pool, Vienna, Austria; (with F. Haydn)

5   Gerald Zugmann

● Ausstellungsstrasse 5/2, Vienna A-1020 Austria Tel: +43 1729 6388 Fax: +43 1729 6752

THE STEINBERG GROUP, ARCHITECTS

www.tsgarch.com

1   John Edward Linden

The Steinberg Group, established in 1953, is an architectural, planning, program management and interior design firm involved in a broad spectrum of building types including civic, residential, educational, religious and commercial facilities.

With offices in Silicon Valley and Los Angeles, the firm is sensitive to the rapidly changing demands of dynamic communities as well as adhering to the needs of clients, local municipalities and historical and social precedents. The Steinberg Group's mission to provide socially conscious architecture that enriches lives has led to the development of innovative and sustainable solutions to complex urban and environmental challenges.

The staff of 100 highly trained architects, designers and support personnel is committed to providing quality design to enhance the residential, educational and cultural experience of clients and end-users. The result is architecture for people that exceeds expectations.

2   Marvin Rand

3   John Edward Linden

4   Tom Bonner

5   Tom Bonner

1 Avalon at Cahill Park, San Jose, California; mixed-use community integrates seamlessly with adjacent neighborhoods
2 Riverside County Historic Courthouse, Riverside, California; honored with multiple awards in historic preservation
3 Fountain Park, Playa Vista, California; first housing component in new Playa Vista community 50% affordable
4 Classic Residence by Hyatt, Palo Alto, California; new senior community, living options within university setting
5 Evergreen Valley College Library and Educational Technology Center, San Jose, California; new landmark building integrates three separate programs

● 60 Pierce Avenue, San Jose, California 95110 USA Tel: +1 408 295 5446 Fax: +1 408 295 5928
606 South Olive Street, Suite 1950, Los Angeles, California 90014 USA Tel: +1 213 629 0500 Fax: +1 213 629 0501

THE STUBBINS ASSOCIATES

www.stubbins.us

1   Greg Murphey

2   Timothy Griffith/Esto

4   Chris Barnes

Established in 1949, The Stubbins Associates has successfully completed an unusually broad range of projects both nationally and internationally. Professional services include feasibility studies, programming and masterplanning, architectural, interior and landscape design, and technical services including construction documentation and construction administration.

The size and structure of the firm are designed for active, hands-on participation by a principal-in-charge, who is assisted by a project manager and project designer to ensure a high degree of communication, coordination, and continuity for each project.

The design process is tempered with a deep respect for the client's needs, aspirations, functional requirements, and constraints.

The Stubbins Associates is one of the few firms to have been awarded the prestigious Architectural Firm Award by the American Institute of Architects, placing it at the highest echelon of the profession. In addition, the firm's projects have won more than 160 awards for design excellence, both nationally and internationally. Some of its better-known projects include Citicorp Center in New York, the Federal Reserve Bank of Boston, the Ronald Reagan Presidential Library in California, Congress Hall in Berlin, and the Landmark Tower in Yokohama, the tallest building in Japan.

3   INSITE

5   Hedrich-Blessing

1 Indiana Historical Society, Indianapolis, Indiana
2 United States Embassy, Singapore
3 Venetian Casino Resort Hotel, Las Vegas, Nevada
4 Amgen Center, Cambridge, Massachusetts
5 Biological Sciences Learning Center and Jules F. Knapp Medical Research Center, The University of Chicago, Chicago, Illinois

● 1030 Massachusetts Avenue, Cambridge, Massachusetts 02138 USA
Tel: +1 617 491 6450 Fax: +1 617 491 7104

THEO. DAVID ARCHITECTS / TDA–KAL

tdanyc@aol.com   www.newyork-architects.com/tdanyc

Theo. David Architects is committed to providing comprehensive, professional design services to each of its clients, while meeting their needs on schedule and in the most imaginative way possible.

The practice is headed by Theoharis David, FAIA. Mr David, a Professor of Architecture at Pratt Institute, enjoys an international reputation as an architect and educator. His architecture has received design awards at city, state, national and international levels.

Projects executed in the New York metropolitan area have ranged from sophisticated medical facilities, to private residences, churches, corporate interiors, retail space design, the restoration of historical buildings, and urban housing.

1   Theo. David

Through his affiliate TDA/KAL headquartered in Nicosia, Cyprus, Theo. David has designed corporate facilities, public schools, civic buildings, athletic stadiums, industrial structures and residential neighborhoods. The practice has developed comprehensive housing and tourism masterplans in Cyprus, the Middle East and West Africa.

The design process of Theo. David Architects places primary importance on understanding the more subtle needs of the client. This process includes direct client input during all phases of programming, design development, and implementation. A hands-on approach at the construction phase is considered essential for the accurate execution of the specifications of each project.

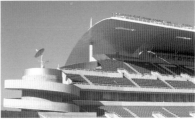

2   Theo. David

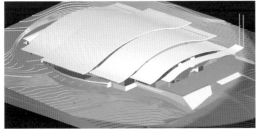

4   D.Kolonis

3   M.Cruzate

1 G.S.P. Pancypria Stadium, Nicosia, Cyprus; Main
   stadium view
2 G.S.P. Pancypria Stadium, Nicosia, Cyprus; Detail
3 G.S.P. Pancypria Stadium, Nicosia, Cyprus, athletes'
   residence
4 Indoor Athletic Center, Limassol, Cyprus; aerial view
5   Y.Kythreotis   5 Cyprus National Theater, Nicosia, Cyprus; entrance

● 170 Duane Street, Suite 2C, New York, New York 10013 USA Tel: +1 212 226 0788 Fax: +1 212 226 7724
Cyprus Tel: +357 2249 9464 Fax: +357 2231 6506

THOMPSON VAIVODA & ASSOCIATES ARCHITECTS, INC.

bob@tvapdx.com   www.tvapdx.com

1   Strode Eckert Photographic

Thompson Vaivoda & Associates Architects, Inc. is a full-service architecture, masterplanning and interior design firm based in Portland, Oregon. Founded in 1984, the firm has received nearly 50 awards for design and construction excellence. The firm has built a strong reputation for providing the highest level of service to clients. The primary focus fueling that reputation lies in a search for balance, where the client's functional, fiscal and aesthetic goals are attained with equal success.

The firm searches for the social, humanistic and community aspects of each commission; client participation in an interactive setting is encouraged with the collaboration leading to a design image that results from a sharing of ideas. The firm has partnered with Nike, Inc. since 1987. Over 15 years, and 2 million square feet of varied building types on the Nike World Campus, the firm has consistently translated the corporate brand to built form and galvanized corporate culture. Similar work has been accomplished for Ericsson, Procter & Gamble and a newly formed bank in Oregon. The firm's strength lies in its ability to connect with the abstract concepts of community, culture, brand and ethos and then express those concepts in a building and plan that inspire and resonate clearly with the user.

2   Strode Photographic

3   Strode Photographic

4   Strode Photographic

5   Strode Photographic

1 Marilyn Moyer Meditation Chapel, Portland, Oregon; north elevation, a man-made insertion to the landscape
2 Nike World Campus, Beaverton, Oregon; partial east elevation, Mia Hamm Center
3 Nike World Campus, Beaverton, Oregon; lounge seating at the Tiger Woods Center
4 Ericsson North American Headquarters, Plano, Texas; living room at level two bathed in natural light
5 Fox Tower, Portland, Oregon; east elevation seen from Pioneer Square

● 920 SW Sixth Avenue, Suite 1500, Portland, Oregon 97204 USA
Tel: +1 503 220 0668 Fax: +1 503 225 0803

THOMPSON, VENTULETT, STAINBACK & ASSOCIATES (TVS)

www.tvsa.com

1   Brian Gassel

2   Brian Gassel

3   Brian Gassel

5   Brian Gassel

Founded in 1968, Thompson, Ventulett, Stainback & Associates (TVS) has grown to a firm of over 260 professionals. With offices in Atlanta and Chicago, TVS provides planning, architecture and interior design services. TVS has distinguished itself throughout its three decades with an ongoing and unrelenting commitment to excellence through responsive design.

The firm's award-winning portfolio includes a broad range of project types, including office buildings, corporate headquarters, retail centers, hotels, resorts, and performing arts centers. TVS is also the leading designer of convention and exhibition centers, having designed over 35 convention centers.

Honored with the National AIA 2002 Architecture Firm Award, TVS has made significant contributions to the architectural profession and to the built environment through its consistent design excellence. TVS is a member of Insight Alliance, serving clients worldwide.

1   Salt Palace Convention Center, Salt Lake City, Utah; cylindrical tower marks main entrance
2   Prince Street Corporate Office, Cartersville, Georgia; sustainable, environmentally responsive corporate facility
3   McCormick Place Convention Center, Chicago, Illinois; world's largest convention and tradeshow facility
4   United Parcel Service World Headquarters, Atlanta, Georgia; world-class corporate campus within a nature preserve
5   New Washington Convention Center, Washington DC; 2.3 million-square-foot center is a new landmark for Washington DC

- 2700 Promenade Two, 1230 Peachtree Street NE, Atlanta, Georgia 30309 USA
  Tel: +1 404 888 6600 Fax: +1 404 888 6700

TIGHE ARCHITECTURE

patrick@tighearchitecture.com www.tighearchitecture.com

Tighe Architecture is committed to creating unique solutions that re-evaluate the way people inhabit their environments. The architecture is not of style, but of process that is driven by influences such as client, site, budget, culture, society, and the environment.

Patrick J. Tighe, AIA is principal of Tighe Architecture. Since its inception in 2000, the firm has won several national AIA awards as well as local AIA honors. The work has appeared in *Architectural Record*, *Architectural Digest*, *The LA Times Magazine*, *Interior Design*, and *LA Architect*.

1   Art Gray

3   Art Gray

2   Art Gray

1 Trahan Ranch, Wimberley, Texas
2 8743 Ashcroft, Los Angeles, California
3 Collins Gallery, West Hollywood, California
4 Jacobs Subterranean, Sherman Oaks, California
5 Live Oak Studio, Hollywood, California

4   Art Gray   5   Art Gray

● 1632 Ocean Park Boulevard, Santa Monica, California 90405 USA
Tel: +1 310 450 8823 Fax: +1 310 450 8273

TOMÁS TAVEIRA, SA

tomas-taveira-sa@mail.telepac.pt   www.tomas-taveira-proj.pt

1   Tomás Taveira

The work of Tomás Taveira has developed to include many different areas of architecture. The latest projects include product design, broadcast design, large urban plans with housing, football stadiums, large public transportation programs such as metro stations, and exclusive housing in a new urban development area in Lisbon called Park Expo (the site of the 1998 World Expo).

The five projects illustrated on this page represent one part of the firm's work over the past four years. The firm has directed its work into the 'free style' field, where modern elements are integrated with classical elements, as well as sculpture, painting and modest high-tech.

The firm aims to apply its vision of art in architecture to all types of buildings, even though the aesthetics of some of the great contemporary architects are difficult to apply to all architectural programs and functions.

2   Tomás Taveira

3   Tomás Taveira

4   F & S Guerra

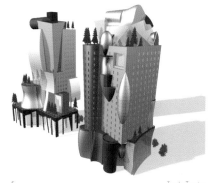

5   Tomás Taveira

1 Casa da Música, Caldas da Rainha, Portugal
2 Albufeira's Marina, Algarve, Portugal
3 Aveiro Stadium, Aveiro, Portugal
4 Civic and Cultural Center, Barrô, Portugal
5 Office Towers, Moscow, Russia

● Av. da República, n°2, 1° Lisbon 1050-191 Portugal Tel: +351 21 313 8770 Fax: +351 21 313 8794

TOMBAZIS (A.N.) AND ASSOCIATES – MELETITIKI LTD

meletitiki@hol.gr   www.tombazis.gr

Nikos Danielides

2   Dimitris Kalapodas

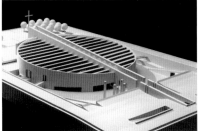

3   Tombazis Associates

4   Nikos Danielides

Alexandros N. Tombazis and Associates Architects was founded in 1963 in Athens, Greece. The firm undertakes architectural, town planning, bioclimatic and low-energy design, as well as interior and furniture design. The practice today employs approximately 70 people.

Work of the office has been honored with prizes in more than 85 national and international competitions. As well as projects in Greece, it has undertaken commissions in Cyprus, Dubai and the Middle East, Portugal, the Netherlands, Bulgaria, Romania and the Ukraine. The production of drawings and documents is fully networked and computerised.

The firm was certified on 18 August 1998, fulfilling the EN ISO 9001 quality assurance system for architectural design, supervision and consulting. It is also a member of the Hellenic Association of Consulting Firms.

1 Office Building for Shipping Company, Athens, Greece; two parallel
   linear wings with shaded atrium between
2 Church of the Most Holy Trinity, international architectural competition
   by invitation, 1st prize, Fatima, Portugal; multipurpose assembly hall
   for 10,000 pilgrims
3 Athens 2004 Olympic Sports Hall for Table Tennis and Rhythmic
   Gymnastics, Galatsi, Athens, Greece; two volumes with curved roofs
   molded into landscape
4 Greek Refinery Headquarters, Aspropyrgos, Athens, Greece; comb-like
   building with enclosed and open air atria
5 Miramare Wonderland Tourist Complex, Island of Rhodes, Greece;
   seaside resort using elements of local architecture

5   Alexandros N. Tombazis

● 27, Monemvasias Street, GR-151 25 Polydroso – Athens, Greece Tel: +30 210 680 0690 Fax: +30 210 680 1005

TOMMILA ARCHITECTS

info@arktom.fi www.arktom.fi

Tommila Architects Ltd. is located in Helsinki, Finland. The practice's commissions focus predominantly on mixed-use buildings, commercial premises, offices and urban design. Generally these deal with combining a range of demanding functional requirements and have been completed in several stages. Many of the commissions have been won in national and international architectural competitions. Each commission has a project manager who oversees the project, from inception to completion, under the direction of principal-in-charge Mauri Tommila, an approach that has been proven in many projects.

The Tommila Architects Ltd. design philosophy aims at realizing architectural designs that meet the changing needs of society. In each project functional and economic factors are weighed and the design is given an architectural expression that favorably reflects its time. The practice maintains active international cooperation with technical experts in various related fields. Through the advanced application of natural illumination, ventilation and energy conservation, Tommila Architects Ltd. is involved in a number of projects in which the ultimate goal is to produce rational, flexible, efficient and functional buildings.

1   Tommila Architects Ltd.

2   Voitto Niemelä

3   Tommila Architects Ltd.

1   IBM Head Office extension, Kista, Stockholm, Sweden;
    view of connecting walkway
2   Radiolinja Group Headquaters, Keilaniemi, Espoo, Finland;
    Radiolinja building viewed from the sea
3   Putten Housing and Office Block, Putten, Stockholm, Sweden;
    exterior night view
4   The Big Apple (Iso Omena) Multipurpose Urban Centre,
    Matinkylä, Espoo Finland; view of main gallery

4   Jussi Tiainen

● Kuusiniementie 5, 00340 Helsinki, Finland Tel: +358 9 477 8100 Fax: +358 9 477 81011

TOSHIKO MORI ARCHITECT

staff@tmarch.com   www.tmarch.com

Toshiko Mori established her firm, Toshiko Mori Architect in 1981. With a background in fine arts, Mori has a unique conceptual and aesthetic approach to each project, complemented by her research-based design process.

Toshiko Mori's intelligent approach to historical context, siting strategy, and the use of materials reflects a creative integration of design and technology. Each project involves extensive studies in the historical precedence, site, and programmatic conditions, in order to provide an architecture that responds dialectically and appropriately.

From commercial interiors, residences, museums, and exhibition design projects, to the specific ecological conditions from Maine to Florida, and her clients, Mori approaches each project with fresh and original insight. Rooted firmly in the tradition of modernist design, each project calls for economy of means and efficiency of structure to give it direction and continuity.

1   Antoine Bootz

2   Paul Warchol

3   Paul Warchol

4   Paul Warchol

1 House, Cushing, Maine; private house built on a pre-existing waterfront compound
2 House on the Gulf of Mexico, Casey Key, Florida; private guest house to an original Paul Rudolph house
3 Museum of Modern Art Structure and Surface Exhibit, New York, New York; exhibit on contemporary Japanese textiles
4 Issey Miyake Pleats Please Store, New York, New York; retail store in downtown NYC landmark district
5 Darwin D. Martin House Visitors' Center, Buffalo, New York; visitors' center for Frank Lloyd Wright residential complex

Portrait Credit: Nana Watanabe

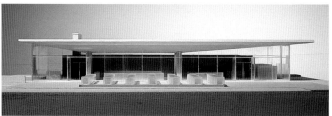

5   Reid Freeman

● 180 Varick Street, Suite 1322, New York, New York 10014 USA
Tel: +1 212 337 9644 Fax: +1 212 337 9647

TRAVERSO-VIGHY

posta@traverso-vighy.com   www.traverso-vighy.com

1   Traverso-Vighy

Giovanni Traverso and Paola Vighy graduated together from the school of architecture at the University of Venice and formed Traverso-Vighy, a small-scale studio, in Vicenza in 1996. The firm's interest lies in the relationship between light and architecture, and the development of detailed construction using innovative materials.

The studio's knowledge of architectural detailing and lighting techniques has allowed it to undertake projects of varying scales and functions: from the lighting fixtures for the Soprana Clockshop in the Palladian Basilica, to the Spidi Sport headquarters.

Traverso-Vighy's projects have been published in national and international magazines and presented at conferences and architecture schools.

2   Traverso-Vighy

3   Traverso-Vighy

1 Salvagnini Technical Center,
   Izumi, Japan; courtyard
2 Clock shop in the Palladian
   Basilica, Vicenza, Italy;
   stair detail
3 The new Spidi Sport
   Headquarters, Meledo, Italy;
   scale model
4 Folotec Industry, Torri di
   Quartesolo, Italy;
   entrance detail
5 Saccardo Studio, Vicenza,
   Italy; interior

4   Traverso-Vighy

5   Traverso-Vighy

● Contrà Della Misericordia 36, Vicenza I-36100 Italy   Tel: +39 0444 929 056   Fax: +39 0444 939 869

TRIDENTE ARCHITECTS PTY LTD

tridente@tridente.com.au

Tridente Architects is a collaborative design team committed to the pursuit of excellence in contemporary architecture. The projects demonstrate a rigorous approach to design and an ability to satisfy clients' needs through innovative solutions. Tridente Architects is highly regarded within the architectural profession, evident by the numerous awards presented to it by the Royal Australian Institute of Architects and private corporations.

The firm works closely with clients, expert consultants and community members to produce appropriate solutions within allocated budgets. This investigative and creative process produces results that exceed expectation.

1   courtesy Tridente Architects Pty Ltd

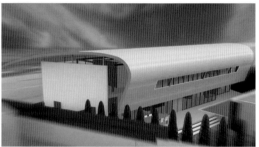

2   courtesy Tridente Architects Pty Ltd

3   courtesy Tridente Architects Pty Ltd

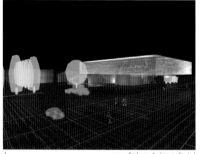

4   courtesy Tridente Architects Pty Ltd

5   courtesy Tridente Architects Pty Ltd

1 Glenelg Apartments, Adelaide, South Australia
2 Keene Residence, Adelaide, South Australia
3 Botanical Gardens Seed Pool, Adelaide, South Australia
4 Gerard Corporation Warehouse, Adelaide, South Australia
5 University of South Australia Student Housing, Adelaide, South Australia

● 203 Melbourne Street, North Adelaide, South Australia 5006 Australia
Tel: +61 8 8267 3922 Fax: +61 8 8267 4946

TRO/THE RITCHIE ORGANIZATION

info@troarch.com   www.troarch.com

1   George Cott

TRO/The Ritchie Organization is a 200-person planning and design firm specializing in healthcare, senior living, corporate/commercial, and educational facilities. Services include programming/feasibility studies, architecture, planning, interior design, and engineering. Based in Boston, TRO has offices in Birmingham, Sarasota, Memphis, and Beijing. Since its establishment in 1909, TRO's volume of work has encompassed more than 500 clients with construction projects totaling more than US$10 billion.

Outstanding client service, and a fundamental understanding of ever-evolving design demands are at the forefront of TRO's business philosophy. Responsiveness, availability, commitment, constant communication, and full team involvement are the cornerstones for its success in project delivery.

TRO works with its clients to define a standard of excellence that responds to their needs with flexibility, imagination, and the highest quality design services. Its measure of success is demonstrated by a record of repeat business—over 90 percent.

2   Edward Jacoby, Jacoby Photography

3   TRO/The Ritchie Organization and A&S International Architecture

4   Gary Kessel   5   TRO/The Ritchie Organization and A&S International Architecture

1   Morton Plant Hospital's Cantonis–ER1 Emergency Department, Clearwater, Florida; emergency room addition
2   Stamford Health System's Daniel and Grace Tully and Family Health Center, Stamford, Connecticut; wellness facility
3   Tianjin First Central Health Plaza, Tianjin, PRC; medical complex
4   Concord Hospital, Concord, New Hampshire; skylight tops three-story atrium
5   Xiamen Women's Hospital, Xiamen, PRC; integrated inpatient and outpatient women's hospital

● 80 Bridge Street, Newton, Massachusetts 02458 USA Tel: +1 617 969 9400 Fax: +1 617 558 0331

TSP ARCHITECTS + PLANNERS PTE LTD

admin@tsparchitects.net   www.tsparchitects.net

1   TSP Architects + Planners Pte Ltd

TSP Architects + Planners Pte Ltd is a long-established regional practice with successful building and urban design projects in Singapore, Malaysia, Indonesia, Brunei, Thailand, and Hong Kong. The practice was founded in 1946 under the name of E.J. Seow. After decades of steady growth, the practice was renamed TSP Architects + Planners in 1988, and it became a licensed corporation in 1995 to facilitate multidisciplinary practice. In 1997, the practice was awarded ISO 9001:1994 certification for its quality management system and further upgraded to ISO 9001:2000 certification in 2002.

The practice has won several design competitions for institutional and housing projects and has received several awards from both the Statutory Board and the Singapore Institute of Architects.

2   TSP Architects + Planners Pte Ltd

3   TSP Architects + Planners Pte Ltd

4   TSP Architects + Planners Pte Ltd

5   TSP Architects + Planners Pte Ltd

1   SunGlade Condominium, Singapore
2   Varsity Park Condominium, Singapore
3   The Belleforte, Singapore
4   French Embassy, Singapore (with Dubus-Richez of Paris)
5   Electronic & Communications Engineering, Singapore

● 30 Robinson Road, Robinson Towers, #08-01, Singapore 048546 Tel: +65 6225 0606 Fax: +65 6323 0353

UCX ARCHITECTS

office@ucxarchitects.com www.ucxarchitects.com

UCX architects is an office with a clear vision and ambition, founded by Ben Huygen and Jasper Jägers. UCX designs, researches, and gives substance to contemporary problems on architectural, urban, and landscape matters, contributing to the cultivation and enrichment of the environment.

UCX's projects are characterized by a propositional clarity—each building seems to rise from itself with the addition of emotion and drama.

1   Rob Kamminga

2   UCX

3   UCX

4   UCX

5   UCX

1 Visser Groen BV, Netherlands; office situated in
   a greenhouse area
2 Apartments, Rotterdam, Netherlands
3 Apartments, Rotterdam, Netherlands
4 Rotterdam Optimism, Rotterdam, Netherlands
5 Adrenalin Tower, Leisure Island, Rotterdam, Netherlands

● Westerstraat 39b, 3016 DG Rotterdam, The Netherlands
  Tel: +31 10 2829 989 Fax: +31 10 2829 998

UN STUDIO VAN BERKEL & BOS

info@unstudio.com   www.unstudio.com

Van Berkel & Bos Architectuurbureau was founded by Ben Van Berkel and Caroline Bos in 1988. In 1998, the firm changed its name to UN Studio, which stands for United Net of specialists in architecture, urban development and infrastructure. Since its inception, UN Studio has developed a structure of advisors to provide additional intelligent and creative input to its projects.

UN Studio's projects range from small to large-scale, and its services include technical drawing services, project supervision, and design consultancy. Work includes civil infrastructure projects such as viaducts, bridges and tunnels; office buildings; research buildings for universities; public buildings such as music halls and museums; and residential projects, including private residences, housing estates, and masterplans.

UN Studio's industrial design commissions range from the design of a coffee and tea set for Alessi, to the development of a standard window.

1   Christian Richters

2   Christian Richters   3   Christian Richters

4   Christian Richters

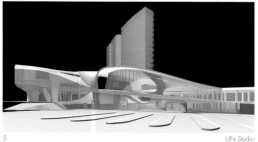

5   UN Studio

1 Möbius House, Het Gooi, Netherlands,
   1993–1998
2 Museum Het Valkhof, Nijmegen, Netherlands,
   1995–1998
3 NMR facilities for the University of Utrecht,
   Utrecht, Netherlands, 1997–2000
4 Erasmus Bridge, Rotterdam, Netherlands,
   1990–1996
5 Masterplan, Arnhem Central, Netherlands,
   1996–2007

Portrait credit: Valerie Bennet

● Stadhouderskade 113, 1073 AX Amsterdam, Netherlands Tel: +31 20 570 2040 Fax: +31 20 570 2041

URBAN OFFICE ARCHITECTURE

uoa@uoa-architecture.com www.uoa-architecture.com

Established in 1998, Urban Office Architecture is a practice-collaboration that exists between two offices in New York City and Milan. Its two founders Carlo Frugiuele and Massimo Marinelli, both graduates of the Milan Polytechnic University in Italy, acquired international experience prior to combining their professional efforts. Carlo Frugiuele, also a graduate from Columbia University GSAPP in New York, now teaches at the Parsons School of Design and the New Jersey Institute of Technology, as well as leading the New York office. Massimo Marinelli has served as Professor at the Milan Polytechnic, and leads the office in Milan.

Prior to establishing UOA, the two principals worked together as design architects for more than 20 firms in Italy, Austria, and the USA. UOA focuses on design excellence and sustainability in an effort to suggest more potential beyond the limitations of site, budget, and style. The firm's solutions are based on cutting edge technologies and the visionary belief that architecture is a process of analogical and inspirational nature, which is able to make art a quotidian necessity.

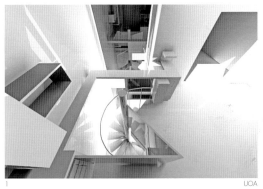

1   UOA

2   UOA

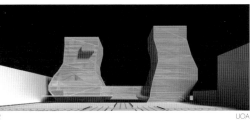

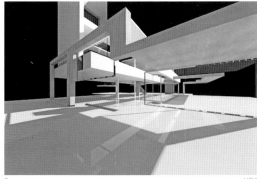

3   UOA

4   UOA

1   YT residence, Hoboken, New Jersey; duplex loft space focuses on "vertical vistas" and rotational perception
2   Public Library of Jalisco, Guadalajara, Mexico; two dizygotic twin-buildings separate the reading from the collection spaces
3   Ideal Villa; exploratory space investigates ambiguous nature of translucent digital environments
4   Elementary School Renovation and New Addition, Trenton, New Jersey; open, semi-open, and enclosed spaces for a diversified learning environment

● 66 West Broadway, Suite 303 New York, New York 10007 USA
Tel: +1 212 233 2290 Fax: +1 212 233 2292

VALODE ET PISTRE ARCHITECTES

info@valode-et-pistre.com   www.valode-et-pistre.com

Valode et Pistre Architectes is an international architectural design firm with expertise in the fields of urban design, interior design and engineering services.

Founded in 1980, the firm is comprised of four different entities: Valode et Pistre Architectes and VP Green in France, Valode & Pistre Arquitectos in Spain, and Valode & Pistre Architekci located in Poland.

For Denis Valode and Jean Pistre, an architectural project is a social act for both client and user, an act based upon original research and reflection, an act of creation in response to a specific program and site.

The office's reputation has grown from projects using this approach—the Museum of Contemporary Art at Bordeaux, the L'Oréal Factory at Aulnay sous Bois near Paris, the Renault Technocentre, Headquarters for Shell and Air France, the University Leonardo de Vinci at La Défense, the Cours Saint-Emilion at Bercy in Paris, and the T1 Tower at La Défense.

1   Georges Fessy

Today, as a result of its expertise, Valode et Pistre has designed and built projects in numerous countries including France, Spain, Italy, the UK, Poland, the Czech Republic, Hungary, Russia, Lebanon, Morocco and Mexico.

2   Georges Fessy   3   Valode et Pistre

4   Georges Fessy   5   Georges Fessy

1 Cap Gemini Ernst & Young University, Gouvieux, France
2 L'Oréal Factory, Paris, France
3 T1 Tower, La Défense, Paris, France
4 Air France Headquarters, Paris, France
5 The CAPC Contemporary Art Museum, Bordeaux, France

Portrait Credit: Patricia Canino

● 115, Rue du Bac, 75007 Paris, France Tel: +33 1 53 63 2200 Fax: +33 1 53 63 2209

VASCONI ASSOCIES ARCHITECTES
GUY BEZ – YVES LAMBLIN – CLAUDE VASCONI

agence@claude-vasconi.fr   www.claude-vasconi.fr

Claude Vasconi received his diploma in 1964 from the Ecole Nationale Supérieure des Arts et Industries of Strasbourg. In 1982, he was awarded the French National Grand prize in Architecture. He has been a member of the French Academy of Architecture since 1991 and an honorable member of 'Bund Deutscher Architekten' since 1996.

He mixes architectural conception with urban reflection, demonstrated in large projects such as cultural buildings (L'Onde, Vélizy; Congress Center, Reims; la Filature, Mulhouse; le Corum, Montpellier), office buildings (Périsud, Paris; Dexia Bank, Luxemburg; Chamber of Commerce, Luxemburg; Ministry of Justice, Grenoble) and malls (Hallen am Borsigturm, Berlin).

Claude Vasconi has been widely published and his work has also been regularly exhibited in Europe, the USA and South America.

He has participated in several juries for international competitions, seminars and architectural awards.

1   Jürgen Hohmuth

2   G. Fessy

3   A. Martinelli

4   Wilmar Koenig   5   Airdiasol/Rothan

1&4   Commercial and Entertainment Center Borsig, Berlin
  2   Congress Center, Reims
  3   Cultural Center "la Filature", Mulhouse
  5   Radar, Grand Ballon des Vosges

● 58 rue Monsieur Le Prince, F-75006 Paris, France Tel: +33 1 5373 7475 Fax: +33 1 5373 7450

VASILKO . HAUSERMAN AND ASSOCIATES, INC.

generaldelivery@vasilkohauserman.com   www.vasilkohauserman.com

1   Craig Dugan/Hedrich-Blessing

2   Bob Shimer/Hedrich-Blessing

Vasilko . Hauserman and Associates, Inc. is an architecture and interior design firm comprised of planners, architects, and interior designers. The firm is deliberate about its work and prides itself on quality projects and long-standing client relationships.

Services offered include architectural and interior design, master planning, programming and space planning, existing building and site due-diligence reports, environmental graphic design and art programs, furniture selection and specification, construction documentation, and construction administration.

Vasilko . Hauserman and Associates, Inc. enjoys the challenge of specialized, one-of-a-kind projects. Its project experience includes athletic and convocation centers, student unions, corporate dining facilities, food courts, computer facilities and cyber cafes, science laboratories, student housing, corporate headquarter campuses, fitness centers, daycare centers, technology classrooms and auditoriums, retail spaces, parking structures, and specialty projects such as habitats for endangered animals.

The firm philosophy is to approach each project with the same fresh interest and diligence, regardless of the project size or complexity. A successful project meets the client's budget, schedule, and design expectations.

3   Bob Shimer/Hedrich-Blessing

4   Craig Dugan/Hedrich-Blessing

5   Craig Dugan/Hedrich-Blessing

1 Café 200, Aon Center, Chicago, Illinois; corporate dining facility at Blackstone Group's landmark building
2 USITE/Crerar Computing Cluster and Cyber Cafe, The University of Chicago, Chicago, Illinois; state-of-the-art computing laboratory
3 Hutchinson Commons, The University of Chicago, Chicago, Illinois; restoration of main dining hall
4 Lincoln Park Student Center, DePaul University, Chicago, Illinois
5 3000 Town Center, Southfield, Michigan; entrance lobby

● One IBM Plaza, 330 North Wabash Avenue, Suite 2123, Chicago, Illinois 60611-3603 USA
Tel: +1 312 755 9800 Fax: +1 312 755 9806

VEAZEY PARROTT DURKIN & SHOULDERS

www.vpdsweb.com

With offices in Indianapolis and Evansville, Indiana, Veazey Parrott Durkin & Shoulders (VPDS) has designed higher education, library, public education, corporate, and cultural facilities throughout Midwest USA. VPDS practices the principles of high-performance design, a long-term, life-cycle design approach that considers the relationship between site, structure, energy, materials, indoor air quality, acoustics, lighting, and technology.

The firm's holistic approach examines each component within a building and then fully integrates these systems into a whole-building design solution. The design philosophy places priority on client service, quality, performance, conservation and innovation. A Midwest leader in sustainable design solutions and applications, VPDS has designed the first LEED-registered corporate facility, library, and public middle school in Indiana.

1   Photics, LLC

2   Photics, LLC

3   Photics, LLC

4   VPDS

5   Jerry Butts Photography

1&2   Old National Bancorp Corporate Headquarters, Evansville, Indiana; catwalk links banking center to administrative tower (with Hellmuth, Obata + Kassabaum)

3   Ivy Tech State College Southwest Campus Expansion, Evansville, Indiana; grand stair in student commons area

4   Indiana University Main Library Masterplan Update, Bloomington, Indiana; cutting into the existing mass creates open, multi-story atrium

5   Oaklyn Library, Evansville, Indiana; circulation desk, with undulating CloudGate (Engberg Anderson Design Partnership)

●   528 Main Street Suite 400, Evansville, Indiana 47708 USA   Tel: +1 812 423 7729   Fax: +1 812 425 4561

VENTURI, SCOTT BROWN AND ASSOCIATES, INC.

info@vsba.com   www.vsba.com

1   Matt Wargo

In 41 years of practice, Venturi, Scott Brown and Associates (VSBA) has earned an international reputation as a world leader in architectural design and planning. The firm's experience ranges from city and campus planning, civic, commercial, and academic architecture to exhibition design and the decorative arts, but all of its projects share a fresh approach to complex and contradictory problems.

Because the designs are generated from the specific imperatives and context of a project, VSBA's completed works have unique identities, derived from careful consideration of its clients' philosophies, traditions, programs, and site characteristics.

VSBA's eye for careful detail and functional excellence are reflected through over 400 projects in the US, Europe, and Asia, including the Sainsbury Wing of the National Gallery in London; the Seattle Art Museum; a regional legislative and administrative center in Toulouse, France; and the Mielparque Nikko Kirifuri Hotel and Spa near Nikko, Japan. In addition, the firm has completed over 75 academic projects on 35 different campuses, including campus and precinct plans, laboratories, campus centers, libraries, museums, performance spaces, residence halls, and athletic facilities. VSBA's clients include Princeton, Harvard, Yale, Dartmouth, UCLA, Bard, and the Universities of Michigan, Ohio State, Kentucky, and Pennsylvania.

2   Matt Wargo

3   Matt Wargo

4   Matt Wargo

The Anlyan Center for Medical Research and Education, Yale University School of Medicine, New Haven, Connecticut (with Payette Associates)
1 Entrance lobby
2 Courtyard
3 Entrance arcade
4 Entrance elevation
5 Street elevation with decorative trees

5   Matt Wargo

● 4236 Main Street, Philadelphia, Pennsylvania 19127-1696 USA
Tel: +1 215 487 0400 Fax: +1 215 487 2520

VERITAS ARCHITECTS SDN BHD

archkl@veritas.com.my www.veritas.com.my

VERITAS was founded in 1987 upon the principles of constant innovation and a commitment to quality. Led by its principals, David Mizan Hashim, Lillian Tay, Shamsuddin Wahap, Azif Nasaruddin, Matthew Torlesse, and Eric Tham, VERITAS is backed by a team that includes more than 40 qualified professionals and 60 support staff. Although VERITAS is primarily an architectural practice, it also offers a full range of design services including interior design, landscape, and project management.

VERITAS is committed to a contemporary architecture founded on the basic principles of modernist design. Beyond building solutions that respond to site and function, VERITAS' work re-examines the recurrent issues of identity and national expression, and explores new spatial interpretations and experiential objectives, to express the emerging consciousness and aspirations of a rapidly evolving contemporary culture in Malaysia. VERITAS seeks to develop a distinctive tectonic language from the conditions of local climate, materials, and socio-cultural traditions, while connecting the larger discourses outside the local context.

1   Vivid Ideas

4   Vivid Ideas

2   KL Ng Photography

3   KL Ng Photography

5   Vivid Ideas

1 Ministry of Natural Resources & Environment, Putrajaya, Malaysia; steel-framed podium façade with movable timber shading screens
2 Western Transportation Terminal, Putrajaya, Malaysia; curved entrance roof canopy
3 Private Residence, Selangor, Malaysia; timber sunshades extend roof eave for more shading
4 ING Center for Performance Development, Selangor, Malaysia; curved podium and expressed wall plane break down overall massing
5 Audi Hangar, Glenmarie, Shah Alam, Malaysia; extensive glazed façades add transparency

● 2nd Floor, Bangunan Getah Asli, 148 Jalan Ampang, Kuala Lumpur 50450 Malaysia
Tel: +603 2162 2300 Fax: +603 2162 2310

VERMEULEN/HIND ARCHITECTS

info@vharch.com www.vharch.com

1   Ben Rahn/Design Archive

2   Ben Rahn/Design Archive

Established in 1992 by founding partners Fred Vermeulen and Mary Jo Hind, Vermeulen/Hind Architects (V/HA) continues to grow and serve its primarily healthcare and institutional clients. With an expertise in the design of oncology facilities, the firm is exploring innovative solutions to technological requirements and expanded ways to meet patient needs and comfort. Currently, with a staff of approximately 20, V/HA provides full architectural, interior, landscape and urban design services for a range of projects.

Vermeulen/Hind Architects recently completed the Windsor Regional Cancer Centre, a new $16.8-million, 73,000-square-meter award-winning facility. The centre, described as 'benevolent, modern architecture', includes three high-energy radiation treatment rooms, a 31-station chemotherapy suite, brachytherapy and simulator suite and multiple examination and counseling rooms. The building also contains a health resource library, research labs, classrooms, conference facilities, and a landscaped patient water garden.

Vermeulen/Hind Architects has completed or is currently working on a number of regional cancer centres for Cancer Care Ontario including: Grand River, Hamilton, Kingston, London, Niagara and Windsor.

3 ·   Ben Rahn/Design Archive

Windsor Regional Cancer Centre
1 Enclosed water garden is viewed from second level chemotherapy suite
2 Exterior view of children's waiting area with limestone cladding and mahogany window frames
3 Projecting elements along west façade are scaled to suit surrounding neighborhood
4 Central fireplace in main lobby provides a calming introduction to centre
5 View of naturally lit radiation waiting area

4   Ben Rahn/Design Archive   5   Ben Rahn/Design Archive

● 15 Foundry Street, Dundas, Ontario L9H 2V6 Canada Tel: +1 905 628 1500 Fax: +1 905 628 6300

VICTOR LÉVY DESIGN & ARCHITECTURE

vlevy@ulb.ac.be

The office began its activities in 1989, when Victor Lévy, after having gained multidisciplinary experience in the Totem studio, created his own practice.

His achievements include: Film Message, the Tintin Shop (Brussels), the Hergé Foundation, Action Video, Tower 66, the Dunn & Hargitt Building and the Bertiau Pharmacy.

Numerous publications and exhibitions in relation to his work have contributed to his becoming well-known by the public.

The work of the office can be characterized by its simplicity of form and concept, material research and sophistication of details.

1   Marie-Françoise Plissart

2   Marie-Françoise Plissart

3   Fabien de Cugnac

1&2   Maison Katz, Brussels, Belgium; house in wood
  3   Action Vidéo, Brussels, Belgium; renovation of an
      existing industrial building
4&5   Pharmacie Bertiau, Brussels, Belgium; interior design
      of a pharmacy

4   Fabien de Cugnac   5   Fabien de Cugnac

● Avenue de l'Université 92, B-1050 Brussels, Belgium Tel: +32 2 647 3216 Fax: +32 2 640 4978

VILIUS IR PARTNERIAI

info@abvp.lt www.abvp.lt

1   Raimondas Urbakavicius

Since its foundation in 1994, Vilius ir Partneriai has undertaken a wide range of activities from a small sauna to high-rise office and industrial buildings, using a detailed knowledge of how to combine the latest design trends with the local vernacular. Today, Vilius ir Partneriai is one of Lithuania's leading architecture firms.

The firm attempts to embody the idea of the purpose of the building, while considering the environment of a development. Much attention is paid to the relationship between color and form, as well as to the design of active details. Structural concepts are clearly exhibited in constructions, sometimes appearing as playful design elements.

2   Gintaras Cesonis

3   Gintaras Cesonis

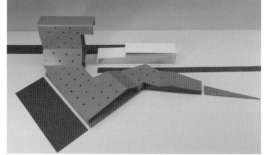

4   Vilius ir Partneriai

1   Villa On Lake Kalviai, Kalviai, Lithuania
2&3 Tennis And Fitness Center, Kaunas, Lithuania
4   Multi-Function Building Complex, Kaunas, Lithuania
5   Villa On Lake Antakmenis, Ciziunai, Lithuania

5   Vilius ir Partneriai

● Vilniaus 22, Kaunas LT-3000 Lithuania Tel: +370 6998 5454 Fax: +370 3742 3232

VINCENT VAN DUYSEN ARCHITECTS

vincent@vincentvanduysen.com www.vincentvanduysen.com

1 Vincent Van Duysen Architects

The architecture and the interiors of Vincent Van Duysen Architects are characterized by a mixture of simplicity and sensuality, and a preference for primary forms and compact volumes. The style can be described with a long line of adjectives: flat, simple, clear; but also pure, elementary, essential, minimal, and silent, quiet, relaxed.

For Vincent Van Duysen Architects, the design is the outcome of a process of progressive refinement in which the raw material— a mixture composed of suggestions, awareness and reminiscence— is gradually purified and ordered until it reaches a final point of stable geometric equilibrium. When called on to renovate a building, the focus is more on the space, always revealing the original structure, than on the furnishing, using a reductionism in design that underlines plastic and communicative values.

The firm's prolific output includes a wide diversity of works and projects worldwide, extending from furniture design, via interior design for houses, apartments, shops and offices, to the planning of single-family housing.

2 Vincent Van Duysen Architects

3 Vincent Van Duysen Architects

5 Vincent Van Duysen Architects

4 Vincent Van Duysen Architects

1 Chair, part of the 'Vincent Van Duysen Collection' designed for B& B Italia
2 Alteration of a Townhouse in L, Belgium
3 Private Residence in W, Belgium
4 Interior Design of the Copyright Art & Architecture Bookshop in Antwerp, Belgium
5 Office Building for Concordia Textiles, Waregem, Belgium

● Lombardenvest 34, 2000 Antwerp, Belgium Tel: +32 3 205 9190 Fax: +32 3 204 0138

VOA ASSOCIATES INCORPORATED

mtoolis@voa.com   www.voa.com

1   Nick Merrick/Hedrich-Blessing

2   Steinkamp/Ballogg, James Steinkamp

3   Steinkamp/Ballogg, James Steinkamp

VOA Associates Incorporated, founded in 1969, is a Chicago-based organization with offices located in Orlando, Florida; Washington, DC; Columbus, Ohio; and São Paulo, Brazil.

VOA offers comprehensive services embracing the disciplines of facility programming, masterplanning, architecture, landscape architecture and interior design. The firm's diversified practice is international in scope and includes: college and university facilities, institutional masterplans, corporate headquarters and offices, law firms, financial institutions, housing, hotels and hospitality related projects, institutional and healthcare facilities, government and transport-related structures. This broad selection of projects allows for a cross-fertilization of ideas and resources that reinforces VOA's commitment to render a superior level of client service. A consistent record of repeat clients is testament to the firm's design philosophy and effective project management.

4   VOA Associates Incorporated

1 Investment Management Firm, Chicago, Illinois; view of lobby/reception area
2 Department of Natural Resources, Springfield, Illinois; view of building with lake reflection
3 White Chapel, Rose-Hulman Institute of Technology, Terre Haute, Indiana; view from water at dawn
4 Student Residence Hall at Lawrence University, Appleton, Wisconsin; site is on Fox River with spectacular southwest views
5 Compensar Fec (XXI Pavilion and Jubilee Plaza), Santafe de Bogota, Colombia; pavilion and plaza looking southeast, with Andes mountains in background

5   Enrique Guzmán

● 224 South Michigan Avenue, Suite 1400, Chicago, Illinois 60604 USA
Tel: +1 312 554 1400 Fax: +1 312 554 1412

VYSEHRAD ATELIER

vysehrad@vysehrad-atelier.cz   www.vysehrad-atelier.cz

1   Filip Slapal

Czech architecture and design studio VYSEHRAD atelier is driven by a sense of harmony and balance between practical use and esthetic beauty.

The firm was founded in 1996 by two partners, Jiri Smolik and Zdenek Rychtarik, and currently comprises seven young architects. VYSEHRAD atelier provides complete architectural services, including new construction design, reconstruction, interior design, urban, and regional planning, with a focus on residential, recreational, administrative, and public buildings.

2   Zdenek Helfert

3   VYSEHRAD atelier

4   VYSEHRAD atelier

5   Filip Slapal

1 Villa, Klanovice, Czech Republic
2 Boarding House, Vacov, Czech Republic; reconstruction and extension
3 Scientific Library in Ostrava, Czech Republic; competition entry
4 Czech Embassy, London, UK; competition entry
5 Villa, Cercany, Czech Republic

● Zeleny pruh 111, 140 00 Prague 4 Czech Republic Tel: +420 241 441 631 Fax: +420 241 441 680

WALKER AND MARTIN ARCHITECTURE

david@walkerandmartin.co.uk   www.walkerandmartin.co.uk

WAM was established by its partners, David Walker and Stuart Martin, in 1995 as an architecture and design practice with a simple agenda and a laid-back attitude. This continues today, even though the practice has grown, now handling a variety of projects up to £5 million in value for a wide variety of clients in Europe (Barcelona and Denmark) and the UK.

The firm prides itself on its informal hands-on approach, taking time to listen to clients and evolve a well-researched brief as the basis for interesting and innovative design solutions. It believes that the quality of the end product relies on the quality of the design concept and its implementation.

WAM is convinced that a successful project is the result of dynamic teamwork, communication, understanding, cooperation, and talent.

David Walker and Stuart Martin are respected among consultants, clients and contractors as being team players, extracting the best from others and producing high-quality architecture within the toughest parameters.

1   WAM

2   Morley von Sternberg

3   Philip Vile

4   Philip Vile

1   Thomas Cook Global Services, Peterborough, Cambridgeshire; high-tech control centre and café combine with a training room under a tensile structure extension
2   Aram Furniture Showroom, Drury Lane, London; refurbishment project creating flagship store for top-of-the range furniture retailer
3   Allgoods, Euston Road, London; showroom and gallery space for high-profile door furniture and ironmongery company
4   Artist studio for Thirza Kotzen, London; art studio and house renovations for international artist based in London
5   Thomas Cook HQ, Maple Street, London; complex refurbishment to form prestige new headquarters building in central London

5   Morley von Sternberg

● Morelands Building, 9–15 Old Street, London EC1V 9HL UK Tel: +44 207 253 8624 Fax: +44 207 253 8625

WALLACE E. CUNNINGHAM INC.

wallace@wallacecunningham.com www.wallacecunningham.com

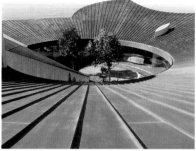

1   Wallace Cunningham

2

Wallace Cunningham

3   Glen Allison

Wallace Cunningham, educated at Chicago Academy of Fine Arts and the Frank Lloyd Wright School of Architecture, began his career in 1978 with the first of several commissions for private residences in southern California.

From the beginning, Cunningham rejected the concept of architectural design as the definition of living spaces within a designated, confining outline. Instead, a conscious effort is made to open the buildings to the surrounding environment through translucent building materials and sculptural forms. They are infused with the transitory and boundless characteristics of the sky, landscape and views. Natural light is manipulated to define, fragment and animate spaces and becomes as important as the constructed forms themselves. The character of each building evolves throughout the course of the year. Just as nature is not static, nor should be the manufactured efforts of man. Such a creation of unconfined space generates a place for the soul to go.

Recent publications include *Architectural Digest*, *Global Architecture Houses*, and *Wallpaper*, and work is presently underway on a book of his work to be published by Yale Press.

4   David Hewitt and Anne Garrison

5   Wallace Cunningham

1 Ray, 1998, La Jolla, California
2 Brushstroke, 1995, La Jolla, California
3 Winghouse, 1979 and 1999, Rancho Santa Fe, California
4 Cityhouse, 1990, La Jolla, California
5 Harmony, 1998, Rancho Santa Fe, California

● PO Box 371493, San Diego, California 92137 USA Tel: +1 619 293 7640 Fax: +1 619 293 0624

WALTER BROOKE AND ASSOCIATES

wba@walterbrooke.com.au   www.walterbrooke.com.au

1   Walter Brooke and Associates

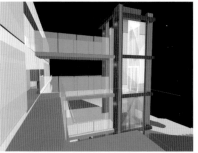

2   Walter Brooke and Associates

4   Walter Brooke and Associates

For 30 years, Walter Brooke and Associates has been at the forefront of the competitive Adelaide market, with an imaginative approach to functional architecture. The firm's experience covers many sectors of the local and national built environment, including commercial, government, educational, recreational, and aged-care facilities.

Each new project is approached with a fresh and creative enthusiasm, behind which lies the certainty of practical experience. Architecture, interior design, and project management teams are led by one of the four experienced directors in the pursuit of creative and innovative time and budget solutions.

Walter Brooke and Associates strives to build unique collaborative relationships with each client, establishing a mutual understanding of the project scope, direction, and desired outcomes. Its client-oriented professional service, ethical business operation, and well-resolved solutions continually exceed expectations, ensuring a satisfied and loyal customer base.

3   Trevor Fox

5   Walter Brooke and Associates

1   Yobar, Norwood Mall, Adelaide, South Australia; retail franchise
2   Graduate Center Lift, University of Adelaide, South Australia
3   Saab Systems, Technology Park, Adelaide, South Australia; corporate offices
4   Cartridge World, Elizabeth City Center, Adelaide, South Australia; retail shop
5   AAMI Stadium, Football Park, West Lakes, Adelaide, South Australia; sports stadium

● 49 Greenhill Road, Wayville, South Australia 5034 Australia Tel: +61 8 8272 4166 Fax: +61 8 8271 7967

WEESE LANGLEY WEESE ARCHITECTS LTD.

dlangley@wlwltd.com   www.wlwltd.com

Since its founding in 1977, Weese Langley Weese has completed a broad variety of projects, but with major emphasis on the not-for-profit client sector—multi-family housing, institutional work, including churches, libraries and schools, and some commercial projects.

Completed works include three separate projects for The Art Institute of Chicago; Coe College Art Museum and Library in Cedar Rapids, Iowa; the Illinois Wesleyan Chapel in Bloomington, Illinois; and the Westminster Presbyterian Church in Peoria, Illinois. More recent work includes the Cullerton Loft Family Housing, St. Andrews Court SRO, a new construction 5-story building, an addition to Winnetka Congregational Church, South Loop Apartments in Chicago's south loop, Deborah's Place rehabilitation on Chicago's west side, and the Wabash YMCA in Chicago's Bronzeville neighborhood.

Weese Langley Weese has won numerous AIA awards. Its work has been published and exhibited in the United States and abroad. The firm has a strong history of housing projects and has strongly supported numerous community groups. Most important however, is the opportunity to work intensely with clients to jointly discover the opportunities inherent in each project.

1   Steve Hall/Hedrich-Blessing

Karant + Associates, Jamie Padgett   3

Steve Hall/Hedrich-Blessing

4   Wayne Cable, Cable Studios

Steve Hall/Hedrich-Blessing

1 Chicago City Day School, Chicago, Illinois
2 The Wartburg Chapel, Wartburg College, Waverly, Iowa
3 Winnetka Congregational Church, Winnetka, Illinois; Fellowship Hall Atrium
4 International Homes, Chicago, Illinois; scattered site housing
5 Allerton Hall Renovation, Department of Prints and Drawings Conservation Lab, The Art Institute of Chicago, Chicago, Illinois

● 9 West Hubbard Street, Chicago, Illinois 60610 USA Tel: +1 312 642 1820 Fax: +1 312 527 5377

WEISZ + YOES

info@wystudio.com www.wystudio.com

1   Albert Vecerka/Esto

Weisz + Yoes is an award-winning architectural and urban design firm specializing in innovative and contextual architectural, site, and environmental design work. The firm engages in work at a variety of scales and is noted for its exploration of the expressive power of architectural form and its relationship to the landscape, as well as the incorporation of new technologies and green design.

Clients include large and small companies, not-for-profit organizations and institutions, public authorities, and individuals. All of the architecture and planning projects are informed by an engaged client process and knowledge of sustainable practices.

The firm specializes in the design of buildings that have a contemporary approach to interior space and modern forms. Weisz + Yoes is an equal opportunity employer and a New York City and State certified Woman-Owned Business Enterprise.

2   Paul Warchol

3   David Sundberg/Esto

4   Paul Warchol

1 Bronx School for the Arts, Bronx, New York; adaptive reuse of a former industrial building
2 House in the Springs, East Hampton, New York; innovative plywood house
3 Museum of Jewish Heritage Visitors Center, New York, New York; dynamic six-sided glass and aluminum building
4 Slate Bar and Billiards Clubs, Queens and New York, New York; series of bars incorporating billiard forms

● 224 Centre Street, 5th Floor, New York, New York 10013 USA Tel: +1 212 219 1953 Fax: +1 212 274 1953

WELLS MACKERETH ARCHITECTS

hq@wellsmackereth.com   www.wellsmackereth.com

'We don't like the restriction of a Design Manifesto, as we believe good design is an unpreconditioned response to create the right solution for each individual situation. So, although we'd shy away from the idea of a 'house style' there's still a recognisable design approach underpinning each project which is based on the following general principles:

The creation of dry static architecture for its own sake leaves us cold; instead we see buildings as living organisms that fluctuate in mood and support the activities of the people within.

Whilst our work is intrinsically modern and abstract we like to combine unexpected materials, intense colours, texture and light to achieve dramatic spatial effects.

We reject the modernist dogma that design should not include reference to other periods and culture; instead we take the opportunity to include subtle references and where possible a little humour.'

1   Keith Parry

3   Wells Mackereth Architects   4   Adam Beaumont-Brown

2   Richard Davies

5   Richard Davies

1   Pringle Flagship Store, London; interior view of ground floor space
2   Stone Island/CP Company Store, London W1, UK; interior of flagship store for Italian sportswear company
3   Triyoga Studios, London NW3, UK; interior view of main yoga studio
4   This Works, London SW3, UK; interior view of flagship aromatherapy products store
5   Goodwin Road Offices, London W12, UK; exterior view

● Unit 14 Archer Street Studios, 10-11 Archer Street, London W1D 7AZ UK
Tel: +44 20 7287 5504 Fax: +44 20 7287 5506

WESKETCH ARCHITECTURE

info@wesketch.com   www.wesketch.com

1   A Harrison

WESKetch Architecture offers total designed environments, from property line to paint, combining site-responsive sustainable design with traditional buildings through an organized process of collaboration, communication and creativity. Expanded professional services include engineering and interior design services, as well as landscape design.

Each project site is carefully studied, unveiling the story of the place to the design team. This thorough understanding of the past, present, and future of the place once evaluated, together with the client's requirements, informs the design team in making sensitive explorations of potential solutions. The results are an eclectic vernacular architecture specifically integrated with site, program, and the client's aesthetic preferences.

WESKetch projects adhere strictly to principles of environmental stewardship. A palette of environmentally friendly materials is assembled with the tender artistry and hand crafted qualities of our forgotten past, creating timeless buildings of distinguished charm and character.

2   A Harrison   3   A Harrison

4   A Harrison   5   Jay Rosenblatt

1 Knollwood, Short Hills, New Jersey; split-level ranch transformed into a shingle-style home
2 Bridle Paths, Bernardsville, New Jersey; open outdoor folly
3 Windsong, Seaside Park New Jersey; restored and renovated Victorian home by the sea
4 Cross Pond Farm, Basking Ridge, New Jersey; interior stone fireplace with custom wooden and iron trusses
5 Edgewater, Short Hills, New Jersey; traditional European Craftsman home with latest high performance building techniques

● 1932 Long Hill Road, Millington, New Jersey 07946 USA Tel: +1 908 647 8200 Fax: +1 908 626 9197

WESSEL DE JONGE ARCHITECTEN BNA BV

info@wesseldejonge.nl   www.wesseldejonge.nl

1   Sybolt Voeten

2   Capital Photos

3   Jan Versnel

4   Sybolt Voeten   5   Fas Keuzenkamp

Founded in 1999, Wessel de Jonge Architecten BNA BV has a fascination with layers of past and present. Experts in rehabilitating existing buildings, even the firm's newly built projects bear some traces of the past. Both new buildings and adaptive re-use are appreciated and successfully interpreted as two sides of the same coin.

Inspiration is drawn from the restrictions imposed on existing buildings, and the degree of modesty that allows buildings to speak for themselves. Simple and quiet architecture that deals with space, light, sophisticated details, and the choice of natural materials, result in sustainable environments in which people like to work and live.

1 Zonnestraal Healthcare Center, Main Building, Hilversum, Netherlands; 1920's sanatorium restored and converted into healthcare facility (with Henket & Partners Architecten)
2 Restaurant and Business Club, Schiphol Airport, Amsterdam, Netherlands; conversion of a former air traffic control tower
3 The Netherlands Biennale Pavilion, Venice, Italy; restoration and upgrade of Rietveld's 1953 exhibition pavilion
4 Van Nelle Design Factory, Rotterdam, Netherlands; masterplan for 1920's factory converted into design studios and offices
5 Dispatch Building, Van Nelle Design Factory, Rotterdam, Netherlands; 1930's dispatch facility converted into design studios

● Van Nelle Design Factory, Van Nelleweg 2330, Rotterdam 3044 BC Netherlands
Tel: +31 10 425 9986 Fax: +31 10 425 9968

WILKIE + BRUCE ARCHITECTS LTD

info@wilkieandbruce.co.nz

1   Stephen Goodenough

Wilkie + Bruce Architects Ltd is a substantial Christchurch practice, established in 1982. Its office complement of 10 staff includes two directors, Alun Wilkie and Alec Bruce, and an associate, John Bennett.

The reputation of the practice has steadily grown to the point where it is recognized as one of the main Christchurch architectural practices. This reputation is based on design skills from concept through to technical detailing, combined with experience in project cost control and planning, strong management skills, clear decision making, professionalism and commitment.

The firm's main workload is commercial, institutional, educational and residential in nature, including interior fit-out work. Repeat commissions from clients are testimony to good client relations as much as the ability to achieve sound design solutions. The firm takes pride in forming positive working relationships to achieve each client's objectives. A key part of its design strategy is to integrate a rational analysis of buildability and cost-efficient construction. This ensures that projects can be completed within often tight time frames and within cost parameters.

The Practice has received a number of New Zealand Institute of Architects design awards.

2   Stephen Goodenough

4   Stephen Goodenough

3   Stephen Goodenough

5   Stephen Goodenough

1 Christchurch Polytechnic Jazz School
2 Nam Yee Retail Development, Christchurch
3 4 Houses, Armagh Street, Christchurch
4 Christ's College Fine Arts and Technology Building,
   Christchurch (in association with Sir Miles Warren)
5 Kennedy house, Christchurch

● 307 Durham Street, PO Box 25-141, Christchurch, New Zealand Tel: +64 3 379 7739 Fax: +64 3 379 5478

WILKINSON EYRE ARCHITECTS LTD

info@wilkinsoneyre.com   www.wilkinsoneyre.com

1   Graeme Peacock

Wilkinson Eyre Architects is one of the UK's leading architectural practices, with a portfolio of national and international award-winning projects.

The practice has designed highly successful projects in diverse market sectors including transport, the arts, commercial, infrastructure, large scale master planning, bridge design, industrial, office, retail, leisure, educational, cultural and residential buildings as well as component and systems design.

Wilkinson Eyre Architects' architecture is based on an informed use of technology and materials and combines a commitment to the spirit of the new with an awareness of context. The approach to design is based on the establishment of a clear brief and a legible working diagram through close liaison with the client from the earliest stages of a project.

The designs of Wilkinson Eyre Architects are widely recognized and have received extensive media, public and professional acclaim and numerous awards including unprecedented back-to-back success in the RIBA Stirling Prize for Architecture, for the Magna Project in 2001 and the Gateshead Millennium Bridge in 2002. The practice's reputation is founded on a commitment to quality, program and value for money, which is demonstrated by a number of repeat commissions for leading clients.

2   Timothy Soar

3   Edmund Sumner

4   Hayes Davidson

1 Gateshead Millennium Bridge, Gateshead, UK; view of new bridge with historic Tyne Bridge in distance
2 Stratford Regional Station, London, UK; exterior view at night
3 Magna, Rotherham, UK; exterior view at night
4 Empress State Building, London, UK; computer rendering
5 Explore-at-Bristol, Bristol, UK; exterior view

5   Ben Luxmoore

● Transworld House, 100 City Road, London E2 8LP UK Tel: +44 20 7608 7900 Fax: +44 20 7608 7901

643

WILLIAM MORGAN ARCHITECTS

wnmorgan@aol.com www.williammorganarchitects.com

1   Robert Lautman

Internationally recognized for excellence in architectural design, the work of William Morgan Architects ranges from the U.S. Embassy in Khartoum, Sudan, and courthouses in Fort Lauderdale and Tallahassee, to condominium apartments on the Maryland shore and a wide variety of residences in diverse settings. The firm consistently strives to create life-enhancing architecture for its clients, the guiding principle of the firm since its founding in 1960.

Educated at Harvard under Walter Gropius and Jose Luis Sert, in the offices of Paul Rudolph, and as a Fulbright scholar in Rome, William Morgan is widely regarded as one of America's foremost architects.

Further details about the firm's numerous architectural design awards, and publications by or written about William Morgan, can be found on its website.

2   Wade Swicord

3   George Cott, Chroma, Inc.

4   Otto Baitz

5   George Cott, Chroma, Inc.

1 Pyramid Condominium, Ocean City, Maryland; view from beach
2 Florida State Museum, Gainesville, Florida; view from downslope
3 Drysdale House, Atlantic Beach, Florida; north elevation
4 Police Administration Building, Jacksonville, Florida; aerial view
5 Root Residence, Ormond Beach, Florida; interior view towards oceanfront

● 220 East Forsyth Street, Jacksonville, Florida 32202 USA Tel: +1 904 356 4195 Fax: +1 904 356 2808

WILLIAM RAWN ASSOCIATES, ARCHITECTS, INC.

info@rawnarch.com www.rawnarch.com

William Rawn Associates, Architects, formed in Boston in 1983, has completed a large number of projects, ranging from complex urban buildings to college campuses, from performing arts facilities to affordable housing. These projects have won national recognition, including six AIA Honor Awards in eight years. Recent projects include an overall campus masterplan and architectural design of the West Campus Residential district at Northeastern University in Boston, an urban hotel in downtown Boston, a Concert Hall and Educational Facility in Montgomery County, Maryland, and a new Center for Theater and Dance at Williams College in Williamstown, Massachusetts.

William Rawn Associates is committed to buildings that participate in the civic or public realm— buildings in the city or buildings in important public landscape settings (like Tanglewood). The firm believes that successful architecture, through the active engagement of its civic context, fosters the values of diversity, meritocracy, and participation that are fundamental to the American democratic experience.

1   Steve Rosenthal

2   Steve Rosenthal

3   Robert Benson

4   Steve Rosenthal

5   Steve Rosenthal

1 Glavin Family Chapel, Babson College, Wellesley, Massachusetts; chapel interior with boat hull form in ceiling
2 Seiji Ozawa Hall at Tanglewood, Lenox, Massachusetts; exterior view of concert hall at dusk
3 Pavilion at Symphony Lake, Cary, North Carolina; pavilion illuminated by 'hanging lantern' element over stage
4 West Campus Residence Halls, Northeastern University, Boston, Massachusetts; night view of glass 'gate-post' dormitory elements
5 Seiji Ozawa Hall at Tanglewood, Lenox, Massachusetts; interior view of concert hall and stage.

● 101 Tremont Street, Boston, Massachusetts 02108 USA Tel: +1 617 423 3470 Fax: +1 617 451 9205

WILLIAMS BOAG PTY LTD

intray@williamsboag.com.au

1   Tony Miller

2   Tony Miller

The firm of Williams Boag Pty Ltd Architects was established in Melbourne in 1975, and over the past 30 years has completed works in the commercial, institutional, historical and residential fields, up to a construction value of A$52 million. Williams Boag is a design-oriented practice based around an active consultative methodology, where design solutions are actively shaped by client and other stakeholders as much as by the architect. Within this consultative framework Williams Boag achieves the highest possible levels of design quality. This is reflected in the 19 awards that have been received, including the national Walter Burley Griffin Award for Urban Design and the Victorian Architecture Medal in 1994, and the Stockholm Partnerships for Sustainable Cities 2002 Award.

Williams Boag has a staff of 20. The firm is part of a national alliance providing the resources of five practices and 120 staff distributed between Melbourne, Sydney, the Australian Capital Territory, Darwin, Brisbane and Perth.

3   Tony Miller

4   Williams Boag Pty Ltd

5   Tony Miller

1 Monash Science Centre, Melbourne; education and exhibition facility utilizing environmentally sustainable principles
2 Blackwell Science Asia, Melbourne; architectural interior fitout for an international publishing company
3 Urban Camp, Royal Park, Melbourne; inner city parkland accommodation facility and activity space
4 Flinders Edge, Melbourne; design proposal for urban mixed-use development
5 McClelland Gallery, Melbourne; award-winning contemporary addition to modernist art gallery

● Level 7, 45 William Street, Melbourne, Victoria 3000 Australia Tel: +61 3 8627 6000 Fax: +61 3 8627 6060

WILLIAMSON POUNDERS ARCHITECTS, PC

www.wparchitects.com

1   Jeffrey Jacobs Architectural Photography

2   Jeffrey Jacobs Architectural Photography

3   Jeffrey Jacobs Architectural Photography

4   Jeffrey Jacobs Architectural Photography

Founded in 1990, Williamson Pounders Architects, PC, of Memphis, Tennessee, provides planning, architecture, and interior design services to civic, religious, educational, and commercial clients. Principals James F. Williamson, AIA, and Louis R. Pounders, AIA, lead WPA's staff of 15 architects and support personnel.

Dedicated to design excellence and superior client service, WPA has earned a reputation for being one of the leading architectural firms in the Mid-South. Recent projects from WPA include Lichterman Nature Center, Metropolitan Inter-Faith Association headquarters, The Law Offices of Burch Porter and Johnson, Ballet Memphis, and St. Thomas More Catholic Church.

WPA's projects have appeared in *L'Arca*, *Chiesa Oggi* and *Stone World*. Over the last decade, the firm has received more than 40 design awards, including honors from the local, state and regional AIA, the Interfaith Forum on Religious Art and Architecture, the Chicago Athanaeum, and the Eugene Potente, Sr. Liturgical Design Competition.

5   Jeffrey Jacobs Architectural Photography

Metropolitan Inter-Faith Association Headquarters, Memphis, Tennessee
1   Façade at night
2   Main lobby area
3   Boardroom opens onto skylight courtyard
4   Natural light enters the boardroom via skylights
5   Second lobby with direct access to loading area

● 88 Union Avenue, Suite 900, Memphis, Tennessee 38103 USA Tel: +1 901 527 4433 Fax: +1 901 527 4478

WIMBERLY ALLISON TONG & GOO

honolulu@watg.com   www.watg.com

Wimberly Allison Tong & Goo (WATG) is recognized as the world's leading architectural firm specializing in hotel and resort planning and design. Since its founding in 1945, WATG has created successful destinations in over 120 countries and territories on six continents from offices in Newport Beach, Seattle, Orlando, Honolulu, London, and Singapore.

WATG has extensive expertise in the planning, design, and renovation of urban and resort hotels; vacation ownership properties; retail, dining and entertainment centers; recreational facilities; golf resorts and clubhouses; mixed-use projects and conference centers.

The firm's policy is to respect the unique environment and cultural heritage of each host country, region or community, and to work in association with local architects to make a positive contribution to the lives and culture of that area.

WATG is a member, along with Callison Architecture and TVS, of Insight Alliance, a global alliance of design industry leaders.

1   Cormier/Malinowski/Insite

2   Milroy & McAleer

3   Ken Kirkwood

1 The Venetian Resort Hotel Casino; voted 'best overall hotel', in association with TSA
2 Hyatt Regency Kauai Resort & Spa; repeatedly rated by guests as the best Hyatt in North America
3 The Movenpick Resort & Spa, Dead Sea; cited as one of the best new destinations in the world
4 Hotel Bora Bora; ranked among the best small hotels in the world
5 Mandarin Oriental, Kuala Lumpur; leads the market in both occupancy and revenue

4   Doug Peebles   5   George Apostolidis

●   700 Bishop Street, Suite 1800, Honolulu, Hawaii 96813 USA Tel: +1 808 521 8888 Fax: +1 808 521 3888

WINTERSGILL

info@wintersgill.net www.wintersgill.net

1   John David Begg
2   Peter Grant

The practice was formed in 1980. The aim then, as now, was to create a soundly managed architectural and design practice with a reputation for high quality work. Wintersgill does not believe in a dogmatic approach; rather, it strives to find appropriate solutions based on careful analysis and working closely with clients, whose interest and commitment is fundamental to every project. The firm offers objective advice that focuses on the client's needs.

Over the years, the firm's skills and experience have expanded into a wide range of activities including architecture, interior design, space planning, space audits, urban design, masterplanning, graphic design, project management, historic building conservation, and planning consultancy. Its production work is fully computerized and the firm has the experience and associations to operate in virtually any part of the world.

3   Peter Cook

4   Peter Cook

1 Heidrick & Struggles, London, UK; office interior
2 Wagamama Restaurant, Nottingham, UK
3 St Mark's School, Shepperton, UK
4 British High Commission, Visa Processing Centre, Islamabad, Pakistan
5 Broadwick Street, Soho, London, UK; office development

5   John David Begg   Portrait credit: John David Begg

● 110 Bolsover Street, London W1W 5NU UK Tel: +44 20 7580 4499 Fax: +44 20 7436 8191

WOLF ARCHITECTURE

info.wolf@wolfarc.com   www.wolfarc.com

1   Gordon Schenck

Project types diverge, scale and scope shift, and programs change, yet the architecture of Harry Wolf is marked by a comprehensible clarity. Walking through the spaces or studying the images, the viewer readily discovers the essence of the architecture.

Comfortably of their culture in form and material, the works are timeless in spirit. The synthesis of the necessities—site, systems, and structure; the result—more like poetry than architecture.

The apparent simplicity of Wolf's architecture is based on a profound understanding of the complexities of building. The formal success of Wolf's lyrical rigor is significant in this era, when tendencies in architecture lean toward non-rectilinear geometries as ends in themselves, and not means toward achieving human environments.

The architecture of Harry Wolf speaks with the optimism of the humanist tradition, where order is equated with liberty and tectonics is equated with truth.

2   The Standard

3   The Standard

4   The Standard

5   Cervin Robinson

1   Mecklenburg Courthouse, Charlotte, North Carolina
2   Kansai International Airport Project, Osaka, Japan
3   Toulouse Regional Government Center, Toulouse, France
4   Disney Resort Guest Parking Structure, Anaheim, California
5   NationsBank (BofA) Tower Complex, Tampa, Florida

●   24955 Pacific Coast Highway, Suite C101, Malibu, California 90265 USA
Tel: +1 310 317 1415 Fax: +1 310 317 1418

WONG TUNG & PARTNERS LIMITED

wongtung@wtpl.com.hk www.wongtung.com

1   Wong Tung & Partners

2   Tsai King Yan

The Wong Tung Group was established in Hong Kong in 1963 and has been practicing under the name of Wong Tung & Partners Limited since 1984. Wong & Tung International Ltd. was formed in 1975 and is represented overseas through affiliated practices. The group's activities in China started in 1978 and since then representative offices were set up in Beijing, Guangzhou, Shanghai and Shenzhen. Wong & Tung Computer Aided Drafting (Shenzhen) Co. Ltd. was formed in 1993 and a joint venture Class A design office, Zhong Tian Wong Tung International Engineering Design Consultants Co. Ltd., was opened in March 1996 in Beijing.

The Wong Tung Group provides a complete range of architectural and planning services ranging from large comprehensive community developments to single building projects.

Wong Tung & Partners Ltd has obtained certification to ISO 9001 by the Hong Kong Quality Assurance Agency since July 1996 for the provision of architectural consultancy services in Hong Kong.

3   Wong Tung & Partners

4   Keith Chan

5   Keith Chan

1 Hong Kong Movie City, Hong Kong
2 Dragonair & CNAC Building, Hong Kong
3 Huawei Research and Industrial Park, PRC
4 The Golden Bay Garden, PRC
5 Les Saisons, Hong Kong

● 5/F Cityplaza 3, Taikoo Shing, Hong Kong Tel: +852 2803 9888 Fax: +852 2513 1728

WOODHEAD INTERNATIONAL

rhopton@woodhead.com.au   www.woodhead.com.au

Originating in Adelaide in 1927, Woodhead International is an international architecture and design firm whose operations span seven offices within Australia and five offices in Asia, including Thailand, Singapore and China.

The key to the firm's success comes from undertaking international benchmarking programs to ensure systems, procedures, methodologies and project design outcomes are second-to-none so clients are presented with products and services of international standard.

Undertaking research and education programs is another important facet that ensures Woodhead International stays abreast of economic and market influences, trends and changing market demands.

Through the investment of resources in understanding and interpreting the needs and sensitivities of local markets and by establishing a supportive and dynamic network of contacts and business associates, Woodhead International is now one of the best-known exporters of professional design services to Asia, increasing offshore earnings by over 320 percent over the past five years.

1   John Gollings

3   Jim Fitzpatrick

2   Woodhead International

5   Woodhead International

4   Woodhead International

1   Karijini Visitors Centre, Karijini National Park, Western Australia, Australia; award-winning weathered steel interpretative centre shaped like a goanna
2   Beijing University of Aeronautics and Astronautics, Commercial Building No 2, Beijing, PRC; high-tech intelligent office building
3   Holdfast Shores Development, Glenelg, South Australia, Australia; extensive beachfront development
4   Lobby Foyer, Shandong Hotel, Jinan, Shandong Province, PRC; 700-room, 5-star official guesthouse for Shandong Province
5   Shandong Tower 2500-seat Congress Hall, Jinan, Shandong Province, PRC; one of the largest concert halls in the world

● 343 Pacific Highway, North Sydney, New South Wales 2060 Australia
Tel: +61 2 9964 9500 Fax: +61 2 9964 9683

WOODS BAGOT

thought.design@woodsbagot.com www.woodsbagot.com

1 Martin Vanderwall

Bringing thought and design together is what distinguishes Woods Bagot.

Woods Bagot's approach to architecture, interior design, urban planning and design and landscape architecture begins with its clients.

Understanding clients' visions, business requirements, brands and culture and applying thought to achieve the right strategic framework.

Intelligent and thoughtful design creates places which are at once inspiring and commercially sustainable.

Woods Bagot's vision is to bring the "design mode of thinking" to the project strategy, which in turn liberates stunning spaces and places.

Founded in 1869, Woods Bagot is a world-leading design business with offices throughout Asia and Australia, and in London and Dubai. From this network, more than 400 dedicated staff service global clients regionally.

2 Patrick Bingham-Hall

3 Hayes Davidson

1 KPMG, Sydney, New South Wales
2 Qantas Club, Singapore International Terminal, Singapore
3 Inacity Tower, Manchester, UK

● Level 10, Wynyard Green, 11–31 York Street, Sydney, New South Wales 1220 Australia
Tel: +61 2 9249 2500 Fax: +61 2 9299 5592

YASKY & PARTNER ARCHITECTS
A. YASKY, J. SIVAN, J. YASKY

general@yasky.co.il

Founded in 1955 by Professor Architect Avraham Yasky, the firm is one of Israel's leading architecture and urban design firms. Through its commitment to technological innovation and design excellence, Yasky & Partners Architects offers a unique combination of creativity and functional solutions, while always keeping in mind the client's objectives and the users' convenience.

The firm's work ranges from urban masterplanning to the architecture of individual projects. Throughout the years Yasky & Partners Architects has designed and executed hundreds of projects that include corporate headquarters; university campuses; research facilities; public buildings; health care facilities; shopping malls; sports and recreation facilities; office towers; and residential projects of different scales. Currently Yasky & Partners Architects is involved in projects in Israel, Europe and Africa.

Over the last 47 years, Yasky & Partners Architects has won numerous design competitions and professional awards such as the Reynolds Award for Architecture.

1

Yaki Assayag

2

Yaki Assayag

3

Yaki Assayag

4

Yaki Assayag

5

Yaki Assayag

1 The Smolarz Auditorium, Tel Aviv, Israel; Tel Aviv University's new main auditorium
2 The Opera Residential Tower, Tel Aviv, Israel; commercial and residential tower on Tel Aviv's beach
3 Platinum Tower, Tel Aviv, Israel; entrance lobby of a new office tower in Tel Aviv
4 Alrov Tower, Tel Aviv, Israel; a new office tower in Tel Aviv's downtown
5 Ocean Suites Hotel, Herzlia, Israel; a suites hotel on the Mediterranean beach

● 6 Meitav Street, Tel-Aviv 67898 Israel Tel: +972 3 568 1515 Fax: +972 3 568 1516

YASUI ARCHITECTS & ENGINEERS, INC.

ysano@yasui-archi.co.jp www.yasui-archi.co.jp

Yasui Architects & Engineers, Inc. is an architectural and engineering firm established in 1924 by Takeo Yasui (1884–1955), well-known architect. Currently, the firm has an in-house professional staff of 309, including 177 licensed architects (1st class "Kenchikushi"). The firm is headed by Yoshihiko Sano (1954–), President and Principal Architect.

Yasui Architects & Engineers, Inc. provides planning, design and supervision of architectural projects, interior decoration, urban/regional development projects and consultancy services. Consultancy services include environment assessments, feasibility studies, renewals, CM, PM and FM.

1   Yasui Architects & Engineers

2   Yasui Architects & Engineers

3   Yasui Architects & Engineers

5   Yasui Architects & Engineers

4   Yasui Architects & Engineers

1 Kasugai Culture Center, Aichi, 1999
2 Tokyo National Museum, Heiseikan, Tokyo, 1999
3 Mori Trust Marunouchi building, Tokyo; under construction, 2003
4 Naha Airport Domestic Terminal building, Okinawa, 1999
5 Urban Redevelopment at North Area of JR Takatuki Station, Osaka; under construction, 2004

● 2-4-7 Shimamachi, Chuo-ku, Osaka 540-0034 Japan Tel: +81 6 6943 1371 Fax: +81 6 6941 4094

ZACK | DE VITO ARCHITECTURE

jim@zackdevito.com   www.zackdevito.com

Zack | de Vito Architecture is a multi-disciplinary design office, providing architecture, interior design, furniture design, and custom building services, led by husband-and-wife team James Zack and Lise de Vito. Projects include restaurants, wineries, commercial and retail spaces, and custom residences. The firm's work has been featured in publications and exhibitions, and is also featured in the collection of the San Francisco Museum of Modern Art.

Zack | de Vito Architecture designs and builds creative, unique structures. The architects have the hands-on experience of builders and furniture makers. A broad knowledge of materials and building techniques gives projects a unique and noticeable attention to detail and craft. The firm's work brings together the designer, client, builders, and fabricators to create site-specific, innovative projects, driven by an exploration of place, the client's needs, and an expression of structure, materials, and craft.

1   Massimiliano Bozonella

2   Zack | de Vito Architecture

3   Massimiliano Bozonella

4   J.D Peterson

5   Roger Casas

1&3   110 Chattanooga Street Duplex, San Francisco, California; modern architecture in the San Francisco vernacular

2   RH Phillips Winery, Esparto, California; wine tasting and conference facility

4   Gordon's House of Fine Eats, San Francisco, California; industrial materials transform 1930's warehouse

5   Kohler Residence, San Francisco, California; residential interior connected by a triple-height steel stair

● 156 South Park, San Francisco, California 94107 USA Tel: +1 415 495 7889 Fax: +1 415 495 7869

ZEIDLER PARTNERSHIP ARCHITECTS

mail@zgpa.net www.zgpa.net

With headquarters in Toronto, and offices in Calgary, West Palm Beach, Berlin, Beijing, and London, Zeidler Partnership Architects has project experience covering virtually the entire range of architectural, urban and interior design. The firm has gained a significant international reputation with such projects as Columbus Center of Marine Biotechnology (Baltimore), Raymond F. Kravis Center for the Performing Arts (West Palm Beach), and the Toronto Eaton Centre.

The firm believes that a building must fulfill the functional and economic requirements the owner intends it to serve. At the same time, it must evoke a positive emotional response from both its users and the public at large. This triple commitment—to the client, their employees and the urban environment at large—comes from an expertise that only years of successful experience can bring. The result is one part necessity and one part invention—and a building that is a pleasure rather than a duty to own.

1   Zeidler Partnership Architects

2   Zeidler Partnership Architects

3   Zeidler Partnership Architects

4   Zeidler Partnership Architects

5   Zeidler Partnership Architects

1 DS-8, Canary Wharf, London, England; 250,000-square-foot mixed-use building
2 Hospital for Sick Children, The Atrium, Toronto, Canada; award-winning 572-bed atrium patient tower
3 Canada Place, Vancouver, Canada; landmark mixed-use building on Vancouver's waterfront
4 Columbus Center of Marine Biotechnology, Baltimore, USA; research and educational facilities at the University of Maryland
5 Torre Mayor, Mexico City, Mexico; 55-story office tower located on the city's main thoroughfare

● 315 Queen Street W, Toronto, Ontario M5V 2X2 Canada Tel: +1 416 596 8300 Fax: +1 416 596 1408

ZEROZERO

studio@zerozero.sk   www.zerozero.sk

zerozero was established in 2002, in Prešov, Slovakia and specializes in architecture, urban planning, and interior design.

The firm embarks on a design process to develop any new project, which includes a study of the community, together with its economic, intellectual, and cultural potential. The result of this process is a design which, when built, is destined for a long interatction with its surrounding context.

1   zerozero   2   zerozero

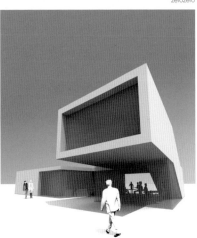

3   zerozero   4   zerozero

1   Slovakian Embassy, Berlin, Germany; competition entry, interior of lobby
2-4   CMYK, Prešov, Slovakia; 190 rental units
5   Pizzeria, Prešov, Slovakia; preliminary restaurant design, street view

5   zerozero

● Požiarnicka 17, 08 001 Prešov, Slovakia Tel: +421 51 7710 741 Fax: +421 51 7710 741

ZIMMER GUNSUL FRASCA PARTNERSHIP

jmitchell@zgf.com   www.zgf.com

1   Nick Merrick © Hedrich-Blessing

Zimmer Gunsul Frasca Partnership is a 385-person architecture, planning and interior design firm nationally recognized for its broad-based design practice. The firm's special talent is the ability to look at the unique qualities of each place and create buildings that respect the existing environment and strengthen, or even heal, the fabric of which they become a part.

Facilitated by offices in Portland, Oregon; Seattle, Washington; Los Angeles, California; and Washington, DC, ZGF is involved in a diverse mix of public and private projects nationwide, ranging from airports, civic centers and regional transportation systems; to commercial developments, high-rises and corporate campuses; to healthcare and research buildings, educational facilities and museums. The firm's work has been nationally recognized for design excellence, most notably as the recipient of the Architecture Firm Award from the American Institute of Architects, with recognition for its 'high standards, humanistic concerns and the unique ability to capture the spirit of a place and the aspirations of its inhabitants.'

2   Courtesy of National Institutes of Health

3   Timothy Hursley

1 U.S. Food and Drug Administration, Irvine, California; 133,000-square-foot replacement laboratory and district office
2 National Institutes of Health, Mark O. Hatfield Clinical Cancer Center, Bethesda, Maryland; 870,000-square-foot addition of a translational research center
3 California Science Center, Los Angeles, California; phase I provides 245,000 square feet of exhibition/education space
4 Cornell University, Duffield Hall Nanofabrication Research Laboratory, Ithaca, New York; 150,930-square-foot nanotechnology research facility
5 Portland International Airport terminal expansion south, Portland, Oregon; 670,000-square-foot final phase of a three-phase expansion program

4   Larry Falke

5   Eckert & Eckert

● 320 SW Oak, Suite 500, Portland, Oregon 97204 USA Tel: +1 503 224 3860 Fax: +1 503 224 2482

ZLG SDN BHD

zlg@streamyx.com www.zlg-design.com

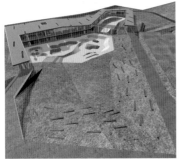

1   ZLG Sdn. Bhd.

ZLG Sdn. Bhd. was founded in 1995, and is led by Huat Lim, Susanne Zeidler Lim, and Project Director Jimmy Wong. ZLG is backed by support staff with diverse international experience.

Inscribed in complex aesthetic values, ZLG's position warrants agility and versatility, and continued awareness of modern trends interspersed with traditional elements exhibited in Asian projects. Its best design solutions are often the simplest, and the search for the essence of an idea permeates all projects. Respect for the natural elements expands the possibilities of place making and carving out of spaces. Mixing natural and artificial elements in all schemes seamlessly creates architecture that is merely an invisible demarcation of comfort, security, and pleasure.

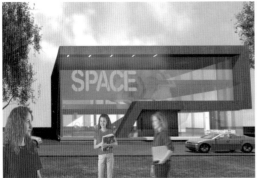

2   ZLG Sdn. Bhd.

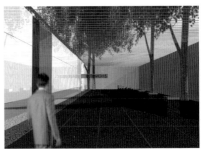

3   ZLG Sdn. Bhd.

4   ZLG Sdn. Bhd.

1   Challenge Park, Putrajaya, Malaysia; roofed elements in complex composition for sports facilities
2   Space Showroom, Kuala Lumpur, Malaysia; minimal façade and canopy design for warehouse and showroom facility
3   Zhongtai Showroom, Beijing, PRC; external view of showroom with mirrored wall and fenced courtyard
4   BOH Visitor Center, Cameron Highlands, Malaysia; pure form articulated to accommodate showroom and F&B facilities
5   Avenue K, Kuala Lumpur, Malaysia; lifestyle development comprising retail and high-end residential towers

5   ZLG Sdn. Bhd.

● Level 3, Bangunan Getah Asli, 148, Jalan Ampang, Kuala Lumpur 50450 Malaysia
Tel: +60 3 2171 2248 Fax: +60 3 2161 2488

ZM ARCHITECTURE

mail@zmarchitecture.co.uk www.zmarchitecture.co.uk

Quantum physics involves small bursts of creative energy that interact continuously, resulting in complex holistic solutions that can also be reduced back to rational manifestations. This conceptual model serves as a metaphor for ZM Architecture's approach.

ZM Architecture delivers work with high standards of total sustainability, social, economic, physical and environmental, within inherently inclusive and researched solutions. Principals have expertise in contract law, development finance, and regulatory procedures and listed building redevelopment. Notable achievements include neighborhood and urban masterplans, the re-use of naval repair yards, former hospitals, and a variety of award winning arts, residential, and leisure projects.

The firm's ambition is to remain adaptable to change and to satisfy its clients' requirements with purpose, energy, and simplicity with the objective of creating appropriate architecture and a sense of culture and place within a small country.

1   Andrew Lee

2   Andrew Lee

3   Andrew Lee

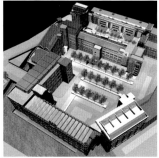

4   ZM Architecture

1 Whale Arts Centre, Edinburgh
2 Tramway Theatre, Glasgow
3 Patrick Burgh Halls, Glasgow
4 Window on the Mac, Glasgow School of Art, Glasgow
5 Templeton business centre, Glasgow

● 62 Albion Street, Glasgow G1 1NY UK Tel: +44 141 572 7001 Fax: +44 141 572 7002

ZNAMENÍ ČTYŘ ARCHITEKTI

architekti@znamenictyr.cz   www.znamenictyr.cz

1   Tomaš Souček

The firm specializes in architectural, urban, and interior design projects at all stages: architectural and volume design, documentation for building permits and zoning procedures, and implementation. The firm also offers clients complete services in building preparation, engineering, and the securing of architectural and technical supervision during construction.

In addition to its architectural activities, Znamení Čtyř Architekti also offers the complete installation of selected interiors. The office works with certified craftsmen, manufacturers, and business representatives.

2   Esther Havlova   3

Esther Havlova

4   Esther Havlova

1   Store, Prague, Czech Republic; interior
2–3 Restaurant, Prague, Czech Republic; interior
4–5 Synagogue, Prague, Czech Republic

5   Tomaš Souček

● Ul. U Pujčovny 5, Prague 1, 110 00 Czech Republic Tel: +420 224 32 21 13 Fax: +420 224 32 21 28

ZONG ARCHITECTS

us@zongarch.com   www.zongarch.com

1   Lim Suat Teng

Established in 1999, Zong Architects is a young and committed firm noted for its cross-disciplinary approach to architecture. The firm offers architecture, interior, art, exhibition, and product design services.

The firm hopes to make a positive contribution to this endeavor, compatible with the needs and visions of its clients.

By synthesizing its values in the shaping of design, both in process and product, the firm ultimately aims to deliver the many possibilities of its multi-layered discipline to its clients.

2   Lim Suat Teng

3   Jancy Rahardja

4   Jancy Rahardja

1 Jau House, Malacca; interior view of living room looking at master bedroom fitness platform
2 Jau House, Malacca; front view of 3-story bungalow
3 Chuan Loft, Singapore; front view of 9 units of 2-story terrace with attic
4 Klebang 8, Condominium, Melaka; model

● 2 Leng Kee Road, #05-11 Thye Hong Centre, 159086 Singapore Tel: +65 6226 0211 Fax: +65 6223 1128

INDEX

UPDATE YOUR FIRM'S ENTRY FOR 2008 EDITION

Ensure that your firm's details are current for the next edition of *2000 Architects*, to be published mid-2008. All aspects of your entry can be updated, including your firm profile, the photographs, and of course, your contact details.

Deadline for updates is 30 November 2006. Please contact us at books@images.com.au or by fax on +61 3 9561 4860 and we will assist with your update.

2008
edition

NOT LISTED IN THIS EDITION?

Did you know that your firm can be listed, free of charge, in the 2008 edition of *2000 Architects*?

The deadline for new entries is 31 October 2006. Please contact us by email at books@images.com.au, or by fax on +61 3 9561 4860 to find out how your firm can be listed in this prime international resource.

NEED EXTRA COPIES?

Additional copies of *2000 Architects* can be obtained from any good bookstore, or directly from The Images Publishing Group.

You can order additional copies by:

- visiting our website: www.imagespublishing.com and completing an order form

or

- emailing us: books@images.com.au

or

- by fax: +61 3 9561 4860

THE MASTER ARCHITECT SERIES

The *Master Architect Series* is a valuable information source and reference to some of the greatest architecture of our time, reflecting each master architect's unique and innovative designs.

Projects selected for inclusion are representative of the most significant works from each stage of the architect's career, including works currently in progress.

Each volume contains color photographs, renderings, drawings and sketches, together with concise chronological lists of buildings and projects, a comprehensive bibliography and a resumé of the partners.

Titles recently released:
KPF Millennium
FXFOWLE Architects
Valode et Pistre Architectes
SITE
Perkins & Will
John Portman and Associates
Payette Associates
Development Design Group Inc.
SCDA Architects
Moore Ruble Yudell
LS3P Associates Ltd
(EEA) Erick van Egeraat
  associated architects
Sasaki Associates
Goettsch Architects
Peter Gisolfi Associates
Mecanoo Architekten

For the complete list please refer to
www.imagespublishing.com

NEO ARCHITECTURE SERIES

While The Images Publishing Group has established a reputation over the past two decades for publishing work of the world's most revered and eminent architects, the dawn of the 21st century has brought a new generation of architects whose work is yet to reach a wide audience.

IMAGES is delighted to introduce the *Neo Architecture Series,* which focuses on the work of this next generation of master architects. Featured works vary widely, from concepts to built projects, elaborate models and competition entries to modest buildings. All are provocative, and represent the vanguard of international architectural practice.

Titles in this Series include:
cj Lim/Studio 8 Architecture
Mark Goulthorpe/DECOI
Jakob & Macfarlane
Manuelle Gautrand Architects
DZO/ITERAE Architecture
Osborn
Push Architecture
HYLA Architects
Studio Downie Architecture

THE INTERNATIONAL SPACES SERIES

The *International Spaces Series,* which has captured design excellence for more than 15 years, now includes almost 40 titles.

As one of the world's most established pictorial collections, each book is complete with dynamic corporate and public interior spaces, as well as intimate and reflective spaces. The Series has provided inspiration to architects the world over.

Firm biographical information is included for many of the featured firms.

Current titles include:
Interior Spaces of the USA and Canada
Residential Spaces of the World
Water Spaces
Courtyard Spaces
Museum and Art Spaces of the World
Retail Spaces
Office Spaces
Industrial Spaces
Sporting Spaces
Health Spaces
Social Spaces
Interior Spaces of Asia and the Pacific Rim
Educational Spaces
Transport Spaces

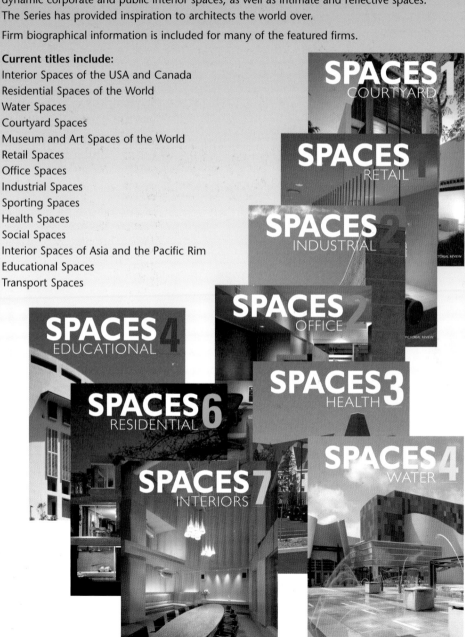

Every effort has been made to trace the original source of copyright material contained in this book. The publishers would be pleased to hear from copyright holders to rectify any errors or omissions.

The information and illustrations in this publication have been prepared and supplied by the entrants. While all reasonable efforts have been made to source the required information and ensure accuracy, the publishers do not, under any circumstances, accept responsibility for errors, omissions and representations expressed or implied.